AGENCY, MORALITY AND LAW

How does law possess the normative force it requires to direct our actions?

This book argues that this seemingly innocuous question is of central importance to the philosophy of law and, by extension, of the very concept of law itself. It advances a position grounded in the secular natural law tradition, and in doing so addresses the two success criteria for this position head on:

- Firstly, that commitment to the existence of a supreme moral principle is required;
- Secondly, that any supreme moral principle must be identifiable through human reason.

The book argues that these conditions are met by Alan Gewirth's Principle of Generic Consistency (PGC), which – through a dialectically necessary argument – locates the existence of universally applicable moral norms in the concept of agency. Given the very purpose of law is to guide action, legal norms must be located in a unified hierarchy of practical reason. It follows that, if law is to succeed in claiming to be capable of guiding our action, moral permissibility with reference to the PGC is a necessary condition of a rule's legal validity.

This strong theory of natural law is defended throughout, both against moral sceptics and positions within contemporary legal positivism.

European Academy of Legal Theory Monograph Series: Volume 17

EUROPEAN ACADEMY OF LEGAL THEORY MONOGRAPH SERIES

General Editors
Professor Mark Van Hoecke
Professor François Ost

Titles in this Series

Moral Conflict and Legal Reasoning
Scott Veitch

The Harmonisation of European Private Law
Edited by Mark Van Hoecke & Francois Ost

On Law and Legal Reasoning
Fernando Atria

Law as Communication
Mark Van Hoecke

Legisprudence
Edited by Luc Wintgens

Epistemology and Methodology of Comparative Law
Edited by Mark van Hoecke

Making the Law Explicit.
The Normativity of Legal Argumentation
Matthias Klatt

The Policy of Law
A Legal Theoretical Framework
Mauro Zamboni

Methodologies of Legal Research
Which Kind of Method for What Kind of Discipline?
Edited by Mark van Hoecke

Objectivity in Law and Legal Reasoning
Edited by Jaakko Husa and Mark van Hoecke

An Introduction to Comparative Law Theory and Method
Geoffrey Samuel

The Tapestry of Reason
An Inquiry into the Nature of Coherence and its Role in Legal Argument
Amalia Amaya

Democracy and Ontology
Agonism between Political Liberalism, Foucault and Psychoanalysis
Irena Rosenthal

Global Constitutionalism and Its Challenges to Westphalian Constitutional Law
Martin Belov

Legal Validity: The Fabric of Justice
Maris Köpcke Tinturé

Paradigms in Modern European Comparative Law: A History
Balázs Fekete

Agency, Morality and Law
Joshua Jowitt

Agency, Morality and Law

Joshua Jowitt

•HART•
OXFORD • LONDON • NEW YORK • NEW DELHI • SYDNEY

HART PUBLISHING

Bloomsbury Publishing Plc

Kemp House, Chawley Park, Cumnor Hill, Oxford, OX2 9PH, UK

1385 Broadway, New York, NY 10018, USA

29 Earlsfort Terrace, Dublin 2, Ireland

HART PUBLISHING, the Hart/Stag logo, BLOOMSBURY and the Diana logo are trademarks of Bloomsbury Publishing Plc

First published in Great Britain 2022

A catalogue record for this book is available from the British Library.

A catalogue record for this book is available from the Library of Congress.

Library of Congress Control Number: 2022944246

ISBN: HB: 978-1-50994-768-3
ePDF: 978-1-50994-770-6
ePub: 978-1-50994-769-0

Typeset by Compuscript Ltd, Shannon

I would like to dedicate this book to my parents, without whose unconditional love and unfailing support I would be nothing.

Thank you.

Contents

Introduction

WERE A TIME traveller from 100 years ago to find herself in our twenty-first century world, she would doubtless be amazed at the technological advances achieved since her journey began. One cannot but think that our world would be almost unrecognisable to the one she left behind. But should our time traveller happen to be interested in legal theory and enquiries into the normative force claimed by legal rules, she may find the terrain of contemporary jurisprudential debate comfortingly familiar. Now, as then, any study that attempts to answer the question of how law comes to create a normative obligation on those to whom it is addressed necessarily takes a position as to whether the moral permissibility of a rule is a necessary criterion of its legal validity. On the one hand, legal positivists claim that no necessary connection exists between the normative force claimed by legal rules and their moral permissibility. On the other hand, natural lawyers (or non-/anti-positivists) argue that such a connection is axiomatic to the very nature of law itself. Yet the fact this debate continues today is not to say that the question is dated; nor does it mean that we should avoid what many consider an indeterminate enquiry and instead focus on questions that are perhaps more popular within contemporary jurisprudence. Rather, the question of whether a rule must be morally permissible in order to be legally valid matters for the reason given by Jules Coleman; it matters 'because law matters, and law matters because it figures in our practical lives – in our determinations of what we ought to do and why.'[1]

This book takes this question seriously and seeks to contribute to the debate by addressing an oft-overlooked theory that considerably expands upon our understanding of the concept of law. It will endorse the natural law theory of legal idealism proposed by Deryck Beyleveld and Roger Brownsword that grounds legal validity in the Principle of Generic Consistency (hereafter referred to as the PGC), a supreme moral principle that twentieth-century moral philosopher Alan Gewirth located within the inescapable fact of our own agency.[2] In defending this position, this work knowingly sails against a prevailing current that seemingly favours a legal positivist understanding of law. But in doing so it attempts to show that, should Gewirth's argument for the PGC be successful, the positions adopted by several prominent contemporary positivists cannot

[1] J Coleman, *The Practice of Principle: In Defence of a Pragmatist Approach to Legal Theory* (Oxford University Press 2001) 70.

[2] D Beyleveld and R Brownsword, *Law as a Moral Judgment* (Sweet and Maxwell 1986); A Gewirth, *Reason and Morality* (Chicago University Press 1978).

explain the normative force necessarily claimed by law unless they abandon their commitment to the positivist position. Furthermore, those that have attempted to engage with the Gewirthian framework have done so in a way that either misrepresents or misapprehends the nature of the claim being advanced. Far from it having nothing but a past, natural law claims such as this one will be shown to be the only way in which legal normativity can be coherently explained.[3]

This introduction will frame the substantive chapters to follow by firstly outlining foundational claims of both the legal positivist and natural law traditions. This is necessary in order to demonstrate points of agreement between both schools and to identify the nexus of the normative disagreement between them. Having done so, we will close with a brief outline of the content of the chapters that will make up the remainder of the book.

1. KEY POSITIONS IN THE DEBATE

If this book is to succeed in successfully demonstrating that positivist theories cannot adequately explain the normative force necessarily claimed by legal rules, we must first establish the position taken by both the positivist and natural law traditions. To this end, the foundational positivist theory of John Austin will first be explored before moving to a Thomist conception of natural law. This overview will be both brief and largely descriptive, but remains necessary in order for us to fully demonstrate the normative disagreement present between them.

1.1. Austin: The Father of Modern Legal Positivism

In his collection of lectures, published in 1832 under the heading *The Province of Jurisprudence Determined*, John Austin attempted to define the scope of what legal philosophy, and by extension, study of law more generally, should concern itself with. He believed that '[t]he matter of jurisprudence is positive law: law, simply and strictly so called: or law set by political superiors to political inferiors.'[4] Whilst this belief is silent on the question of whether a rule must be morally permissible in order to be legally valid (provided it is created by the relevant political superior whose job it is to *posit* the law) any such link is rejected by Austin towards the end of Lecture V:

> The existence of law is one thing; its merit or demerit is another. Whether it be or be not is one enquiry; whether it be or be not conformable to an assumed standard, is a

[3] W Lucy, 'Natural Law Now' (1993) 56 (5) *Modern Law Review* 745.

[4] J Austin, *The Province of Jurisprudence Determined* (first published 1832, WE Rumble ed, Cambridge University Press 1995) 18.

> different enquiry … Now, to say that human laws which conflict with Divine law are not binding, that is to say, are not laws, is to talk stark nonsense.[5]

By this definition, rules that require behaviour that would be morally impermissible are still laws insofar as they have been posited by our political superiors. They acquire their legal validity by dint of being created according to the law making procedure of the jurisdiction in which they have been posited, rendering any discussion of their moral permissibility ancillary. Austin sees valid law as necessarily instructive insofar as 'Every *law* or *rule* … is a command. Or, rather, laws or rules, properly so called, are a *species* of commands.'[6] As commands they generate a correlative duty on those to whom they are addressed to comply with their requirements, making it axiomatic of valid law that it claims to be able to direct our actions. Failure to comply with this duty legitimises the imposition of a compliance encouraging sanction.[7] It is this logical chain, starting with a rule being posited by a competent political authority, which Austin believes can explain the origin of the normative force claimed by law.

One of the reasons upon which he grounds his rejection of the claim that a rule's moral permissibility is a necessary condition of its legal validity is his belief that it is difficult, if not impossible, to identify a universally acceptable test for moral permissibility. He considers this to be self-evident given the fact that people, both historically and in his own time, disagree over the content of moral standards:

> The respective moral sentiments of different ages and nations, and of different men in the same age and nation, have differed to infinity. This proposition is so notoriously true, and to every instructed mind the facts upon which it rests are so familiar, that I should hardly treat my hearers with due respect if I attempt to establish it by proof.[8]

He goes on to claim that, given '[t]here is no broad sun destined to illumine the world, but every single man must walk by his own candle.'[9] In doing so, he grounds his positivism firmly in what he holds to be the inescapable fact of moral pluralism; if no objective and universal test for moral permissibility can exist, then it is impossible for such a test to be used to ascertain the legal validity of a rule. Yet, as will be shown, this will be a characterisation of the nature of moral claims that thinkers in the natural law tradition would reject.

1.2. Natural Law and Practical Reason

An example from the law of England and Wales may help us ascertain why a natural lawyer would reject Austin's portrayal of the nature of moral claims.

[5] ibid 157–158.
[6] ibid 21.
[7] ibid 22.
[8] ibid 89–90.
[9] ibid 90.

Let us consider Sir Leslie Stephen's famous claim, made in connection with the doctrine of Parliamentary Sovereignty, that it is within the law making power of Parliament to create a law that mandated the execution of all blue-eyed babies at birth.[10] Should they do so, Austin appears to suggest that such a rule would be legally valid despite the claim that we in our own society would view its directive as clearly morally impermissible.[11] A natural lawyer would respond that this is to mischaracterise the nature of moral claims, which are by necessity overriding of all other reasons for action. This would require them to ground this claim in a way that makes an objective test possible, and one way of doing so would be to trace such a test to a divine command.[12] Such claims have been made since antiquity, such as the following from Cicero:

> True law is right reason, consonant with nature, spread through all people. It is constant and eternal; it summons to duty by its orders, it deters from crime by its prohibitions ... it is not permitted to abrogate any of it; it cannot be totally repealed. We cannot be released from this law by the senate or the people, and it needs no exegete or interpreter ... There will not be one law at Rome and another at Athens, one now and another later; but all nations at all times will be bound by this one eternal and unchangeable law, and the god will be the one common master and general (so to speak) of all people. He is the author, expounder, and mover of this law; and the person who does not obey it will be in exile from himself.[13]

According to Cicero then, legal obligations must be in conformity with the demands of reason and rationality; these are gifts from the gods, and as we have an overriding obligation to behave according to their will, we should ensure our positive law is in compliance with this requirement. This standard is universal, unchangeable through time and, for Ulpian, equally applies to all species:

> [Law is that] which nature has taught all animals ... But we shall disregard so general an acceptation and consider the meaning of it essentially in relation to matters which are proper to the human race alone.[14]

Note here, however, that the connection between legal validity and moral permissibility is not due to a deity *per se*, but is instead connected with the conformity of the legal rule with the demands of practical rationality. This connection was also claimed by perhaps the most famous exponent of the natural law position in the Christian tradition, St Thomas Aquinas. He characterises law as 'a kind of direction or measure for human activity through which a person is led to

[10] Sir L Stephen, *The Science of Ethics* (first published 1882, Cambridge University Press 2011) 143.

[11] Austin (n 4) 92.

[12] AP d'Entrèves, Natural Law; *An Introduction to Legal Philosophy* (first pub 1951, Hutchinson & Co., 1970) 38.

[13] Cicero, *On the Commonwealth and On the Laws* (J Zetzel tr, first pub 1999, Cambridge University Press 2002) Book III, 71–72.

[14] d'Entrèves (n 12) 38.

do something or held back' and as 'nought else than an ordinance of reason for the common good made by the authority who has care for the community and promulgated.'[15] These positions are summarised by Paul Sigmund – that law is 'an ordination of reason for the common good promulgated by one who is in charge of the community.'[16] At this point we should note that a Thomist natural lawyer would accept Austin's claim that legal rules must necessarily be posited by a political superior. They would also agree that law takes the form of a command and is thus designed to encourage or discourage certain behaviour. Yet from here, the natural law and positivist positions would diverge. In categorising law as 'a dictate of practical reason'[17] Aquinas is referring to more than just rationality; he is referring to practical reason as a teleological and goal-orientated standard aimed at ensuring human flourishing. Rules not in compliance with this standard of practical reason are somehow deficient, and are 'not straightforwardly a law, but rather a sort of crooked law'[18] because 'Every law aims at this, to be obeyed by its subjects. It is plain, therefore, that leading its subjects into the virtue appropriate to their condition is a proper function of law.'[19]

Here, then, is a key distinction between the Thomist position and Austinian positivism. Aquinas notes that because legal rules exist to be followed, tyrannical rules are not law because they cannot provide a reason as to *why* they should be followed. He thus identifies reason and rationality as essential for the task of ascertaining the validity of a legal rule; given the purpose of law is to direct our actions, any rule that cannot provide an overriding reason to act without the threat of sanction cannot be a legally valid rule. This claim is universally applicable in its scope, and thus overcomes Austin's objection from moral pluralism; for if all human beings are equally rational, rationality could serve as a basis upon which we could identify a 'true' version of natural law:

> So then in questions of theory, truth is the same for everybody, both as to principles and to conclusions, though admittedly all do not recognise truth in the conclusions, but only in those principles which are called 'common conceptions … So then it is evident that with respect to general principles of theory and practice what is right is the same for all and is equally recognised. With respect to specific conclusions of theory the truth is the same for all, though all do not equally recognise it: for instance some are not aware that the angles of a triangle together equal two right angles.[20]

Put another way, the truth of a concept that can be rationally justified is in no way affected by its acceptance. This is as true for a moral standard as it is for the fact that the inner angles of a triangle add up to 180°.

[15] T Aquinas, *Summa Theologiae Vol.28, IaeIIae 90–97*, (T Gilby OP tr, Cambridge University Press 2006) Q.90 Art 1, 5; Art 4, 17.

[16] P Sigmund, 'Law and Politics' in N Kretzmann and E Stump (eds), *The Cambridge Companion to Aquinas* (Cambridge University Press 1993) 222.

[17] Aquinas (n 15) Q90 Art 1, 5.

[18] ibid Q92 Art 1, 45; Q95 Art 2, 105.

[19] ibid Q92 Art 1, 43.

[20] ibid Q94 Art 4, 89.

This identification of practical reason as a potential source of tests for the moral permissibility of action is one that remains present in contemporary natural law claims. Though Aquinas argued that a large reason behind the prioritisation of practical reason is that it was given to us by God, one need not endorse this view in order to accept his conclusion that 'reason gets its motive force from the will, as we have shown. For it is because a person wills an end that his reason effectively governs arrangements to bring it about.'[21] The secular natural law claim would thus take the following form: 'natural law is a plea for reasonableness in action' and that only legislative acts that in accordance with the requirements of practical reason can guide our action and, thus, function as law.[22]

2. THE NEXUS OF NORMATIVE DISAGREEMENT

The importance of fully understanding the nature of the normative claim made by law can be seen when we consider the role of legal officials and the adjudication of disputes. Such official do not have unlimited discretion to act as they see fit in such a role; rather: 'Given the nature of a legal system, the officials in that system are subject to distinctive constraints of rationality. There is, in this sense, an *inner rationality of law*.'[23] As subjects against whom legal rules are applied, it is therefore important for us to know that those whose job it is to apply those rules are applying the law correctly according to this inner rationality of law. One of the functions subject to this inner rationality is the ability of such officials to identify which rules are legally valid to begin with, and thus ought to be applied in legal disputes. If a debate exists with regards to whether a rule's moral permissibility should factor within this deliberation, then it is a debate that matters.

Though legal positivists and natural lawyers disagree as to whether a rule must be morally permissible in order to be legally valid, they agree that legal rules need to be created by a law-making body that is charged with that task, and that – in certain circumstances – sanctions to encourage compliance are permissible. They also agree that legal rules necessarily attempt to guide our actions by instructing us to behave, or refrain from behaving, in a certain way. In this sense, the dispute can be seen to be one that is clearly normative in character. It is for this reason that this work will limit itself to discussing normative, as opposed to non-normative theories of legal positivism; that it appears axiomatic that law simply does issue a normative claim. Any theory of legal obligation that

[21] ibid Q90 Art 1, 9.

[22] d'Entrèves (n 12) 77–78.

[23] ME Bratman, 'Reflections on Law, Normativity and Plans' in S Bertea and G Pavlakos (eds) *New Essays on the Normativity of Law* (Hart 2011) 73.

suppresses or otherwise denies law's normative claim, for Hart, 'fails to mark and explain the crucial distinction between mere regularities of human behaviour and rule-governed behaviour.'[24] This is a position that Postema has called 'The Normativity Thesis':

> We understand law only if we understand how it is that laws give members of a community, officials and law-subjects alike, reasons for acting. Thus an adequate general theory of law must give a satisfactory account of the normative (reason-giving) character of law.[25]

When one accepts that law necessarily makes a normative claim, a point agreed by foundational positivist and natural law theories alike, one also accepts that the legal rules must be capable of providing a valid reason for us to accept their normative claim as valid. This, then, is the nexus of disagreement between positivists and natural lawyers; positivists would argue that this normative claim is valid by dint of the legislative process, whereas natural lawyers argue that a rule cannot issue a binding directive if it is morally impermissible. Natural lawyers would argue this claim is necessary because of the nature of a normative claim, an assessment of whose validity requires an agent to factor in all relevant considerations; for to be an agent means to make choices in order to pursue our ends, and it is these choices and ends that legal rules seek to constrain. Our capacity to make choices is an unavoidable statement of our condition; as Korsgaard rightly identifies, 'Human beings are *condemned* to choice and action'[26] because 'self-constitution through action is our essential function as rational agents'.[27] We simply cannot escape our capacities as rationally autonomous agents, and legal rules address themselves to us at this normative level.

To exclude moral considerations from this assessment is, for the natural lawyer, to misunderstand what it means to be an agent, and thus arbitrarily limit the scope of any enquiry into the operation of normative claims. This claim can be demonstrated if we consider a thought-experiment offered by Scott Shapiro, in which he asks us to consider a man who is instructed to buy butter despite preferring margarine. If he buys butter anyway, Shapiro suggests that the reason for his choosing this action despite preferring another is his reliance on the special status of authority:

> Legitimate authority is a good thing.
>
> I ought to obey the authority's commands.
>
> The planners have asked me to buy butter.

[24] HLA Hart, *Essays in Jurisprudence and Philosophy* (Clarendon Press 1983) 13.

[25] GJ Postema, 'Coordination and Convention at the Foundations of Law' (1982) 11 *Journal of Legal Studies* 165.

[26] C Korsgaard, *Self-Constitution: Agency, Identity, and Integrity* (Oxford University Press 2009) 1.

[27] ibid 42.

The planners are the authority.

I ought to obey the planners' commands.

Conclusion: I ought to buy butter.[28]

Shapiro thus attempts to show why it can be rational to disregard one's own agential autonomy and submit to the will of a legislator. This may hold in connection to what many perceive to be the morally neutral proposition of buying butter over margarine, but it is not obvious that the same logical chain follows should we replace this choice with one that requires our actor to behave in a way which he knows to be morally impermissible. Shapiro's claim that it may remain rational for an agent to behave in a morally impermissible way because participating in coordinated social activity increases our chances of survival may seem persuasive,[29] but cannot overcome the logical necessity that – when faced with a binding moral directive – an agent has an overriding reason to comply with its requirements against all other reasons. To claim otherwise is to mischaracterise the normative hierarchy at play, and fail to acknowledge that categorically binding normative claims are stronger reasons for action than all others. The natural lawyer thus concludes that, if a legal rule must be able to provide a reason as to why we should see it as making a valid directive, any such directive cannot conflict with categorically binding moral reasons.

If a positivist were to respond that an effective system of sanctions can enforce compliance then, as Hart puts it, this is to concede that a legal system generates normative claims in the same way as the bank robber who declares 'Hand over the money, or I will shoot.'[30] If the only means by which a system can ensure compliance is through violent coercion, such a system is nothing more than a gunman writ large. Unless positivists would endorse this conclusion, their characterisation of law as nothing more than a social planning mechanism artificially limits the scope of the normative enquiry being undertaken.[31] Rather than it being axiomatically true, this book views the positivist exclusion of moral claims as nothing more than a reflection of a historical situation, that 'the modern state has assumed a monopoly of law and the making of law.'[32] This historical peculiarity leads scholars to assume that the state has unlimited power to create legal norms, without questioning whether the rules that emerge from the legislative process are capable of making the valid normative claims that law must necessarily make.

[28] V Rodriguez-Blanco, 'The Moral Puzzle of Legal Authority; A Commentary on Shapiro's Planning Theory of Law' in S Bertea and G Pavlakos (eds) *New Essays on the Normativity of Law* (Hart Publishing 2011) 94.

[29] ibid 97.

[30] HLA Hart, *The Concept of Law* (3rd edn, Oxford University Press 2012) 19.

[31] K Schaubroeck, 'Legal Normativity and the Instrumental Principle' in Stefano Bertea and George Pavlakos (eds) *New Essays on the Normativity of Law* (Hart 2011) 109.

[32] d'Entrèves (n 12) 187.

It is this mistake that the present work attempts to address. It will do so through a defence of the strong natural law position identified by Beyleveld and Brownsword: that Gewirth's argument, if successful, requires us to accept that the moral permissibility of a rule with reference to the PGC is necessarily a criterion of its legal validity.[33] The book will be divided into two main parts, the first of which is comprised of two substantive chapters and will deal with the philosophical validity of the PGC. Chapter 1 will begin by introducing the PGC and the argument by which it claims to act as a supreme moral principle that is capable of guiding all action, before defending it against some philosophical objections as to its validity that might be made from relevant sceptical positions. Chapter 2 will use the framework of deliberative rationality and practical reasons outlined by Joseph Raz in order to demonstrate that the PGC necessitates the recognition of a unified conception of practical reason in which the spheres of moral and legal normativity cannot be seen as distinct but must necessarily overlap. This philosophical groundwork in part one of the book is necessary in light of the nature of the natural law claim that moral reasons for action necessarily override all other non-compliant reasons for action – including morally impermissible directives claiming to be law. The only means by which this natural law claim can overcome the common positivist observation that practitioners rarely seek to trump black-letter legal arguments with purely moral ones because law 'necessarily claims to *trump* moral and other reasons for action'[34] is if we can first demonstrate that a supreme moral principle can be identified and that it sits at the top of a unified conception of practical reason.

Having defended the philosophical validity of the PGC, part two of this monograph will move on to apply our conclusion to the question of whether a rule's moral permissibility with reference to the PGC is a necessary condition of its legal validity. Chapter 3 will begin with what it is hoped is an uncontroversial claim: that natural lawyers and legal positivists must begin their debate from a starting point upon which both positions can agree. This is the functional claim that that law is a directive and, as such, must necessarily be capable of guiding action. In light of the unified conception of practical reason demonstrated in Part One, this requires us to accept that a legal directive must be morally permissible with reference to the PGC in order for it to claim to be capable of guiding our action. The natural law claim that a rule's moral permissibility with reference to the PGC is a necessary condition of its legal validity will therefore be shown to be necessary for any internally coherent theory of legal validity. The chapter will close with a discussion of the necessity of this conclusion by demonstrating that, in light of the argument for the PGC, the paradigmatic

[33] Beyleveld and Brownsword (n 2). Beyleveld and Brownsword refer to their theory as one of 'legal idealism' rather than 'natural law'.

[34] Torben Spaak, 'Kelsen and Hart on the Normativity of Law' in Peter Wahlgren (ed), *Perspectives on Jurisprudence; Essays in Honour of Jes Bjarup* (Stockholm Institute for Scandinavian Law 2005) 399–400.

positivist theories of Kelsen and Hart cannot provide a non-moral explanation of the normative claim of law.

Chapter 4 will return to the writings of Joseph Raz, and address whether his theory of legal positivism remains internally coherent in light of the conclusions previously reached with regards to his theory of reasons for action and deliberative rationality. In doing so it will address Raz's conception of the nature of law and legal reasoning, the importance of points of view, legal normativity, systemic functionality and obligations to obey the law. It will be demonstrated that Raz's conclusions on each of those topics can only remain compatible with his conception of reasons for action if he abandons his commitment to legal positivism and accepts that a rule's moral permissibility with reference to the PGC is a necessary condition of its legal validity.

Chapter 5, the final substantive chapter, will critique three further contemporary theorists who can be more uncontroversially categorised as inclusive in their positivism. These are the formalism of David Lyons, the 'incorporationism' of Jules Coleman and Matthew Kramer's 'moderate incorporationism'. These will be shown to be incapable of explaining the normative source of law unless they accept that moral permissibility of a legal rule is a necessary criterion for its legal validity; yet in recognising the connection with moral normativity to be necessary as opposed to be contingent, they cease to be theories of inclusive positivism and become theories of natural law. Thus, in recognising the relevance of moral norms to legal deliberation on even a contingent basis, they allow the Trojan horse to enter which leads to their necessary collapse.

This book will therefore defend a simple claim – that the PGC properly understood provides an inescapable reason to accept that the moral permissibility of a rule is a necessary connection of its legal validity. It is not anticipated that this work will conclusively end the debate between the legal positivist and natural law claims. It does, however, hope to address some misconceptions with regard to the natural law position upon which the claims of much contemporary positivism rest. Both schools accept that law is necessarily created and does not appear in isolation. Both accept that law necessarily makes a claim to direct our action in some way. And both recognise that normative conflict is sometimes inescapable. The disagreement is about how this conflict can be resolved, with reference to the normative claim made by legal rules themselves. It is hoped that this book will show that the moral permissibility of the rule cannot be overlooked when making this call.

Part 1

Establishing the PGC as a Supreme Moral Principle

1

The PGC as a Supreme Moral Principle

1. INTRODUCTION

AT THIS POINT I would like to bring us back to our hypothetical time-traveller and that, although she may find the terrain of contemporary jurisprudential debate familiar, the same could not be said of the rest of the world around her. Technological advancements in areas such as transport, communications and entertainment, which we take for granted, appear almost unimaginable when viewed from the perspective of a mind formed by the nineteenth century. I note this point in particular because, as our technological capacities have increased, so have the means by which we are able to detrimentally interfere with one another's existence. The number of interactions we have with one another, and the planes on which they take place, mean that there has never been more scope for legal rules to govern them.

The debate between legal positivists and natural lawyers has therefore never been more relevant. Now more than ever before, a rigorous exploration of ethical principles and the extent to which moral permissibility is a necessary criterion of a rule's legal validity is needed. In his 1978 book *Reason and Morality*, American philosopher Alan Gewirth, the author whose works will form the foundation of the strong theory of natural law that the remainder of this volume seeks to defend, put the point succinctly:

> In a century where the evils that man can do to man have reached unparalleled extremes of barbarism and tragedy, the philosophic concern with rational justification in ethics is more than a quest for certainty. It is also an attempt to make coherent sense of persons' deepest concerns about the principles that should govern the ways they treat one another.[1]

The extent to which a moral theory such as that proposed by Gewirth is genuinely of use to a theory relating to the normative force claimed by legal rules is, of course, far from settled. Like many others, Spaak believes empirical reality shows us that law and legal rules 'necessarily claims to *trump* moral and

[1] A Gewirth, *Reason and Morality* (University of Chicago Press 1978) ix.

other reasons for action' insofar as, in a courtroom situation where the conduct required by a legal rule is viewed as morally impermissible, the court will rarely see this as sufficient reason to aside the legal rule.[2] Let us frame this dispute in the abstract, and consider the existence of a legal rule that directs us towards an end that is morally impermissible. We have here a normative conflict: a rule claiming to be a legal norm (R_L) asks us to behave in a certain way (Φ), and a moral norm (R_M) directs us to refrain from undertaking that act ($-\Phi$). How ought we to resolve this dilemma, since it is clearly impossible that both ($R_L\ x, \Phi$ & $R_M\ x, -\Phi$) can operate at the same time? If the positivist claim is correct and a rule's moral permissibility need not be a condition of its legal validity, then Spaak's observation is correct and ($R_M\ x, -\Phi$) < ($R_L\ x, \Phi$). Or if we accept both Austin and Aquinas' position that the whole point of law is that it exists to guide our conduct, does this require us to acknowledge that R_L can only succeed in this enterprise if its directives are substantively limited by R_M?

This book seeks to establish that the second of these two statements is true, which first requires us to identify a supreme moral principle that is capable of providing the test that this connection requires. Part 1 of this work will argue that the PGC, developed in Gewirth's '*Reason and Morality*'[3] is capable of serving as such a test. Chapter 1 will begin with an outline the workings of the PGC and endorse the claim that, by a dialectically necessary argument, it successfully establishes a test by which we can ascertain the moral permissibility of any action. This is a test that all agents are required to accept by the fact of their being an agent, meaning the PGC acts in a way that is analogous to a categorical imperative and restricts the range of morally permissible actions to those that are in conformity with its requirements. Such a position relies on a Kantian conception of the person, and this assumption – and the validity of the conclusions reached by adopting it – will then be addressed, before the chapter closes with a defence of the PGC against common arguments against its validity. Thinkers that will be engaged with directly are Williams, Friedman, Foot and Nietzsche; all can be broadly categorised as being from the sceptical tradition, and each of their rebuttals will be assessed for their success in defeating the PGC. The chapter will close by addressing the writing of David Enoch. His claim that logical contradiction is not a charge that would trouble an agent who decides that they should not be bound by the PGC could be a troubling line of argument for Gewirthian Ethical Rationalism, but Enoch's argument will be

[2] T Spaak, 'Kelsen and Hart on the Normativity of Law' in P Wahlgren (ed), *Perspectives on Jurisprudence; Essays in Honour of Jes Bjarup* (Stockholm Institute for Scandinavian Law 2005) 399–400. This is an account of the positivist view of legal rules that appears to be dominant in legal practice. Some theorists, of course, disagree and hold that judges have a duty to disregard immoral legal rules if a certain threshold of impermissibility is crossed. See G Radbruch, 'Statutory Lawlessness and Supra-Statutory Law (1946)' (2006) 26(1) *Oxford Journal of Legal Studies* 1; R Alexy, *The Argument from Injustice* (S Paulson and B Paulson tr, Oxford University Press 2009).

[3] Gewirth, *Reason and Morality* (n 1).

shown to be a straw man that does not substantively engage with the argument for the PGC at all. Taken together, these defences of the philosophical soundness of the PGC will provide the ground work required for chapter two, which will seek to locate the claim made by the PGC in a unified hierarchy of reasons.

2. THE DIALECTICAL NECESSITY OF MORALITY

As was previously noted with regards to Austin, and will be demonstrated with regards to other authors to be considered throughout this book, a large part of the positivist denial that a rule's moral permissibility is a necessary condition of its legal validity can be traced to the widely held belief that it is impossible to find an objective and universally applicable test for moral permissibility that all individuals would accept regardless of their subjective beliefs. In formulating the PGC, Gewirth attempts to overcome this problem by grounding his test for the moral permissibility of action in the unavoidable fact of our individual agency. In doing so he identifies a critical morality; one that is mind-independent, and not the contingent collective morality that a given society may extrapolate from its own subjective cultural requirements.[4] He suggests that such an abstract principle remains valid in light of its mind-independence by offering the following definition of what features a norm need possess in order to be considered moral in character:

> … [A] morality is a set of categorically obligatory requirements for action that are addressed at least in part to every actual or prospective agent, and that are concerned with furthering the interests, especially the most important interests, of persons other than or in addition to the agent or the speaker. The requirements are categorically obligatory in that compliance with them is mandatory for the conduct of every person to whom they are addressed regardless of whether he wants to accept them or their results, and regardless also of the requirements of any other institutions such as law or etiquette, whose obligatoriness may itself be doubtful or variable.[5]

Of note here is Gewirth's direct opposition to the claim endorsed by Spaak in the introduction of this chapter: whereas many hold the view that legal norms necessarily override moral norms, Gewirth suggests that a true understanding of the operation of a supreme moral principle would require us to argue the reverse. This section will address the first stage needed to show the correctness of this natural law claim: if we are to prove that moral rules constrain the substantive content of legal rules to directives that are morally permissible, the PGC needs to be shown to be capable acting as a test by which we can ascertain the moral permissibility of all action. It will be shown to be capable of this function, and ought to be accepted as valid.

[4] ibid ix–x.

[5] ibid 1.

2.1. The Argument for the PGC

Gewirth believes that moral judgements cannot rely on empirical facts or observations, such as whether a given society agrees that certain conduct is moral, to demonstrate their truth and objectivity. To accept this claim at face value is to beg the question and accept the moral judgement in question as correct simply because it is already seen as correct. He calls this problem that of 'the independent variable'; that without the existence of an independent and external benchmark against which moral judgements can be assessed, their correctness can never truly be determined.[6] To find an independent benchmark that can serve this purpose and also be accepted by all societies is, of course, a difficult task. Gewirth acknowledges this and suggests that to be universally accepted, such a benchmark must be located and grounded in something that is universally possessed by all individuals against whom moral claims can be made. He argues that the very concept of action, and the bare agency required for its pursuit, should be suitable for this given that – as was previously noted and is widely accepted – human beings are simply 'condemned to choice and action'[7] because 'self-constitution through action is our essential function as rational agents'.[8] The concept of action is itself constructed from two further concepts, each of which possesses features relevant for moral discourse:

(a) Voluntariness: Conduct must be externally sourced (i.e.: not caused by reflex or disease) an not caused by either direct or indirect compulsion; and
(b) Purposiveness: Actors have goals which constitute their reason for acting.[9]

This grounding of the PGC in bare agency forms the beginning of a sequence of claims, each of which flows logically from the previous claim and applies to any action that is undertaken purposively and voluntarily. Gewirth's argument is therefore dialectically necessary; the fact of our agency means that we are required to accept the conclusion reached – namely, the test of moral permissibility expressed by the PGC.

Gewirth presented the argument for the PGC in various formats of varying complexity over the years,[10] but it was broken down in to three main claims by Beyleveld in his own work defending the Gewirthian position.[11] Given the

[6] ibid 5.

[7] C Korsgaard, *Self-Constitution: Agency, Identity, and Integrity* (Oxford University Press 2009) 1.

[8] ibid 42.

[9] Gewirth, *Reason and Morality* (n 1) 27–37.

[10] ibid; A Gewirth, *Human Rights: Essays on Justification and Applications* (University of Chicago Press 1982); A Gewirth, 'Replies to my Critics' in E Regis Jr (ed), *Gewirth's Ethical Rationalism* (University of Chicago Press 1984); A Gewirth, *The Community of Rights* (University of Chicago Press 1996).

[11] D Beyleveld, *The Dialectical Necessity of Morality; An Analysis and Defense of Alan Gewirth's Argument to the Principle of Generic Consistency* (University of Chicago Press 1991) 14.

clarity brought to the dialectically necessary progression of the argument by Beyleveld's three-stage presentation, it will be adopted as the framework for the present account. Stage one of the argument for the PGC begins with a statement of what it means to be an agent from the internal viewpoint of the agent themselves: that I act purposefully and voluntarily to bring about a given end. This statement entails several value-neutral, implicit and interconnected statements. Firstly, that the agent must view the end sought as being subjectively good or of benefit to them – were this not to be the case, the agent would have no reason to attempt to attain it.[12] Secondly, that an agent requires a minimum degree of both freedom and well-being in order to pursue the end being sought;[13] for without a minimum degree of freedom or wellbeing, any purposive or voluntary action that seeks to progress from the internalization of the desire that is the reason for action (and which is therefore beyond mere reflex or natural impulse) cannot be carried out.[14] Freedom and well-being should therefore be recognised as instrumentally necessary goods in order for any end to be achieved, and can legitimately be referred to as 'Generic Conditions of Agency' (GCAs).[15]

Stage two of the argument for the PGC continues from the identification of these GCAs. As GCAs are necessary for any end to be achieved, any agent must, from their own internal point of view, see interference with their GCAs without their consent as undesirable. If the agent must view such non-consensual interference as unjustifiable, this is analogous to a belief that they have a claim-right that their GCAs ought not to be interfered with without their consent.[16] It should be noted, however, that at this stage in Gewirth's argument, the 'right' and 'ought' are not, in and of themselves, moral claims. They may have other normative foundations, such as pragmatism or aesthetics; for until the consideration of others' interests outside the agent, without the principle of reciprocity and interaction, no moral principle is brought into play.[17] It may be asked, then, why such claims to freedom and wellbeing should be classified as rights and not as merely egoistic demands. Gewirth suggests that is because rights, unlike demands, require certain criteria be fulfilled which are supplied by the PGC:

(a) Rights claims must be grounded in a valid, legitimate and justifiable claim based on entitlement.

[12] A Gewirth, 'The Normative Structure of Action' (1971) 25(2) *The Review of Metaphysics* 238, 242.

[13] For Gewirth's purposes, freedom and wellbeing are defined thusly: 'freedom consists in controlling one's own behaviour by one's own unforced choice while having knowledge of relevant circumstances, and well-being consists in having the other general abilities and conditions required for agency.' See: A Gewirth, 'The Basis and Content of Human Rights' in JR Pennock and JW Chapman (eds), *Human Rights – Nomos XXIII* (New York University Press 1981) 125.

[14] The source of the initial motivation for action is of secondary importance; it is the internalisation of the reason for action as a valid reason for undertaking the action that is the important focus here for the progression of the argument.

[15] Gewirth, *Reason and Morality* (n 1) 22–63, esp. 48–52.

[16] ibid 63–103.

[17] ibid 69.

(b) Such entitlement must be grounded in valid rules or other identifiable reasons.
(c) Rights claims require a community to be addressed towards which understands the legitimacy of the rules or reasons upon which the rights claim is based.
(d) Such a community must be both legal and political in nature.[18]

The initial claim-right therefore exists because the goods of freedom and well-being are not necessary for a specific act (E) but are required for action itself. It is therefore impossible to waive these specific rights and remain an agent; since non-interference is therefore necessary for action itself, the four conditions above are met and GCAs can be legitimately claimed as rights.[19] This conclusion flows directly from the point at which stage one of the argument ends: given that an agent must recognise their GCAs as instrumentally necessary goods, universally necessary for any end, that they must make prudential claim-rights to them is a logical necessity. It is this inescapable progression of the argument, that one is bound to accept stage two if one also accepts stage one, demonstrating the dialectically necessary structure of Gewirth's claim.

From this necessary conclusion, stage three of the argument attempts to universalise the rights-claim made from the internal viewpoint of one agent to all other agents. For if I must necessarily claim my GCAs as rights because of the inescapable fact of my own agency, then so too must all other agents. I am required to accept this conclusion because it is self-reflexive. Refusal to acknowledge that other agents are capable of making rights-claims because of their agency means one of two things: either I reject agency as the foundation of my own rights claim and conclude I cannot claim rights to my GCAs, which is irrational insofar as it rejects the dialectically necessary argument presented to this point, or I deny that I am an agent at all. As both denials require the agent to use their agency, and thus rely on their GCAs, the denial cannot be successful: it relies on a paradox where the criterion whose importance they seek to deny is essential for the denial itself to be successful. To deny this conclusion is a logical contradiction and should be rejected. It is dialectically necessary that an agent must accept that all other agents are capable of making equally valid claim-rights against non-consensual interference with their GCAs, for no other reason than the fact that they are an agent.[20] If the claims made by all agents are equally valid, then all agents are bound to respect the claims of all other agents in order to maintain the validity of their own claim. The argument therefore creates a prescriptive normative obligation restricting the permissible behaviour of all agents to that which does not interfere with the rights of other agents without their consent.[21] It is at this final stage of the argument, through

[18] ibid 71–72.
[19] ibid 77.
[20] ibid 104–198, esp 104–128; Beyleveld, *The Dialectical Necessity of Morality* (n 11) 44–45.
[21] Gewirth, *Reason and Morality* (n 1) 63–64.

becoming other-regarding,[22] that the prudential 'ought' contained in previous stages of the argument becomes a prescriptive moral 'ought'.[23] The PGC can therefore be summarised as follows: 'Act in accord with the generic rights of your recipients as of yourself.'[24] This statement provides a universally applicable test for the moral permissibility of all actions, regardless of the subjective preferences of the agent.

2.2. Universal Morality and Cultural Pluralism

A common mistake made by those who seek to dismiss the PGC is to assume that Gewirth attempts to prove a categorical imperative. This is not his task; rather, his argument is dialectical in that it seeks to show that an agent contradicts themselves if they choose not to act in accordance with the PGC.[25] This results in an outcome that is admittedly similar to moral principles that *do* claim the status as a categorical imperative, such as those discerned by Kant,[26] but which differs in two important ways. Firstly, rather than Kant's open-ended indeterminism, the PGC seeks to protect two generic yet specific and identifiable rights.[27] Secondly, where a categorical imperative can be critiqued from the point of view of the moral relativist the PGC cannot, insofar as it proceeds dialectically from the internal, cognitive standpoint of the agent.[28] The PGC is universalisable based on the logic that if a Predicate (P) belongs to a Subject (S) because of a Quality (Q), all S who have Q possess P.[29] Therefore, all S who are agents possess generic rights to freedom and wellbeing. Such a statement is dialectically necessary in that it is relative to what all agents must logically accept for themselves,[30] and universal in that all human beings are capable of rational autonomy and are thus agents for this purpose.[31]

At this point, an objection might be raised that not all human beings are agents capable of being covered by the requirements of the PGC; it is not

[22] ibid 1; A Gewirth, 'The "Is-Ought" Problem Resolved' (1973) 47 *Proceedings and Addresses of the American Philosophical Association* 34, 54; P Allen III, '"Ought" from "Is"? What Hare and Gewirth Should Have Said' (1982) 3(3) *American Journal of Theology and Philosophy* 90, 94.

[23] This 'ought' is in line with the commonly accepted view that moral norms are prescriptive (ought to be followed), rather than obligatory (impossible to not be followed) in nature. See D Beyleveld, 'The Principle of Generic Consistency as the Supreme Principle of Human Rights' (2012) 13(1) *Human Rights Review* 1, 4 n 7.

[24] Gewirth, *Reason and Morality* (n 1) 135.

[25] Beyleveld, *The Dialectical Necessity of Morality* (n 11) 15.

[26] I Kant, *Groundwork of the Metaphysics of Morals* (M Gregor tr, Cambridge University Press 1998) 4:421; 4:429; 4:431; 4:439.

[27] Gewirth, *Reason and Morality* (n 1) 169.

[28] ibid 161.

[29] ibid 105.

[30] Gewirth, *The Community of Rights* (n 10) 16.

[31] Gewirth, *Reason and Morality* (n 1) 138.

apparent, for example, whether newborn infants or those temporarily or permanently lacking consciousness, as but two examples, are capable of acting purposively or voluntarily. On a strict reading, this would exclude them from being able to benefit from the imperative Gewirth has identified. It is at this stage, however, that a precautionary principle necessarily comes into play. This can be seen to be necessary when we restate the imperative provided by the PGC: that we are required to avoid breaching its requirements in every situation when such a breach is a possible consequence of our actions. If an observer is required to decide whether the individual before them is also an agent, then the following is true:

(a) If the being is an agent, then:
   (i) If the observer treats them in a way that is PGC compliant, then the observer's behaviour is morally permissible.
   (ii) If the observer treats them in a way that is *not* PGC compliant, then the observer's behaviour is morally impermissible.

(b) If the being is not an agent, then:
   (i) If the observer treats them in a way that is PGC compliant, then the observer's behaviour is morally permissible.
   (ii) If the observer treats them in a way that is *not* PGC compliant, then the observer's behaviour is morally permissible.

The PGC requires us to avoid behaviour which is not compatible with its requirements in all circumstances, meaning that the course of action we are categorically required to avoid in the above scenario is option (a)(ii). If the agential status of the person in question is in anyway uncertain – even minimally so – an agent is required to treat them in a way that is PGC compliant as this is the only way to guarantee that the agent avoids course of action (a)(ii). The PGC thus requires us to see all beings who could conceivably be agents – hereafter prospective agents – as being of moral concern, and as being covered by its imperative.

Being a prospective agent is thus sufficient for us to see the individual in question as being of moral concern, and we ought to guard against mistakenly treating them as though they were non-agents 'to the extent that it is possible and meaningful for agents to do so'.[32] This is referred to as the 'Argument for the Sufficiency of Agency'.[33] It could be countered, however, that this claim means that the PGC becomes a categorical imperative – something Gewirth wished to avoid – rather than a moral claim grounded dialectically in universally applicable instrumental reason. This will make many sceptical of the Gewirthian

[32] Beyleveld, 'The Principle of Generic Consistency as the Supreme Principle of Human Rights' (n 23) 10.

[33] Gewirth, *Reason and Morality* (n 1) 110–14.

position given the difficulties involved in presenting objective moral claims to a world that seems – as a matter of social fact – morally pluralist. In order to address this critique, Gewirth argues that it is important to distinguish two different senses in which the term 'moral' is used in different areas of discourse. Positive, or collective, morality concerns itself with rules or directives held as categorically obligatory and is often found in customary ways of acting which are empirically identifiable. By contrast, normative, or critical, morality concerns mind-independent moral precepts, rules or principles that are demonstrably valid and ought to be upheld regardless of whether they are accepted as such. Unlike customary positive moralities, normative precepts exist independently of personal belief and are rationally identifiable through reason. Certain standards of moral rightness, such as the PGC, are simply universally valid; no alternative principles of what is genuinely morally right that conflict with the requirements of the PGC can coexist with its dialectical necessity.[34]

To further insist on collective moral pluralism in light of a critical moral standard such as the PGC entails one of two arguments. Firstly, one may argue that normative morality cannot exist; the only standards are a series of positive, collective moralities as is demonstrable by empirical observation. This can be countered with two main arguments. One could respond to the objection, as Gewirth does, by pointing out that prioritising positive, collective morality, requires us to see cultures as homogenous wholes; this is clearly not the case, as can be observed by the fact of value pluralism within cultures.[35] Or, one could point out that a rejection of critical, normative moral standards such as those provided by the PGC do not meaningfully engage with the argument in favour of seeing them as valid; they merely double down on a pre-existing scepticism without giving any reason as to why the PGC should be rejected:

> The argument depends on the recognition that *action* is the universal and necessary context of all moralities and indeed of all practice. For all positive moralities and other practical precepts, amid their vast differences of specific contents, are concerned, directly or indirectly, with telling persons how they ought to act, especially toward one another. In addition, all persons are actual, prospective or potential agents, and no person can reject for herself the whole context of agency, except, perhaps, by committing suicide; and even then the steps she takes to achieve this purpose would themselves be actions. The general context of action thus transcends the differences of the various positive cultures and moralities.[36]

The second reason for which the PGC might be rejected in favour of an argument for collective moral pluralism may be that the PGC, by appealing to an idealised 'rational' individual, shows that it is itself culturally grounded in western

[34] A Gewirth, 'Is Cultural Pluralism Relevant to Moral Knowledge?' (1994) 11 (1) *Social Philosophy & Policy* 22, 22–24.
[35] ibid 25–26.
[36] ibid 27.

moralities that are more prone to valuing individual rights over those that might exist at the community level. Any moral principle that emerges from it is therefore itself culturally grounded in this western prioritisation, rather than being of a truly neutral and universal value. This point can again be rejected insofar as it does not fully engage with the argument in favour of accepting the PGC and – as with the first objection – merely doubles down on a pre-existing scepticism as to the existence of normative moral standards. It thus demonstrates either a refusal to engage with, or a misunderstanding of, the operation of the dialectically necessary argument for the PGC.[37] Community values are necessarily a product of the choices and acts of individuals acting together, so a community right cannot exist unless we see its purpose as being the protection of the individuals that comprise the community in question. To criticise rights as individualistic therefore misses the point.[38]

A final point should be made at this stage as to the purpose of the test provided by the PGC; that it is not a test of moral obligatoriness. It does not seek to demonstrate that every moral question only has a single possible answer. Rather, it serves as a test for moral permissibility. It is therefore perfectly compatible with the concept of cultural pluralism; cultures and societies are free to engage in practices that diverge significantly from one another and can even raise them to the level of a positive and collective morality. The only thing that is impermissible is for these standards to fall below the line of impermissibility provided by the PGC. And what is true of cultural pluralism is also the case for attempts to apply the PGC to the question of legal validity; as will be shown in section 2.3 of Chapter 3, the PGC is compatible with the pluralism of legal reality.

2.3. Justifying Gewirth's Starting Point

The dialectically necessary progression of the argument requires us to accept its requirements for no other reason than its starting point of the bare agency of its subjects. The success of the enterprise thus rests on the validity of this starting point, and it is this that the final part of the present section will seek to justify. Gewirth's starting point is a simple one: that to be an agent is to act purposefully and voluntarily to bring about a given end. This statement is in accordance with the standard view of what it means to be an agent and was chosen for this purpose. Our default justification for this starting point could therefore be that, though many alternate conceptions of what it means to be an agent have been offered since he first conceptualised the PGC, none have successfully replaced the standard view adopted by Gewirth to become a new, superior understanding

[37] ibid 33-35.
[38] ibid.

of the concept of agency. As such, the view should be accepted as valid in the absence of a viable alternative.[39] If it is a starting point we ought to accept, we can begin to turn to Gewirth's reasons for adopting it: that its very inescapability means it is prima facie capable of grounding any universal principle that would apply to all agents.[40] It seems doubly suitable given that, as moral claims are necessarily connected to the permissibility of a given action, the concept of agency is necessarily engaged in all moral deliberation.[41] It follows from this that, if certain conditions are necessary for our agency, then the principle of instrumental necessity requires us to see that it is *these* conditions that are capable of being universalised. Put in Kantian terms, 'Whoever wills the ends also wills (insofar as reason has decisive influence on his actions) the indispensably necessary means to it that are within his power.'[42] If this point can be proven, then it would follow as a matter of logic that our moral identity is inseparable from our bare agency.[43] It is for this reason that Gewirth identifies bare agency as a suitable and desirable starting point for any attempt to identify a supreme moral principle.

The starting point is one that has pedigree. Like Gewirth, Kant also believed that the authority claimed by moral norms must depend on features that are inherent within rational agents.[44] His Categorical Imperative from the Formula of Universal Law provides a test against which the permissibility of actions is to be assessed: 'Act only according to that maxim through which you can at the same time will that it become a universal law.'[45] For Kant, that practical reason is capable of providing a foundation for the existence of a supreme moral principle is axiomatic: 'One must *be able to will* that a maxim of our action become a universal law: this is as such the canon of judging it *morally*.'[46] Yet such a statement is far from controversial, and its critics hold that it reduces moral judgments to an abstract test that ignores the reality of human existence.[47] Both Kant's categorical imperative and Gewirth's PGC appear to fall within the scope of these criticisms; yet a Kantian would reject both criticisms by noting that

[39] For a comprehensive defence of this standard view of agency, see MS Archer, *Being Human: The Problem of Agency* (Cambridge University Press 2000).

[40] Gewirth, 'The Basis and Content of Human Rights' (n 13) 120; On the unavoidability of agency see: Korsgaard, *Self-Constitution* (n 7) 1.

[41] Gewirth, 'The Basis and Content of Human Rights' (n 13) 124.

[42] Kant (n 26) 4:417. For a deeper analysis of this principle see: K Schaubroeck, 'Legal Normativity and the Instrumental Principle' in S Bertea and G Pavlakos (eds) *New Essays on the Normativity of Law* (Hart 2011) 117.

[43] Korsgaard, *Self-Constitution* (n 7) 42, 129–130.

[44] Kant (n 26) 4:389-90, 4:400, 4:427, 4:442-3.

[45] ibid 4:421.

[46] ibid 4:424.

[47] Mill, for example, thought that any such theory 'fails, almost grotesquely' in reducing moral enquire to logical permissibility. See JS Mill, *Utilitarianism* (R Crisp ed, Oxford University Press 1998) 51–52. See also G Hegel, *Elements of the Philosophy of Right* (HB Nisbet tr, A Wood ed, Cambridge University Press 1991) §135; H Sidgwick, *Methods of Ethics* (7th edn, Macmillan 1907) 379.

they do not properly engage with the central argument behind the argument: that substantive moral verdicts simply *can* be derived from practical reason and formal normative deliberation.[48] To be valid, such moral verdicts must possess three features:

(1) Inescapability, in that their application does not depend on their being convergent with the agent's own interests.
(2) Authority, in that their being requirements of reason renders non-compliance prima facie irrational.
(3) Supremacy, in that they operate to exclude all non-compliant conduct on the ground of irrational contradiction.[49]

This section is designed to show that Gewirth's starting point can lead us to a principle that meets these requirements and should be accepted as valid. Firstly, let us turn to three central principles that are essential to any understanding of the operation of practical reason in order to demonstrate what kind of reason the PGC purports to provide to those against whom it applies. The first is the principle instrumental reason, which holds that an agent has a reason to perform an action that will allow her to attain her ends. This reasoning is sometimes explained through the medium of a hypothetical imperative; if I want to attain E, then I have a reason to do X. The second form of principle within practical reasoning is the principle of prudence, which holds that I always have a reason to do what is in my best interest. This principle can also be expressed through a hypothetical imperative: that if E is in my best interests, then I have a reason to do X. The final principles are moral principles; these take the form of a categorical imperative for the three reasons outlined above, and thus hold that whatever my own subjective E, I must always X.[50] Thus the PGC operates in a way that is analogous to a categorical imperative; it is dialectically necessary that whatever an agent's E, their ability to X means they are required to accept its requirements.[51] And since all three principles of practical reason – including the moral reasons provided by the PGC – operate at the deliberative stage, Gewirth's starting point of bare agency can be seen to be an appropriate starting point for our enquiry.

We can now ask in what sense any directive emerging from this starting point of practical reason and deliberative rationality can be normative. We will begin with a commonly accepted statement of what it means to act rationally: '[T]o be rational is to deliberately conform one's will to certain rational truths, or truths

[48] M Timmons, *Significance and System: Essays on Kant's Ethics* (Oxford University Press 2017) 84.

[49] D Brink, 'Kantian Rationalism: Inescapability, Authority, and Supremacy' in G Cullity and B Gaut (eds) *Ethics and Practical Reason* (Clarendon Press 1997) 255.

[50] ibid 215–218.

[51] ibid 218; D Beyleveld, 'Gewirth versus Kant on Kant's Maxim of Reason: Towards a Gewirthian Philosophical Antropology' in Per Bauhn (ed) *Gewirthian Perspectives on Human Rights* (Routledge 2016) Ch 1.

about reasons, which exist independently of the will.'[52] To follow the directives of practical reason, for this statement, is a rational thing to do. Yet Korsgaard points out that this claim is circular; it does not provide us with any real justification as to why we should act rationally and follow the guidance of our will.[53] This statement might be true of the three main aspects of practical reason above, yet the dialectical necessity of the argument for the PGC, proceeding from the starting point of bare agency, allows it to provide the reason we need to accept its requirements. As noted earlier in the chapter, by rejecting the direction of the PGC, an agent either rejects agency as the foundation of her own rights claim, meaning she is happy to have her GCAs interfered with to the point where no action is possible, or she denies she is an agent at all. Both denials require the agent to use her agency to deny the importance of her agency; a paradox is thus created whereby the criterion whose importance she seeks to deny is essential for the denial to be successful. This paradox demonstrates that the PGC must be accepted by all agents, thus providing the normative reason Korsgaard says is required to act rationally and follow the requirements of instrumental reason.[54] It may be countered that this remains circular; that one is simply restating the rationality of following reasons rather than providing why a normative reason exists to do so.[55] Further, rationality cannot provide these reasons: all that can be created is an infinite regress which fails to address why an agent ought to internalise and comply with the claim that to act rationally and follow reasons is something they ought to do.[56] This objection may succeed against a categorical imperative, but misunderstands the unique claim made by the PGC; the dialectical progression of the argument requires all agents to internalise the principle, as a failure to do so results in the paradox previously outlined. Even if an agent were to reject the PGC by denial of their agential status, this cannot succeed without the use of their agency – thus requiring them to internalise the principle they seek to reject. The unique form of reason thus provided by the PGC not only provides a reason as to why it should be internalised, but also provides an inescapable normative obligation to do so. It thus overcomes the objection and succeeds in demonstrating that the reflective nature of human consciousness is capable of serving as the source of, and solution to, normative dilemmas.[57]

A final and connected objection might be raised based on the ascription of universal scope to the moral principles thus identified. The objection would hold that universalisability can only demonstrate that what is rational for me is to be

[52] Brink (n 49) 218–219.
[53] ibid.
[54] ibid 220.
[55] ibid 240.
[56] ibid 241–242.
[57] C Korsgaard, 'Reflective Endorsement' in O O'Neill (ed) *The Sources of Normativity* (Cambridge University Press 1996) 49–50; T Nagel, 'Universality and the Reflective Self' in O O'Neill (ed) *The Sources of Normativity* (Cambridge University Press 1996) 200.

self-interested, and that subsequently I must agree that you must also view the pursuit of self-interest as rational. If this is at the heart of the moral claim, then it is empty of normative content and is incapable of generating the normativity that has been claimed here.[58] Such a claim, however, appears to be grounded in the assumption that the claims being made regarding the respect of other agents are not necessary, but somehow optional. This is not the case. The PGC demonstrates that it is necessary for all agents to respect the Generic Conditions of Agency possessed by other agents, at risk of contradiction. Such a claim is consistent with the instrumental rationality principle previously defended, and thus is a principle that is capable of generating norms in the way this objection attempts to deny. We should therefore dismiss the objection as being grounded in a misunderstanding of the argument of the PGC, as it is perfectly acceptable to ground the moral permissibility of acts in a test of universalisation that itself relies on the general requirement of following instrumental hypothetical imperatives.[59] Since this is the foundation of the PGC, we can accept it as a valid test by which to identify moral norms as the Kantian notion of agency upon which it is built holds that agents are able to 'transform contingent values into necessary ones by valuing the humanity that is their source.'[60] Since the PGC provides a dialectically necessary rather than an optional reason to do this, our conclusions as to its universal applicability as a moral standard are sound.

3. PHILOSOPHICAL CRITICISMS OF THE PGC

Before the defence of the PGC can begin, it is worth reminding ourselves of two distinct types of moral claim. Positive, or collective, moral claims are those that are practice dependent, insofar they can be identified by asking what moral rules a given society accept as valid. Yet this thesis is concerned with normative, or critical morality; those moral principles which can be demonstrated to be philosophically sound regardless of their acceptance by a population. The two may overlap, but it is only the latter which is capable of generating the objective normative claim required for true moral and, for natural lawyers, legal authority. Yet within critical, normative morality, there are a significant number of mutually exclusive theories that each claim to have identified a universal test for the moral permissibility of all action. We must therefore justify why we seek to identify the PGC as our preferred point of moral reference rather than any other theory. The remainder of this chapter will therefore introduce various theories which could be used to attack the validity of the claim to dialectical necessity made by the PGC. It will show that none are capable of rebutting the argument

[58] C Korsgaard, 'Reply' in O O'Neill (ed) *The Sources of Normativity* (Cambridge University Press 1996) 220.
[59] ibid 231.
[60] ibid 240.

or its conclusions, and that the PGC should therefore be accepted as a supreme moral principle that is capable of providing a universal test for the moral permissibility of all action.

3.1. Bernard Williams

The first thinker upon whom our spotlight will turn will be Bernard Williams. Williams is well known for reviving Aristotelian conceptions of the good life in modern analytic philosophy, and his belief that the only ethical belief that might survive the challenge of reflective endorsement put forward in our previous chapter would be the claim that 'that a certain kind of life was the best for human beings.'[61] Note first that, by his own admission, this claim is devoid of any substantive content that lets us know what kind of life *is* best for human beings. He would therefore likely be sceptical of the claim to universality present within the PGC. This is not to say that Williams is dismissive of claims of moral truth; on the contrary, he believes that the very fact of moral disagreement presupposes that a correct answer to moral problems does exist. Were there no correct answer, he suggests a moral disagreement would be exactly the same as two men on a boat – one of whom is seasick and one who isn't – disagreeing as to the merits of ocean travel. The fact that moral statements necessarily contain a truth claim and do not merely reflect the speaker's own attitude sets them apart from subjective perceptions such as this.[62] Williams' position should therefore be seen as one which recognises that critical, normative morality exists – but that it is practically impossible to discern its requirements to a degree where they were seen as uncontroversial. It is for this reason that he would be inclined to subject the PGC to scrutiny.

Williams' first objection might be to criticise the formalism of the PGC; that the level of abstraction taking place in the identification and application of such a test robs the agent to whom it should apply of the subjective features necessary for a meaningful standard of moral deliberation.[63] Any formal, impartial principle is simply too impersonal and, by extension, is unrealistic given the personal interaction necessary for moral deliberation to take place:

> Of course, in general a man does not have one separable project which plays this ground role: rather, there is a nexus of projects, related to his condition of life, and it would be the loss of all or most of them that would remove meaning.[64]

In locating individual actions in the abstract and removing them from the personal context in which they arise, Williams suggests we are no longer

[61] B Williams, *Ethics and the Limits of Philosophy* (Fontana 1993) 154.
[62] B Williams, *Morality: An Introduction to Ethics* (Cambridge University Press 1972) 29–30.
[63] B Williams, *Moral Luck* (Cambridge University Press 1981) 4.
[64] ibid 13.

undertaking something that can be recognised as realistic moral deliberation. The moral project exists to give direction and meaning to life and must therefore necessarily reflect the lived experience.[65] Abstraction thus undermines the entire enterprise. To give an example of the subjective experience he considers essential for moral deliberation, Williams suggests that it is an incontrovertible fact that individuals gain attachments to other agents over the course of their lives. Given it seems natural that one would be inclined to behave more sympathetically to a close friend or family member than to somebody seen in a neutral or negative light, Williams argues that to claim that moral deliberation can take place in the abstract is to deny value in lived human existence and should be rejected.[66] This objection is powerful, but does not engage on a substantive level with the normative argument presented by the PGC. Williams' point is an example of collective morality; an empirical account of how agents interact with one another based on their subjective preferences. This is a different meaning of what it means to act morally than that which is the focus of the argument for the PGC, and presents a standard which cannot be assessed for its normative validity. Since the two enquiries are qualitatively different, Williams' attack does not hit its target and should be rejected.

Williams might contend that this is exactly the point – that morality is not something which lends itself well to critical analysis such as that which forms the basis of the Gewirthian project. Yet it is difficult to see how this rejection can be reconciled with Williams' own observation that moral disagreement is suggestive of moral truth;[67] if moral truth is something which exists, then a tool must exist for its identification. Any such test for moral permissibility must necessarily be impartial in order to be universally acceptable to all, necessitating the level of agential abstraction employed by Gewirth in choosing to construct his argument for the PGC from the inescapable fact of human agency. Reasons provided by such a test for the permissibility of action must necessarily be internalised by the agent to provide a reason for them to act,[68] which requires the agent to apply it to a particular motivation for action.[69] And since the PGC applies to all agents, it must be internalised by agents and applied to all conceivable action equally. The internalisation required in order for a principle to exert reason-giving force on an individual that Williams requires is therefore achieved through deliberative reasoning on how to act, thus meeting his own requirements for the internalisation of any reason.[70] He may reject this, arguing that any such internal statement is falsified by 'the absence of an appropriate element from [the agent's motivation],'[71] but as the dialectically necessary reason to

[65] ibid.
[66] ibid 18.
[67] ibid 75.
[68] ibid 101.
[69] ibid 102.
[70] ibid 104.
[71] ibid 102.

comply with the PGC is contained in the fact of bare agency, the only way that the falsification claimed by Williams can exist is if no agent were ever to act ever again. Since agents do act, the internalisation is compliant with Williams' own conception of action – the reasons for which must be internal or no action would take place.[72] In thus locating action on the internal plane, Williams is bound to accept the rules of deliberative rationality that this internalisation requires. He is thus bound to acknowledge the operation of the PGC, or else he misunderstands the nature of action itself.

Williams might suggest that this is but a neat sidestep of the argument he originally raised; that any principles which derive from the abstract level are too imprecise to be applied to moral dilemmas in the real world, and therefore are of no real use to the resolution of moral conflict. In locating morality at the level of practical reason, Gewirth's formula is limited to the production of 'general and formal principles to regulate the shape of relations between rational agents' that are unrealistic in their rigidity.[73] This objection can still be rejected, however, as it is incompatible with Williams' own characterisation of action and the possibility of location value within what it means to be an agent. This can be seen in Williams' belief that all agents necessarily possess a general desire not to have their freedom frustrated. This can be identified in that agents necessarily desire the outcome of their actions as, without this desire, they would possess no reason to act. In Williams' own words: '*[O]mne appetitum appetitur sub specie boni*'; everything pursued is pursued as something by dint of the agent's perception of it as desirable.[74] Agents thus necessarily desire that their actions are not interfered with as, without this, any action would be impossible.[75] This claim is the same as that offered by the PGC, requiring a closer examination of why Williams might reject Gewirth's conclusions.

This rejection can be summarised thus: that our shared starting point, the fact all agents necessarily claim their freedom to act should not be interfered with, does not in itself give an agent a reason to see this as a right. Williams instead characterises the value an agent places on their action as purely pragmatic, and argues formalistic principles are incapable of generating the universalising step necessary to transform this pragmatic claim into a rights-claim.[76] It cannot provide one agent with a coherent reason as to why they should refrain from interfering with others' ability to act. This may seem a clear and coherent position to take, but one need only take it to its logical conclusion in order to show why it is misplaced. This would be that Williams must concede that other agents also do not possess adequate reason to refrain from interfering with his capacity to act – meaning that he would be happy to accept that there is no reason

[72] ibid 107–111.
[73] Williams, *Ethics and the Limits of Philosophy* (n 61) 54–55.
[74] ibid 58.
[75] ibid 56.
[76] ibid 60–61.

why his will could be constantly frustrated by agents who want to ensure he can never achieve any end at all. He would reject this characterisation by arguing that his lack of proscription is not permission for others to interfere, but rather silence on the matter;[77] yet this riposte is clearly unsatisfactory and can be rejected on two connected grounds.

Firstly, in claiming that lack of proscription is not analogous to permission to interfere, Williams in effect asks the interfering agent to decide whether they see a reason to interfere with his capacity to act. Shifting the burden in this way assumes that the agent whose actions might be interfered with would be entirely neutral as to whether their ends are frustrated, thus contradicting Williams' own starting point that all agents necessarily have a pragmatic reason to value that their ability to act remains unimpeded. An agent would clearly be aggrieved if another agent were to frustrate their ends against their will, which is precisely the reason Williams suggests agents see a pragmatic value in their ability to act in the first place. Thus, if Williams wishes to claim that an agent should be neutral as to whether another agent has a reason to frustrate their ends, he must abandon his own starting maxim of '*[O]mne appetitum appetitur sub specie boni*'; to do this would be to abandon the standard view of what it means to be an agent. The objection can therefore be seen to be founded on a mischaracterisation of the very concept of action itself.

A second reason as to why we should reject Williams' claim that a lack of proscription is not the same as permission for others to interfere would take the following form. Even were we to grant that an agent can be disinterested enough in their ends to be neutral as to the desirability of allowing another agent to frustrate them, a decision must still be made as to whether the interference should take place. All Williams has done is shift the burden of assessing the desirability of interference away from the original actor, onto the interfering agent. The interfering agent thus has two options open to them. If she does interfere, she concedes that the principle of non-interference is purely pragmatic and accepts that she also ought to be neutral with regard to whether others are able to legitimately frustrate her ends. If she decides that she ought not to interfere, then she is accepting that her own pragmatic claim would be damaged by her choice to ignore the pragmatic claim made by the original actor. If she decides that she wishes to protect the foundation of her own pragmatic rights claim, she is acting in accordance with the PGC; that if I make a pragmatic claim that I value non-interference with my GCAs because of the fact of my own agency, then all agents necessarily make the same claim. The universalisation Williams is sceptical of has taken place, thus allowing the claim to be legitimately characterised as a right. Williams' objection cannot overcome the argument presented by the PGC and can be rejected.

[77] ibid 62.

Such a conclusion is clearly undesirable for Williams. For although he recognises that moral conflict is indicative of moral truth, he is sceptical about the extent to which rational deliberation can solve ethical dilemmas.[78] This arises from his characterisation of moral deliberation, which begins with the observation that perceived moral obligations frequently *do* conflict.[79] It follows that the conflict must be grounded in options that are perceived as equally valid, otherwise the conflict would be easily resolved and would not exist.[80] Williams thus concludes that a certain degree of moral relativism must exist, meaning that rationality cannot fully identify moral truths.[81] If this conclusion is true, the PGC necessarily fails. The claim must therefore be explored further to test its validity. Williams' scepticism is connected to his belief that acts can never be concretely linked to a given end due to the inherent uncertainty which exists in the world. Luck inevitably plays a role in the ability of an individual to successfully execute their will; yet the nature of luck means that individuals cannot predict whether it will operate in a given situation. If luck cannot be planned for in the execution of our actions,[82] one can never adequately predict whether our actions will lead to a given end. This introduces a level of arbitrariness and indeterminacy in all action, which in turn makes deliberation ultimately arbitrary and indeterminate itself. It follows that if one cannot adequately predict the outcome of an action, then one cannot use reason and rationality to assess whether the outcome is morally permissible. Reason and rationality thus cannot ground moral norms. Williams would here find an ally in Hannah Arendt, who similarly argues that the unknowability of whether our ends will ultimately be attained both renders our desires imprecise and uncertain and renders the will incapable of generating normative claims.[83] These statements seem sound, but do not succeed when directed at the claim made by the PGC. This is because they express a scepticism grounded in causation and the ability of an end to be realised, rather than in the rational formulation of the end itself. The PGC operates at the level of desire formulation at the level of deliberative rationality itself, not at the stage of the attempted execution of the will. Moral obligations thus arise at the conception of the will, not at its execution as characterised by Williams and Arendt in the above objections. The criticism is therefore not engaging substantively with the argument for the PGC and can be rejected. Agency and rationality can, as shown by Gewirth, be used to identify binding moral norms capable of resolving moral conflicts.

This subsection has attempted to demonstrate that Williams' scepticism with regard to the ability of rationality to identify moral norms is misplaced.

[78] Williams, *Moral Luck* (n 63) 75.
[79] ibid 125.
[80] ibid 139.
[81] ibid 142.
[82] ibid 26.
[83] Hannah Arendt, *The Human Condition* (2nd edn, University of Chicago Press 1998) 230–232.

It is either founded on a mischaracterisation of the arguments that do make this claim, or relies on a differing conception of what is meant by the term 'moral' that prioritises the empirical observation of collective belief over sound normative arguments. Not only do these positions not engage substantively with the argument for the PGC, but both also operate on assumptions that instead presuppose that the starting point of bare agency, from which the PGC is derived, is itself legitimate. In thus accepting the PGC's starting point, Williams ought to accept its conclusion. His scepticism is ultimately concerned with doubt,[84] and the argument for the PGC can satisfy this doubt by providing rationally inescapable justification for its practical applicability.[85] If Williams is to stand by his own view of what it means for a demand to be rationally inescapable, that it is 'one that a rational agent must accept if he is to be a rational agent,'[86] then he should accept the PGC as valid.

3.2. Nietzsche

Many view Nietzsche as the ultimate moral sceptic, and it is for this reason that the ability of the PGC to overcome the Nietzschean position will be addressed. His position begins from a subjective characterisation of the good, in which he argues that the concept of 'value' is only good insofar as it allows us to preserve a certain type of life.[87] By extension, something can only be of moral value if it helps the agent preserve a certain type of life that they see as valuable: '[A person's] morality which provides decidedly and decisively *who he is* – that is, in what hierarchy the innermost drives of his nature are arranged.'[88] Morality is thus necessarily reflective of a person's subjective priorities arising from their own lived experiences, meaning moral norms are themselves subjective insofar as they are dependent on the value preferences of the agent. Thus, an agent only has reason to accept a moral principle if to do so would further their own subjective interests.[89]

This subjective position appears incompatible with the claim that the PGC serves as a test for the moral permissibility of all action, regardless of the preferences of the individual agent. This section will argue that this need not be the case, and that the PGC is actually compatible with Nietzsche's characterisation of the bindingness of moral obligations. This becomes apparent when one accepts that Nietzsche is best regarded as an ethical naturalist; he holds that

[84] B Williams, 'Ethics and the Fabric of the World' in T Honderich (ed), *Morality and Objectivity: A Tribute to JL Mackie* (New York University Press 1981) 204.

[85] B Williams, 'History, Morality, and the Test of Reflection' in O O'Neill (ed) *The Sources of Normativity* (Cambridge University Press 1996) 213.

[86] Williams, 'Ethics and the Fabric of the World' (n 84) 206.

[87] F Nietzsche, *Beyond Good and Evil* (Marion Faber tr, Oxford University Press 1998) para 3.

[88] ibid para 6.

[89] ibid para 188.

moral principles can be identified *if* they are correlated to pre-ethical facts of those who espouse them.[90] The PGC does precisely this by correlating its requirements to facts that are pre-ethical for all agents: the very fact of their agency itself, and the pragmatic value they must place on their GCAs to undertake any action whatsoever. By thus identifying a pre-ethical fact that is necessarily valuable for all agents regardless of their subjective preferences Gewirth has shown that the PGC's requirements should be accepted by all agents, as only by doing so can an agent ensure that they are able to further their own subjective interests. On Nietzsche's own terms, then, it can legitimately claim moral authority over all agents and can be used to suppress non-compliant actions.[91] It can also do so whilst maintaining Nietzsche's commitment to value pluralism. It is perfectly acceptable for collective moral claims to be made by a society or an individual, provided these requirements are themselves compatible with the PGC. Its requirements are not a ceiling, but a floor – and any and all action is permissible provided it does not fall below the requirements of this critical test for moral permissibility. Nietzsche's conception of value pluralism does not, therefore, damage the validity of the PGC.

Nietzsche would likely object to this suggestion given that he downplays the possibility of identifying moral norms through use of practical reason, characterising it as 'a scheme that we cannot throw off' that places excessive importance on impersonal, formalistic principles that are not reflective of real-world moral deliberation.[92] This can be rejected for two reasons. Firstly, the claim belies the fact that Nietzsche is conflating collective and critical moral claims and is thus directed against a straw-man characterisation of the claim being made by the PGC. Pluralism is possible, provided it does not directly undermine the agent's dialectically necessary interests – something that Nietzsche ought to accept. Secondly, the claim highlights a logical paradox in Nietzsche's own project. If Nietzsche rejects reliance on formal principles of rationality and logic as being essentially interpretive and incapable of grounding truth claims, then we have no reason to accept his conclusions on his own terms. For we can presume that in writing his thesis, Nietzsche was concerned with discerning and communicating concepts that he believed to be *true*; were this not the case, then he would not have put pen to paper as his attempt would have been dismissible as merely subjective belief. The very fact that Nietzsche wrote his claims down is an exercise that relies on rational justification in order to advance a truth claim.[93] Thus, if Nietzsche's claim that rationality is merely one of many possible interpretations possessing no independent value, then this very claim can itself be dismissed as either paradoxical or void. A Nietzschean objection to the PGC necessarily fails.

[90] S May, *Nietzsche's Ethics and his War on 'Morality'* (Clarendon Press 1999) 10.
[91] Nietzsche, *Beyond Good and Evil* (n 87) para 220.
[92] F Nietzsche, *The Will to Power* (W Kaufman and RJ Hollingdale tr, Vintage 1968) para 522.
[93] May (n 90) 139–49.

3.3. Friedman and Foot

Having shown that the PGC ought to be accepted by the sceptical positions endorsed by both Williams and Nietzsche, this chapter moves on to consider two further arguments that might be raised. We will firstly turn to a general criticism of the structure of the dialectical argument of the PGC presented by Richard Friedman, who argues that the argument for the PGC mistakenly conflates an argument based on dialectical necessity with one of rational choice.[94] He argues that the dialectical necessity of an argument does not necessarily make it one that a rational agent would accept, asking why an agent should claim her rights are grounded in logical necessity over other grounds that she may be more inclined to endorse.[95] This argument fails on its own terms. Firstly, and purely pragmatically, Friedman does not present a convincing reason why an agent would *not* want to endorse a claim that her rights were logically necessary, given that the alternative would be that her rights were contingent or could be otherwise disregarded. Since the argument for the PGC shows that an agent necessarily values her rights by the fact she is an agent, this alternative is one that she should be motivated to avoid if she wishes to undertake any action at all. She therefore has a strong reason to endorse a rights claim grounded in logical necessity. Secondly, the argument fails for a misunderstanding of the scope of the PGC. An agent could conclude that the argument is not one she wishes to accept or endorse and concedes that she does prefer an alternative grounding for her rights claim. Yet in so doing she uses the GCAs whose importance she seeks to deny, thus showing that agential will is not, in itself, enough to deny the truism that, by acting, she is acknowledging the importance of these rights to her agential status. Friedman's critique therefore does not address the fact that, in rejecting the dialectically necessary argument, the agent is using the agency whose importance she attempts to deny. The rejection is a logical contradiction and fails accordingly.

Having addressed this methodological concern, we can now move to address Philippa Foot's scepticism as to the possible existence of any categorical imperative. Whilst happy to accept that moral norms can take the form of a hypothetical imperative, in that they are contingent on a particular desire or action, she believes that it is practically impossible to identify a categorical imperative given that this would require proof of an overriding constraint. She uses the example of rules of etiquette to demonstrate the difficulty in establishing categorical claims;[96] we make normative claims when discussing demands of etiquette, yet their bindingness remains hypothetical in that it is contingent on

[94] RB Friedman, 'The Basis of Human Rights: A Criticism of Gewirth's Theory' in JR Pennock and JW Chapman (eds), *Human Rights – Nomos XXIII* (New York University Press 1981) 150.
[95] ibid 152–153.
[96] P Foot, 'Morality as a System of Hypothetical Imperatives' (1972) 81(3) *The Philosophical Review* 305, 308.

us wishing to be seen to comply.[97] Moral claims, she argues, behave in a similar way – their claims only possess normative character insofar as we care about being moral agents:

> The fact is that the man who rejects morality because he sees no reason to obey its rules can be convicted of villainy but not of inconsistency. Nor will his action necessarily be irrational.[98]

For this reason, Foot would be sceptical about the claim that the PGC necessarily acts as a test for the moral permissibility of call action. This is a similar claim to one made by David Enoch later in this chapter, so the full range of objections will not be addressed here. Two rebuttals specific to Foot's position will instead be presented. The first takes the following form: that based on her own characterisation of moral deliberation, Foot ought to accept Gewirth's argument as sound. She accepts that the circumstances in which an action is undertaken are relevant for its moral permissibility:

> [T]he moral character of an action is on occasion affected by the position of the agent on the causal nexus; by the fact that he is on the one hand the initiating agent of a sequence or happening, or by contrast merely one who does not intervene.[99]

She thus accepts that the capacity of an agent to act, and the circumstances in which they do so, are relevant considerations when assessing the moral permissibility of a given act. Foot therefore accepts that questions around the moral permissibility of action are raised within the process of deliberation and are thus questions of practical reason. Her starting point for moral deliberation is therefore the same as Gewirth's and, given the dialectically necessity of the argument for the PGC from this shared starting point of agency, she ought to accept its conclusion.

We may, here, turn to a second arena of Foot's scepticism: that the claim made by the PGC appears to be a categorial imperative, rather than one that is purely hypothetical and contingent on a particular desire or action. As noted previously, Foot believes that moral claims are necessarily hypothetical in that they are contingent on certain facts – meaning that any imperative claiming to be categorical must be rejected. This argument does not apply to the PGC because, as previously addressed, it is not a true categorical imperative; rather, it behaves in a way analogous to one in that it is dialectically necessary that when an agent desires E, their ability to X requires they accept its requirements. Foot's scepticism as to the possibility of a categorical imperative is thus entirely compatible with an acceptance of the PGC.

[97] ibid 309.

[98] ibid 310.

[99] P Foot, 'Morality, Action and Outcome' in T Honderich (ed), *Morality and Objectivity: A Tribute to J. L. Mackie* (New York University Press 1981) 25.

3.4. Enoch

The final sceptic to be addressed in this part of the chapter will be David Enoch, who would claim that the PGC fails because it assumes an agent should care about their agential status; if an agent does not care that non-compliance would contradict the fact of their own agency, then they have no reason to comply with the PGC. This argument will be shown to be misguided, but before this can take place, an account of Enoch's views on the nature of morality is required to contextualise his objection. He is a moral realist who believes that moral norms require us to reject morally impermissible behaviour.[100] Like Williams, he sees the existence of moral dilemmas as evidence that normative facts exist; if this were not the case, there would be no dilemma as it would not matter which outcome was chosen.[101] Such facts require an epistemic justification, and this must ultimately be grounded in our capacity to formulate a belief about the permissibility of a given action.[102] Enoch thus locates assessments as to the moral permissibility of all action within the broader context of deliberative reasoning: meaning for Enoch, moral reasoning is carried out by the agent when deciding on whether they ought to act in a given way. He thus accepts that, if reasoning is an inescapable feature of our existence, moral discourse is equally inescapable.[103] He also accepts that the fact of moral deliberation presupposes normative reasons that necessarily bear on this deliberation; and that as such deliberation is an inescapable feature of what it means to be an agent, all agents must commit themselves to seeing acceptance of the result of this deliberation as non-optional.[104] To argue otherwise is, for Enoch, prima facie irrational:

> (1) If something is instrumentally indispensable to an intrinsically indispensable project, then we are (epistemically) justified (for that very reason) in believing that that thing exists.
> (2) The deliberative project is intrinsically indispensable.
> (3) Irreducibly normative truths are instrumentally indispensable to the deliberative project.
> (4) Therefore, we are epistemically justified in believing that there are irreducibly normative truths.[105]

Up to this point, Enoch is entirely in agreement with Gewirth's own characterisation of moral deliberation and the bindingness of the outcome; both seem to accept that the inescapability of agency means that agents are committed to recognising the existence of irreducibly normative truths that restrict the scope of permissible action.

[100] D Enoch, *Taking Morality Seriously* (Oxford University Press 2011) 23–24.
[101] ibid 50.
[102] ibid 60.
[103] ibid 63–64.
[104] ibid 61.
[105] ibid 83.

The first indication of a difference in their position is in Enoch's claim that some tests for the permissibility of action are non-moral in nature, and that an imperative to behave rationally is one of these.[106] As compliance with the PGC is a rational requirement for all agents, Enoch would therefore deny that it can be characterised as a moral in character. This denial can only be fully understood if we examine his earlier work, in which he outlines his scepticism more fully. He again accepts that the inescapabilty of agency means that deliberation is central to our existence; and that this inescapability means that any reasons for action that are grounded in in agential deliberation must be seen as a priori universal in their application as opposed to dependent on subjective desires.[107] But Enoch goes on to question why breaching such a principle ought to bother an agent; if agency is inescapable, then it would not be affected by the agent choosing to act in a way that would – as a matter of logic – contradict or otherwise undermine this status. Choosing to act in such a way would therefore have no practical consequences for the agent, meaning that they have no compelling reason to see such a requirement as making a normative claim that they ought to respect.[108]

A preliminary objection could be raised here that Enoch's claim could be applied to all moral codes. Regardless of the nature of the moral code, it is not the practical difference that breaching it would have on the individual that should direct them to follow its requirements. Rather, it is the normative direction provided by the principle itself. By emphasising the consequences of non-compliance, Enoch is conflating the existence of a moral principle with the outcome of having breached it, and obscuring the existence of real normative obligations that he himself accepts can be grounded in rational deliberation. Yet we will grant the singular focus of his objection as exclusively applicable to moral principles derived from agency *arguendo*. This is because Enoch anticipates three possible replies to his position that could be made by advocates of such agent-derived moralities and undertakes to show why each of these does not overcome his objection. If the theory advanced by this book is to succeed, it must therefore be demonstrated why his dismissal of agent-derived moralities cannot overcome the argument for the PGC.

Firstly, Enoch suggests that those who might defend agent-derived moralities would argue that the moral principle in question is normatively valid purely because it is constitutive of agency itself; and given the inescapability of agency, any moral principles derived from it are non-arbitrary and normatively valid. This is the claim made by the PGC – that the necessity of our GCAs for all action means that we must necessarily see them as rights; that the fact this claim is derived from the inescapable fact of our agency means that all agents must be equally capable of making the same claim; and that if all agents are capable

[106] ibid 94.

[107] D Enoch, 'Agency, Shmagency: Why Normativity Won't Come from What Is Constitutive of Action' (2006) 115 (2) *The Philosophical Review* 169, 174.

[108] ibid 178–81.

of making the same claim, we have a reason to respect this claim otherwise we undermine our own claim to the importance of our own GCAs. Enoch would reject this position, simply by asking why the fact that a principle is constitutive of agency renders it non-arbitrary.[109] This dismissal should be rejected, in that it does not engage with the argument being presented to the contrary; he merely repeats his original sceptical claim as if an alternative argument had never been made. The reason why such principles possess non-arbitrary normative value is because one must necessarily accept the claim if one is to undertake any deliberation as to the desirability of action whatsoever. Since Enoch accepts in his later work that deliberative reasoning is capable of producing normative claims if the norm is 'instrumentally indispensable to an intrinsically indispensable project',[110] he ought to endorse the validity of the argument for the PGC. The objection can be dismissed.

The second defence of agent-derived moralities anticipated by Enoch is the claim that we should care if we act in a way which rejects the importance of our own conditions of agency, as it is axiomatic that they do matter to us. Again, this claim is central to the PGC, and is dismissed by Enoch with the claim that it is far from clear that agents do value these conditions.[111] Enoch's argument against the PGC can again be rejected in that, rather than engaging with the argument being made, it merely restates his original claim. In choosing to act, an agent necessarily must value the conditions which allow her to do so as, without these conditions, she would be unable to act. These conditions are again 'instrumentally indispensable to an intrinsically indispensable project',[112] and, as such, are capable of generating legitimate normative claims on Enoch's own understanding of the nature of such claims. Enoch's objection is, again, demonstrably false.

The third and final defence of agent-derived moralities anticipated by Enoch is connected to the second, in the claim that agency as a concept is self-vindicating; reason is therefore unavoidable, and important for an agent to protect. This claim is one that is also made by Gewirth's argument for the PGC, and it is one that Enoch again disputes by suggesting that it is perfectly legitimate for a sceptic to use logic to avoid accepting a logical necessity.[113] The fallacy within this claim can be seen if one were to swap the word 'logic' for 'paint'; doing so demonstrates that Enoch's claim is directly analogous to a painter using paint to demonstrate that paint is not essential for the act of painting. Such a statement is clearly absurd. The objection thus fails for the same reason as the previous two arguments advanced by Enoch: agency is 'instrumentally indispensable to

[109] ibid 181.
[110] Enoch, *Taking Morality Seriously* (n 100) 83.
[111] Enoch, 'Agency, Shmagency' (n 107) 182.
[112] Enoch, *Taking Morality Seriously* (n 100) 83.
[113] Enoch, 'Agency, Shmagency' (n 107) 184.

an intrinsically indispensable project'[114] and can generate legitimate normative claims on Enoch's own depiction of the concept.

As all three objections fail, we can conclude that, based on Enoch's own understanding of what features of practical reason can generate legitimate normative claims, the argument for the PGC is successful. Yet he does have one final line of argument that needs to be addressed: that principles such as the PGC do not apply universally to all agents, but instead apply contingently on their acceptance. Enoch draws the analogy with a game of chess; as one only has a reason to accept the rules of game of chess if one has a reason to play chess, an agent need only value her GCAs, and thus accept the moral constraints of the PGC, if she sees a reason to be an agent. The necessity of the situation is irrelevant as, in the same way that one could play chess disinterestedly and not care about the pursuit being undertaken, one could equally be a disinterested agent.[115] This analogy fails for three reasons. Firstly, the very fact that Enoch's disinterested chess player is playing chess at all suggests that they still have a reason to play; were this not the case, they simply would not be playing. Yet Enoch accepts that whether an agent wishes to be an agent is not a relevant consideration in the same way, as agency is an inescapable fact. Thus, the demands of the PGC are unavoidable whereas playing chess can be avoided. Secondly, the claim that one could be a disinterested agent in a way that is analogous to disinterestedly playing chess cannot be supported, as even a disinterested agent remains an agent. By choosing to act disinterestedly an agent is still making use of – and must necessarily place value upon – their GCAs. It is thus impossible to be a disinterested agent in the manner suggested by Enoch. His final objection is that an agent could accept that to breach the requirements of the PGC would contradict their own agency, but that the agent could re-categorise them as a non-agent (or 'shmagent') to avoid their agential duties. This semantic change does not overcome normative reality; the concept being conveyed by the two terms is the same, in the same way as 'the snow is white' has the same meaning as 'der Schnee ist weiß'. An agent remains an agent regardless of their self-classification; as previously acknowledged by Enoch, our agency and the norms that can be derived from it are inescapable.[116] The objection therefore fails.

Enoch's denial that the PGC is incapable of providing moral norms has therefore been demonstrated to be false, based largely on his own acceptance of the importance of practical reason in identifying valid normative restraints on action. This chapter now moves on to address two paradigmatic theories of legal positivism, to demonstrate that they are incapable of grounding the normative claim necessarily made by law unless all legal rules that emerge are morally permissible with reference to the PGC.

[114] Enoch, *Taking Morality Seriously* (n 100) 83.
[115] Enoch, 'Agency, Shmagency' (n 107) 185–86.
[116] Enoch, *Taking Morality Seriously* (n 100) 63–64.

4. CONCLUSION

This chapter has sought to establish the argument for the PGC is sound. It has been shown that an inescapable Kantian conception of the person is the foundation on which instrumental reasons to act, which are the starting point of the PGC, are universalisable to all agents. If this is true, then the PGC can ground normative obligations with its requirement to respect the GCAs necessarily claimed by all agents as rights in the fact of the bare agency of the agent. It then defended this position against the sceptical positions taken by Bernard Williams, concluding that his scepticism as to the validity of the principle is misguided and based on mischaracterisations of the dialectically necessary argument. The same has been shown to be true for Nietzsche, Friedman, Foot and Enoch. In the absence of any valid philosophical objections to the contrary, the PGC should therefore be seen to be capable of acting as a supreme moral principle that is properly grounded in practical reason. Having undertaken this philosophical defence, Chapter 2 of this work can move on to show why the directive provided by the PGC necessarily sits at the top of a unified hierarchy of reasons for action – and thus provides a stronger reason for action than all non-PGC compliant legal directives.

2

The PGC in Raz's Hierarchy of Reasons

1. INTRODUCTION

HAVING UNDERTAKEN THIS philosophical defence, Chapter 2 of this work moves on to show why the directive provided by the PGC necessarily sits at the top of a unified hierarchy of reasons for action – and thus provides a stronger reason for action than non-PGC compliant legal rules. It will do so using the framework of reasons present in the work of Joseph Raz, whose account has been chosen given his commitment to the legal positivist claim that the moral permissibility of a rule is not a necessary condition of its legal validity. If it can be shown that the PGC necessarily sits at the top of a Razian hierarchy of reasons for action, then his own commitment to legal positivism – and that of others influenced by his work – will be open to question. Firstly, we shall explore Raz's ideas of what it means to undertake action at all, with specific focus on how reasons impact our decisions as to what course of action we ought to take. This will lead into a discussion of Raz's conception of normativity, and the extent to which the guidance provided by normative reasons differs from that provided by non-normative reasons for action. Once any differences between the strength of such reasons have been identified, the chapter will conclude with an overview of Raz's account of how these competing reasons form a hierarchy of deliberative rationality so as to indicate to an agent which, out of many conflicting reasons for action, should be the one upon which she decides to act. It will be shown that Raz's account of reasons requires him to accept that the PGC is valid, and, as such, must sit at the top of any hierarchy of reasons for action for his theory of action to remain internally consistent.

However, before this substantive engagement can take place, we must acknowledge that Raz has elsewhere attempted to dismiss the argument for the PGC. The reasons he provides should themselves be rejected insofar as they do not constitute a serious engagement with the Gewirthian position.[1] Raz begins his attempted dismissal by focusing on what he claims to be the Gewirth's ultimate stated goal: to identify the existence of universally applicable human rights.

[1] J Raz, 'Human Rights Without Foundations' in S Besson and J Tasioulas (eds) *The Philosophy of International Law* (Oxford University Press 2010).

Raz comments that the claim that we can possess rights for no other reason than our status as human beings has 'long been recognised to be logically flawed'.[2] This point can be rejected outright for two reasons. Firstly, and most damningly, Raz has incorrectly framed the quotation he engages with as a statement of the Gewirthian position, rather than a question that Gewirth originally posed in his preface to Chapter One of *Human Rights*:

> We may assume, as true by definition, that human rights are rights that all persons have simply insofar as they are human. But are there any such rights? How, if at all, do we know what they are? What is their scope or content, and how are they related to one another? Are any of them absolute, or may each of them be overridden in certain circumstances?[3]

The full quotation thus shows us that what Raz frames as a statement of the Gewirthian position is actually a statement of scepticism with regards to the enterprise. Secondly, even had this statement been an accurate representation of the Gewirthian position rather than a misquote upon which Raz built a straw man, Raz does not give any reasons at all as to why the argument for the PGC is logically flawed. He merely states that it is. Nowhere in the essay does he actually engage substantively with the Gewirthian position; instead, he chooses to criticise general features he believes traditional theories justifying the existence of human rights can be seen to possess:

1. Human Rights are derived from a basic feature possessed by humans which is necessary to all value in human life.
2. Human Rights claim to be basic moral rights.
3. Traditional theories pay too little attention to the difference between the status of a claim as being valuable and its being a right.
4. Traditional theories are individualistic in nature and pay too little attention to the existence of community rights.[4]

Raz suggests that such theories necessarily fail because of a conflation around what it means to value something and it being claimed as a right.[5] In this vein, he suggests that Gewirth 'ignores [the] possibility of believing that certain conditions are essential to our life, and even of striving to secure such conditions, without either claiming or having a right to them.'[6] Unhelpfully for his argument, he neither provides examples of what such conditions might be nor successfully demonstrates why Gewirth's extensive defence of the claim that our GCAs must necessarily be seen as rights is incorrect.[7] He instead claims that

[2] ibid 323.

[3] A Gewirth, *Human Rights: Essays on Justification and Applications* (University of Chicago Press 1982) 41.

[4] Raz, 'Human Rights Without Foundations' (n 1) 323.

[5] ibid.

[6] ibid 324.

[7] See section 2.1 of Chapter 1.

our GCAs are not essential for action in the way claimed by Gewirth by raising the example of slavery: the fact that slaves are still capable of exercising agency is, Raz claims, evidence that freedom is not a necessary condition of human purposive action.[8] This claim can be rejected on the grounds that Raz is adopting a different definition of freedom to Gewirth. Gewirth argues that freedom requires an agent to act both purposively and voluntarily;[9] the fact that Raz's slave might not be acting voluntarily in their actions means that they are not necessarily free at all in the sense envisaged by Gewirth. Furthermore, the fact that Raz's slave lacks the capacity to act freely in this way is precisely the point being made by Gewirth; that the forcible restriction of freedom is the reason why we ought to see slavery as impermissible. Raz has thus erected a straw man rather than engage with the substantive point with which he takes issue. He has therefore given no valid reason as to why we ought to reject the dialectical necessity of the PGC and the conclusions that flow from it.

2. RAZ ON THE NATURE OF REASONS

If the Gewirthian position is correct, the simple statement of 'I do *X* for purpose *E*'[10] requires us to accept that the PGC, as a supreme moral principle, must sit at the top of any hierarchy of reasons for action in order for any subsequent theory of legal authority to remain coherent. It is for this reason that the present chapter begins from this starting point; if an agent acts in order to attain a purpose *E*, how does Raz believe reasons compete to influence an agent's decision to attain *E* in the first place? He was correct to note in his early work that, in ordinary conversation, agents very rarely state that a single reason exists for a course of action; it is more common to state several reasons to act for a given end, dictated by pragmatic considerations such as the nature and scope of the end in question.[11] He suggests that a complete, perfect reason for agent p to undertake action x (R(Φ)p, x) only exists if the same reason exists for agent q to y (R(Φ) q, y).[12] Raz argues these perfect reasons are extremely rare if not impossible, as even a reason that trumps all other reasons cannot exist in isolation: it must necessarily defeat a conflicting reason, thus requiring a second, weaker reason to exist in order for it to be discarded. From this observation, Raz concludes that reasons for action are not clear cut and frequently – if not always – conflict.

We could infer from this that Raz may also be sceptical of the simplicity of the first step of the argument for the PGC: that if an agent must *X* for

[8] Raz, 'Human Rights Without Foundations' (n 1) 324.

[9] A Gewirth, *Reason and Morality* (University of Chicago Press 1978) 27–37.

[10] D Beyleveld, *The Dialectical Necessity of Morality; An Analysis and Defense of Alan Gewirth's Argument to the Principle of Generic Consistency* (University of Chicago Press 1991) 14.

[11] J Raz *Practical Reason and Norms* (2nd edn Oxford University Press 1999) 22.

[12] ibid 24.

purpose *E*, this renders the desire of attaining *E* the ultimate reason for her to *X*. The purpose of this section is therefore to examine Raz's writing on the nature of reasons to ascertain whether Gewirth's starting point is one he ought to accept. It will do so by first considering the problem of whether false beliefs are capable of being valid reasons for action before moving on to discuss Raz's conception of differing types of reasons. This is necessary to identify the logical foundation of Raz's work on how conflict between reasons for action are resolved that will be discussed later in the chapter.

2.1. Reasons Founded on False Belief

Bruno Celano invites us to consider the following scenario: 'If John takes an umbrella because he believes it will rain, is the reason for his taking it his belief it will rain or the fact it will rain?'[13] This raises a reasonable point with regards to the Gewirthian project: to what extent an individual can be truly said to perform action *X* for purpose *E* if their desire to attain *E* is founded on a false belief, instead of upon an objective fact. Raz is equally aware of this problem, and suggests that to ground action upon belief rather than fact may affect the validity of the reason for which the action is taken. He does this by approaching the problem from the opposite direction to Celano, noting that the fact an agent is unaware that a reason to *X* exists does not mean that they have no reason to *X*; they may have a strong reason to *X*, albeit one about which they are unaware.[14]

Celano suggests that, taken to its logical conclusion, this statement commits Raz to the claim that an objective fact would trump a mistaken belief as a reason for action even if the agent were unaware of the truism in question – and that this demonstrates that Raz is mischaracterising how agents normally behave. He suggests that Raz's claim cannot account for the clear connection that exists, in ordinary agential action, between reason statements (I have a reason to Φ)[15] and judgements of practical rationality (my Φ-ing was rational). Celano concludes that, because agents tend to believe there is a connection between reason statements and those of practical rationality, agential beliefs around their perception of their circumstances are more likely to act as reasons for action rather than true facts about which they may or may not be aware.[16] This does seem like a more accurate account of how agents choose to act; it seems unrealistic to claim, as Raz does, that an agent ought to accept that a reason for action that she is unaware of overrides the reason for action, albeit founded in mistaken belief, that they do accept.[17] This does not seem to be how agents behave; rather,

[13] B Celano 'Are Reasons for Action Beliefs' in LH Meyer et al. (eds), *Rights, Culture, and the Law: Themes from the Legal and Political Philosophy of Joseph Raz* (Oxford University Press 2003) 25.

[14] Raz *Practical Reason and Norms* (n 11) 17.

[15] To Φ is to undertake action X for purpose *E*.

[16] Celano 'Are Reasons for Action Beliefs' (n 13) 25.

[17] ibid 28.

Celano suggests that if asked whether they Φ because of a belief in p or the fact that p exists, most agents would choose the former. This is because an expression of belief in p is generally equivalent to a claim that the agent believes p is true as, were this untrue, we would not hold it as a belief.[18] Celano concludes that this means that reasons for action are determined from the internal viewpoint of the agent, and not against an external and objective standpoint per Raz's account.[19]

For a Gewirthian however, this argument is moot. It does not matter whether the belief that forms a reason to Φ is objectively verifiable or false; all that matters is that it serves as motivation for the agent. For it is the essence of action itself, rather than the nature the motivation behind it, that grounds the PGC. The neutrality of the PGC with regards to the truthfulness of the motivating reason for action can again be shown with reference to Celano's attempted rebuttal of Raz's position, in which he presents three hypothetical motivations for an agent to Φ:

1. An agent has no reason to Φ, she believes she has one, and she Φs
2. An agent has a reason to Φ, she believes she has that reason, and she Φs
3. An agent has a reason to Φ, she doesn't believe she has one, and she Φs[20]

Hypotheses 1 and 2 demonstrate how Celano believes an agent would behave; the first is an account of an agent acting on a false belief, and the second an agent acting on a true belief. The third is Celano's account of Raz's position: that a true reason to Φ overrides the false belief which of the agent, leading them to Φ despite believing they have no reason to do so. He concludes this situation is absurd, meaning that Raz's account should be rejected.

This, however, misrepresents Raz's point; he does not argue that an agent would be motivated to act by a reason of which they are unaware, which is how Celano portrays the claim in the third hypothetical scenario. Rather, Raz's argument is that if an agent undertakes Φ based on a false belief when they have a stronger reason to not- Φ about which they are unaware, their ignorance of the stronger reason does not mean that it does not exist; merely that they are unaware of it. Raz's claim is thus that, if they were aware of it, then they ought to have chosen to not- Φ. Celano thus appears to be attacking a straw man rather than Raz's true position, which is as follows:

> 3. (Modified) An agent has a reason to Φ, she doesn't believe she has one, so does not Φ. This does not mean the reason does not exist, had she been aware of the reason to Φ, she ought to have Φ.

Once this mischaracterisation is taken into account, we can see that all three hypotheses presented by Celano are potentially accurate descriptions of how an

[18] ibid 29.
[19] ibid 30.
[20] ibid.

agent would act. All three are therefore able to generate action that is covered by the remit of the PGC, meaning that false belief is as equally capable of guiding action as true belief. The first stage of the PGC is entirely value-neutral with regard to the action being undertaken; all it requires is that a desire exists which an agent acts upon in order for it to be satisfied. Any objection based on the rationality or reasonableness of the desire or the truth or falsehood of the motivating belief is equally redundant – all that matters at this initial stage is that the desire exists and is acted upon.

2.2. Differing Types of Reasons

The concept of a plurality of reasons is central to Raz's work, and the purpose of this section is to identify the many types of reason that Raz believes to exist. He defines reasons for action as '[F]acts that constitute a case for (or against) the performance of an action',[21] thus locating them prior to action because any decision as to whether Φ can only take place after a process of deliberation during which competing reasons to either Φ or not- Φ vie with one another for primacy. If reasons can compete in this way, it follows for Raz that a hierarchy of reasons must exist, some of which possess more weight than others. He proposes three broad categories:

1. Conclusive Reasons: R is a conclusive reason for an agent to Φ iff there is no stronger reason that overrides R.
2. Absolute Reasons: R is an absolute reason for an agent to Φ iff there cannot be a stronger reason capable of overriding R.
3. Prima facie Reasons: Those reasons which are neither conclusive nor absolute.[22]

These three types of reasons compete against each another until an agent decides which one comes out on top of the hierarchy. Any reason that is not pertinent to their deliberation is defined by Raz as auxiliary, and any that an agent does consider is an operative reason.[23] Operative reasons can be, prima facie, normative or complete in their character.[24] They can either be ones ultimately relied on when deciding to Φ, or ones that are discarded along the way as being outweighed by a reason to not Φ. An operative reason will only be relied upon if an agent sees it as, all things considered, undefeated.[25]

[21] J Raz, *From Normativity to Responsibility* (Oxford University Press 2011) 36.
[22] Raz *Practical Reason and Norms* (n 11) 27.
[23] ibid 32–33.
[24] ibid 34–36; As stated at the beginning of section 2 of this chapter, such complete reasons are rare. Normative reasons are a special type of reason which will be discussed in much more detail in section 2.4 of this chapter.
[25] ibid 40.

A second way of differentiating between reasons that Raz endorses is that of first and second order reasons. First order reasons for action are those for which we undertake a given action; second order reasons are reasons to act, or refrain from acting, on first order reasons. One should therefore only accept an operative reason as being capable of guiding our action as an undefeated, first order reason iff this reason can be supported by second order reasons that justify it and there are no second order reasons that prevent us from choosing that course of action. Such secondary reasons against accepting a primary reason may take the form of exclusionary reasons, a full discussion of which will take place in section 2.3 below; for present purposes, it is enough acknowledge that, should an exclusionary reason exist, then it is not only operative on an agent's choice on how to act but should also be viewed as an absolute reason not to Φ.

In his later work, Raz argues that reasons can be either epistemic or empirical in origin. He gives the example of a right to vote to support this point; if all citizens are entitled to vote and an agent is a citizen, she has a reason to see herself as able to vote. Raz argues this is a non-normative reason and is thus not epistemic in origin.[26] As an empirical reason, it is simply self-evident and does not need further elucidation to be seen to exist. Because empirical reasons are self-evident, they are necessarily first order reasons as they fall within the realm of practical reason generally. They are presumed to be sufficient unless proved otherwise.[27] The same is not true of epistemic reasons. They must necessarily be attached to a primary reason, given they are concerned with ascertaining the truth of the belief in the empirical reason. They are thus necessarily secondary reasons in all cases, insofar as they can only be used to support or defeat a primary reason.

Once an agent has balanced operative reasons to identify a conclusive or absolute reason to Φ, Raz believes they are committed to recognising that this claim is logically equivalent, if not entirely synonymous with, a statement to the effect that they ought to Φ.[28] This appears to be an epistemic jump in that Raz is suggesting that there is normative value in empirical, first order reasons that are either conclusive or absolute with reference to second order epistemic reasons. This move from 'is' to 'ought' is one which Raz addresses head on: 'Statements of facts which are reasons for the performance of a certain action by a certain agent are the premises of an argument the conclusion of which is that there is reason for the agent to perform the action or that he ought to do it.'[29] This claim seems to rely on the same instrumental reasoning that can be found in the PGC; that if an agent does Φ, they are committed to the claim that they see action X as necessary for their end E. A self-reflexive 'ought' is therefore created where,

[26] Raz, *From Normativity to Responsibility* (n 21) 41.
[27] ibid 45.
[28] Raz *Practical Reason and Norms* (n 11) 29.
[29] ibid 28.

if an agent desires *E*, they ought to do *X*.[30] Given that stage one of the PGC is logically equivalent to Raz's explanation of the justification of action, the imperative contained within the PGC is therefore applicable to all deliberative reasoning that takes place within the Razian hierarchy of reasons. Compliance with the PGC thus becomes a universally applicable secondary order epistemic reason; all primary order reasons must be compliant with its requirements to be either conclusive or absolute. This requires us to accept that compliance with the PGC is itself an absolute secondary order reason, insofar as any primary reason that does not comply with its requirements is necessarily overridden and ought to be discarded. To insist otherwise is to misunderstand the nature of what it means to act, based on Raz's own starting point.

2.3. Exclusionary Reasons

A type of reason within Raz's categorisation yet to be discussed is the exclusionary reason. These are any second order reasons that are used to reject a first order reason during the deliberative process.[31] Exclusionary reasons may be moral in nature, but only provide a prima facie reason to behave in accordance with a moral norm.[32] This is a much weaker classification than we might expect from Raz given our previous conclusion that compliance with the PGC is a universally applicable second order epistemic reason that requires all primary reasons to be permissible according to its requirements in order to be capable of being either conclusive or absolute. Adopting the language of exclusionary reasons, PGC compliance is itself an *absolute* exclusionary reason, as any primary reason that is incompatible with its requirements is necessarily excluded and cannot serve as an absolute or conclusive reason to Φ. A discussion of Raz's own characterisation of exclusionary reasons as necessarily prima facie is therefore required to demonstrate why his own conclusion is misplaced, and that his own understanding of what it means to be an agent requires him to accept that compliance with the PGC is an absolute exclusionary reason against all non-compliant action.

This first requires us to consider his views on the nature of moral reasons for action. In his most recent writing on the place of moral deliberation in exclusionary reasoning, Raz neither endorses a particular moral principle, nor does he explore the issue of what form any potential exclusionary moral reason might take. He instead suggests a list of virtues that he claims are self-evidently morally valuable: things that are good for people and experiences which will improve their lives are but two examples.[33] A moral principle could function as

[30] Beyleveld *The Dialectical Necessity of Morality* (n 10).

[31] M Moore 'Authority, Law, and Razian Reasons' (1989) *Southern California Law Review* 827, 829–30.

[32] ibid 829.

[33] Raz, *From Normativity to Responsibility* (n 21) 221.

an exclusionary principle if it could be shown that the proposed action would be bad for people and could thus trump reasons to behave in a damaging way. The problem here is that Raz fails to provide any reason why an agent ought to accept this particular example as morally valuable, instead relying on the claim to self-evidency.

Raz's reluctance to commit to a particular moral framework may in part be grounded in his previous distinction between first and second order reasons. We will recall that Raz categorises exclusionary reasons as definitionally second order, in that they provide us with a reason to disregard a primary order reason. If an exclusionary reason is to be absolute and apply to all primary order reasons, then the reason is behaving in the same way as a categorical imperative in that it applies universally to all actions. An epistemic foundation is therefore necessary in order to provide the normative grounding for a test against which the permissibility of any and all action can be assessed; however, Raz is sceptical as to the existence of any such principle, as he believes that language is too flexible and context-dependent to be capable of supporting such a test.[34] Even though previous sections of this work have shown that the PGC is prima facie capable of serving as a test, we will still concede this point *arguendo*. Let us assume that Raz is correct and that semantic vagueness is problematic with regard to the identification of any functioning test for moral permissibility within the broader realm of practical reasoning, and instead ask what exactly Raz means when he speaks of 'practical reasoning' in this sense. He appears to endorse John Broome's Aristotelian view:

> Aristotle took practical reasoning to be reasoning that concludes in an action. But an action – at least a physical one – requires more than reasoning ability; it requires physical ability too. Intending to act is as close to acting as reasoning alone can get us, so we should take practical reasoning to be reasoning that concludes in an intention.[35]

Such a position appears sound for our present purposes. Based on this definition, Raz's claim could be that forming an intention is simply too subjective and variable to generate an objective and universal 'ought'. This appears inconsistent, however, with his endorsement of the principle of instrumental necessity; that an agent recognising absolute or conclusive reasons to Φ is logically consistent to, if not synonymous with, the agent recognising that they ought to Φ. Raz could attempt to circumvent this contradiction by saying that instead of creating an objective ought, the best that a practical reason can do is to generate a rational ought – that 'we rationally ought to do what we have best reason to believe we have best reason to do'.[36] Yet even this is something about which Raz is sceptical elsewhere, claiming that the incommensurability of some reasons

[34] ibid 107.

[35] J Broome, 'Practical Reasoning' in J Bermúdez and A Millar (eds) *Reason and Nature: Essays in the Theory of Rationality* (Clarendon Press 2002) 85.

[36] Raz, *From Normativity to Responsibility* (n 21) 108–109.

means that even a rational 'ought' is frequently impossible. By extension, any normative exclusionary reason itself grounded in practical reasoning cannot be absolute, as incommensurability means that, in some situations, a deliberation on reasons would remain balanced and no one course of action is preferable to another.

This objection to the possibility of the existence of an absolute exclusionary reason fails on two counts. Firstly, on a practical level, the incommensurability described by Raz simply does not describe how agents act. The example he provides to illustrate his point is that of 'Jackson Cases', or the more easily relatable problem of having to choose between identical cans of soup.[37] He claims that both of these situations are ones of true incommensurability, as no reason exists to choose one outcome more than another; it thus follows that if a situation exists in which an exclusionary reason cannot apply, then an absolute exclusionary reason cannot exist. If Raz were correct here, however, then when an agent decided to buy soup and was confronted with a row of identical cans, then they would be stuck forever in a soup-based limbo – condemned for eternity to an inability to choose between which one to purchase. The fact our supermarkets are not filled with souls condemned to this fate is enough to demonstrate that the situation described by Raz is a fiction; when faced with a row of identical cans of soup, agents do tend to choose one as being preferable to the others. It may be the closest can, the one on a higher or lower shelf or one chosen at random. Yet in picking one up, for whatever reason, an agent has demonstrated that they *do* have a reason to prefer one over all the others, even if the reason has been subsumed into a secondary bout of reasoning resulting in a decision to choose a random can. Were this not the case, our agent would still be in front of the shelf or would have walked away soupless. If an agent does the latter, they are presumably doing so because the equilibrium provided by incommensurable reasons becomes an exclusionary reason against acting arbitrarily, thus breaking the claim of incommensurability in any case. The fact that we act at all in such situations suggests Raz's conclusions on incommensurability are false.

Yet even were we to concede the point of incommensurability, a second reason for rejecting Raz's conclusions exists in the observation that it is founded on a misunderstanding of what an exclusionary reason grounded in a rule akin to a categorical imperative is designed to do. The PGC, in particular, is not designed to provide a reason to act in a certain way, but to refrain from certain types of impermissible behaviour. Framing the PGC as providing a negative duty means that, when presented with incommensurable reasons that are permissible, then it simply does not matter which course of action is chosen. There does not, therefore, appear to be a valid reason to agree with Raz that practical reasoning is too linguistically subjective or otherwise context dependent to provide a normative basis for an absolute exclusionary reason for action. We again must return to the

[37] ibid 120–28.

position that, given Raz's endorsement of the principle of instrumental necessity, he is required to endorse the PGC as exactly the sort of absolute exclusionary reason which, he attempts to argue, is conceptually incapable of existing.

Having established that incommensurability of reasons is no barrier to the PGC acting as an absolute exclusionary reason applicable to all practical reasoning, let us turn consider the implications of this on another aspect of Raz's work, namely the 'facilitative principle'. This holds that if a reason for action is not trumped or overruled by an exclusionary reason, then a reason exists to facilitate that action.[38] Note that this appears to be a weaker claim than the earlier statement that an agent's recognising absolute or conclusive reasons to Φ is logically consistent to, if not synonymous with, the agent recognising that they ought to Φ. We must therefore confront the possibility that Raz has dropped his commitment to the principle of instrumental necessity in his later work, meaning that the claim that he ought to endorse the PGC no longer holds. This conclusion can be shown to be false, however, and that even on the weaker 'facilitative principle' he still has two reasons as to why he ought to endorse the PGC based on his own understanding of the nature of reasons. Firstly, the 'facilitative principle' is not weaker at all, but still contains a commitment to the principle of instrumental necessity. For if an agent accepts that they have a reason to facilitate end *E*, and action *X* is the means by which *E* is attained, then the agent remains logically committed to viewing *X* as instrumentally necessary for them to attain *E*. They still therefore have a reason as to why they ought to Φ.

Secondly, even were we to concede *arguendo* that the 'facilitative principle' is weaker, an agent still must use their GCAs to act to facilitate the end in question meaning that the PGC remains a valid absolute exclusionary reason. Raz's own characterisation of his concept of facilitative reasons encompasses Gewirth's argument that all agents must necessarily value their GCAs:

> To have an end involves believing that it is worth having (at least other things being equal). That belief explains why people pursue ends. They take what they believe to be reasons for the ends as reasons to pursue the ends, and, as explained by the facilitative principle, to take steps to facilitate them.[39]

If GCAs are instrumentally necessary for all action, then Raz must concede that an agent must value them in the way indicated by Gewirth. This would be true even if he did not go on develop his own point into the stronger claim that agents are obliged to do *X* for *E* only when to not do *X* would be irrational.[40] This move places the operation of exclusionary reasons back firmly within the sphere of practical rationality in the same sense as all other reasons for action.[41] Given that Raz's previous objections to the operation of the PGC have been shown to not hit their target, he has not provided any reason for us to reject

[38] ibid 144.
[39] ibid 150.
[40] ibid 158.
[41] ibid 165.

it; since non-compliance with the PGC is definitionally irrational, Raz's own claims require him to accept that an agent is bound to accept the PGC as an absolute exclusionary reason. He must therefore abandon his claim that exclusionary reasons can only be prima facie in nature so that his broader theory of reasons for action can remain internally consistent.

2.4. Normative Reasons

The purpose of the preceding section was to outline Raz's account of different types of reasons and how they interact with one another. It demonstrated not only that the PGC is capable of operating within his framework of deliberative rationality, but also that – based on his own commitment to either the principle of instrumental necessity or the potentially weaker facilitative principle – Raz is committed to recognising and endorsing compliance with the PGC as an absolute exclusionary reason against any and all non-PGC compliant action. The section will strengthen this claim by integrating it with Raz's account of reasons for action that are specifically normative in character.

We will begin by returning to an uncontroversial observation: that reasons for action frequently conflict with one another. The fact that action occurs suggests such conflicts can be resolved, which in turn implies a hierarchy of reasons – a conclusion Raz suggests is inevitable because some reasons are simply stronger than others.[42] This, in turn, implies the existence of an objective test against which the respective strength of reasons can be ascertained. This is necessary because, as was previously established, the same rules of practical reason – including with regard to exclusionary reasons – must apply equally to all agents.[43] Any reasons to act that come out on top of the hierarchy, undefeated by exclusionary secondary reasons, are ones we ought to pursue based on the 'facilitative principle' or the principle of instrumental necessity.[44] This logical progression has necessitated the conclusion that practical reason is subject to mandatory normative claims that direct behaviour away from that which is provided for by other reasons. Such 'oughts' are a special type of reason, perhaps more accurately described as a rule than a bare 'ought', that are deserving more in-depth discussion. Raz defines these specific normative reasons as follows:

> Aspects of the world are normative in as much as they or their existence constitute reasons for persons, that is, ground which make certain beliefs, moods, emotions, intentions, or actions appropriate or inappropriate.[45]

[42] Raz *Practical Reason and Norms* (n 11) 25.

[43] H Frankfurt, *Necessity, Volition, and Love* (Cambridge University Press 1999) 162.

[44] Raz *Practical Reason and Norms* (n 11) 29; R Bittner, 'Stronger Reasons' in LH Meyer et al. (eds), *Rights, Culture, and the Law: Themes from the Legal and Political Philosophy of Joseph Raz* (Oxford University Press 2003) 17.

[45] J Raz, *Engaging Reason: On the Theory of Value and Action* (Oxford University Press 1999) 67.

This definition of normativity is incredibly broad. Raz could be interpreted as believing that all reasons are normative insofar as they make a claim to truth which is capable of directing an agent to one course of action over another. Explaining the concept of normativity is therefore the practice of explaining what it is to be a successful reason for action.[46] The true depth of his definition can be seen more clearly, however, when Raz applies the definition to the concept of rationality – the ability to recognise and respond to such normative demands – and his claim that rationality is the very foundation of personhood.[47] Raz claims that a conceptual connection between rationality and normativity can be demonstrated by four main observations. Firstly, the fact that we need capacities which do not directly contribute to rationality – such as our perceptual abilities or a bare minimum ability to control our bodily movements – to act upon our rational decisions. Secondly, that the idea of rationality is not only the ability to reason but also to understand inferences and premises as reasons for action in an abstract sense. Thirdly, rationality goes beyond our ability to engage in deliberative reason and applies reasoning to all functions which we undertake. Lastly that rationality is a unified concept which is identical in its operation regardless of whether it is directed towards practice, theory, substantive or procedural ends.[48] Thus, if reasons are normative aspects of the world, rationality is conceptually linked with how an agent responds to these reasons.[49] All reasons, including those stemming from emotion, desire, intention or belief, are sources of normativity in that they motivate us to act according to a given directive.[50] The link between rationality and normativity has, for Raz, been established.[51]

It is worth briefly addressing at this point that there are several similarities here between Raz's account and the Gewirthian position. Both seem to endorse the view that rationality, as expressed through agency, is the foundation of a special status that can be legitimately used to distinguish us from non-agential beings. In addition, the capacities Raz identifies as essential for the exercise of agency play the same function in his theory as the GCAs do for Gewirth. This substantive overlap between the two means that Raz ought to have no conceptual problem with the possibility that the PGC might ground normative claims that guide action in a way that protects the interests of all agents. It is also worth briefly addressing that Raz's unified theory of rationality is not universally accepted. Derek Parfit, for one, argues that there is a big difference between substantive and procedural rationality; the former requires us to value certain things (such as our own wellbeing), whereas the latter merely obliges

[46] ibid.
[47] ibid.
[48] ibid.
[49] ibid 75.
[50] ibid.
[51] Raz, *From Normativity to Responsibility* (n 21) 13.

us to follow certain methods of reasoning regardless of our ends.[52] The dialectically necessary argument for the PGC shows us why this separation should be rejected, however; a core facet of any and all action is that it is impossible without a minimum level of freedom and wellbeing. Agents are thus committed to a minimum level of substantive rationality that preserves their freedom and wellbeing, as without this any action would be impossible; if a minimum substantive content of rationality is necessary in all forms of deliberation, then Parfit's separation is false. Raz rejects Parfit's separation on remarkably similar lines, showing another similarity between his and Gewirth's positions. He claims that rational beliefs can be identified by reference to the opposite concept of irrational beliefs, which are definable as existing 'if and only if holding [such beliefs] displays lack of care and diligence in one's own epistemic conduct'.[53] This is analogous to the Gewirthian claim that to act in a way that is non-PGC compliant is to contradict one's own agency. The only difference between the two positions appears to be in their construction; whereas Gewirth builds his claim using the dialectically necessary method, Raz makes the weaker claim of self-evidence. Yet our conclusion must, once again, be that Raz cannot object to the argument for – or conclusions of – the PGC, given that he is already committed to both by his own conception of rational agency and its necessary connection with normative claims.

An objection to Raz's claimed link between rationality and normativity could be raised as follows; if all reasons can be normative insofar as they are action focused, how can normative 'oughts' carry different strengths? In particular, how can exclusionary reasons overrule other reasons for action if all can trace their normative force back to the same source of rational agency? Here, Raz turns to John Broome to draw attention to a different means of categorising reasons beyond his own original tripartite classification of conclusive, absolute and prima facie. Broome suggests two types of reasons exist. Firstly:

> [A] perfect reason for you to Φ is … a fact that explains why you ought to do Φ.' Other reasons are *pro tanto* reasons: 'A *pro tanto* reason for you to Φ is a fact that plays the for- Φ role in a potential or actual weighing explanation of why you ought to Φ, or in a potential or actual weighing explanation of why it is not the case that you ought to Φ and not the case that you ought not to Φ.[54]

Broome suggests that these reasons are respectively explanatory and normative, and that normative *pro tanto* reasons cannot exist independently of a specific desired outcome. Raz endorses this distinction – only with reference to a specific outcome can a balancing act of reasons truly take place.[55] These normative

[52] D Parfit, 'Reason and Motivation', *Aristotelian Society*, 71 (1997), 99, at 101.

[53] Raz, *Engaging Reason* (n 45) 75.

[54] J Broome, 'Reasons' in RJ Wallace et al (eds) *Reason and Value* (Oxford University Press 2004) 41.

[55] Raz, *From Normativity to Responsibility* (n 21) 22.

reasons for and against the action in question outweigh one another, in case of conflict, by simple mathematics:

> [T]here are reasons for you to Φ and reasons for you not to Φ. Each reason is associated with a number that represents its weight. The numbers associated with the reasons to Φ add up to more than the numbers associated with the reasons not to Φ. That is why you ought to Φ.[56]

This account should be questioned for two reasons. Firstly, Broome's distinction between perfect and *pro tanto* reasons appears analogous to Raz's own differentiation between epistemic and empirical reasons discussed in the previous section. This differentiation was shown to be false, insofar as it is impossible for a reason to be purely empirical because of the self-reflexive 'ought' generated by the principle of instrumental necessity that accepting such empirical reasons necessary entails. Broome's distinction can be rejected for the same reason. Secondly, it is not immediately apparent how Broome proposes the relative value weightings to his *pro tanto* reasons are assigned. If, as his distinction suggests, these reasons are only conceptually sound when proffered with regard to a specific end, are they, then, to be judged by reference to this end? If so, what measure is being used to assess the desirability of the end in question? Value is therefore either presupposed by Broome as self-evident, or a reference point for normative value external to the distinction is necessary. To identify what this might be, we should look back to Raz to ask whether any absolute 'oughts' are capable of existing. He suggests there are only two – definitionally conceptual truths and absolute moral truths.[57] Raz here welcomes that an absolute moral truth, if identifiable, could act as such a reference point against which such *pro tanto* reasons could be assessed for their validity. Given that it has been previously shown that Raz ought to accept the PGC's operation as an absolute exclusionary reason in light of several similarities between Gewirth's position and his own, we should again note that the PGC could act as this reference point.

This section has so far been constructed using the connection that Raz claims exists between rationality and normativity. He holds that normative reasons are those which guide agents' actions. Yet Raz later performs a U-turn with the claim that normativity and rationality are not conceptually linked given there is no reason why an agent ought to act rationally.[58] To demonstrate why Raz's later claim is not one we should necessarily accept, we will instead continue to address Raz's earlier, opposite position: that he is committed to recognising a normative reason to act rationally, as per the PGC, in order for his broader writing on the nature of reasons to remain consistent. A point of support for the claim that normative reasons are necessarily connected to the concept of rationality is the empirical claim that, for an agent to recognise the motivational

[56] Broome (n 54) 36–37.
[57] Raz, *From Normativity to Responsibility* (n 21) 24.
[58] ibid 94–95.

force present within a given norm, they must first engage in a process of rational deliberation.[59] A reason cannot motivate action, and by extension, claim normative force, if to follow it would be irrational; reason and rationality are therefore conceptually linked. Early Raz partially accepts the definition of reason provided by Paul Grice to arrive at this conclusion:

> No less intuitive than the idea of thinking of reason as the faculty which equips us to recognize and operate with reasons is the idea of thinking of it as the faculty which empowers us to engage in reasoning ... Indeed if reasoning should be characterizable as the occurrence or production of a chain of inferences, and if such chains consist in (sequentially) arriving at conclusions which are derivable from some initial set of premises, and for the acceptance of which, therefore, these premises are, or are thought to be, reasons, the connection between these two ideas is not accidental.[60]

A process of rational deliberation is thus necessary for reasons to be recognised as possessing normative force. In opposition to this claim, Raz defines irrationality thus: '[W]hen and because one non-accidentally fails to respond appropriately to reasons, and the failure is, is due to, a failure or malfunction of one's rational powers.'[61] Some may criticise this idea of irrationality as being derived from external stimuli. To circumvent this criticism, Raz expands on his definition to demonstrate that irrationality is non-derivative:

> People who recognize a conclusive reason to Φ ... and who fail to respond to it at all, fail ... to form an intention to Φ, have no positive attitude at all towards Φ-ing, do not respond appropriately to other people Φ-ing, etc., are non-derivatively irrational.[62]

This definition clearly places irrationality within the plane of reasoning, rather than as merely derivative of a value ascribed to a given end. As this definition of non-derivative rationality can be applied to normative claims, we can see that Raz ought to maintain that there is a strong connection between rationality and normativity in that to disregard a sound normative claim is prima facie irrational.

This conclusion is strengthened when we return to our earlier observation that Raz's commitment to either the principle of instrumental necessity or the potentially weaker facilitative principle requires him to recognise the validity of the PGC. Raz's scepticism with regard to the existence of a test for moral permissibility that applies equally to all action was alluded to earlier – but he does concede that, were one to be identifiable, it would be capable of generating an absolute normative 'ought'.[63] In light of our claim that he ought to accept the PGC as an absolute exclusionary reason given his own conception of deliberative rationality, he is thus committed to the claim that to ignore the requirements

[59] ibid 27; 86.
[60] P Grice, *Aspects of Reason* (Oxford University Press 2001) 5.
[61] Raz, *From Normativity to Responsibility* (n 21) 89.
[62] ibid 93.
[63] Raz, *Engaging Reason* (n 45) 67.

of the PGC an agent denies their own agential status. To deny the normative requirements of the PGC is therefore definitionally irrational. His claim that there is no reason why an agent should act rationally[64] must be abandoned in light of the absolute and exclusionary reason provided by the PGC. This is necessary given Raz's own account of what character a normative requirement must possess in order to be mandatory: that they must be a deontic operator which directs a subject towards a given act under certain circumstances.[65] Such mandatory norms might be more accurately referred to as rules, and these are different to normal reasons in that they provide a valid absolute and exclusionary reason regardless of whether they are ultimately followed by the agent to whom they are addressed.[66] Raz does, however, note that such mandatory norms must necessarily be issued or supported by an authority which can provide the exclusionary force required.[67] They are successful in guiding action when the following circumstance is true:

> A person follows a mandatory norm only if he believes that the norm is a valid reason for him to do the norm act when the conditions for application obtain and that it is a valid reason for disregarding conflicting reasons, and if he acts on those beliefs.[68]

This statement could be read in one of two ways. Firstly, that mandatory norms only apply when the circumstances under which they should be followed pertain – a point that is axiomatic in the definition of what a mandatory norm is. A second interpretation would be the claim that although a mandatory norm is practice-independent, an agent need only see it as truly exclusionary if they see a valid reason to accept it as such. If this second interpretation holds, which seems likely as the first reading is a tautologous restatement of what it means to be a mandatory norm, then we are required to see that the validity of a mandatory norm, like all other reasons, is subject to the requirements of practical reason and deliberative rationality. Given that the PGC identifies moral normativity within deliberative rationality itself, Raz again ought to accept that it is a valid mandatory norm and capable of generating an absolute and exclusionary reason against non-compliant behaviour.

3. RESOLVING CONFLICTS BETWEEN REASONS

The purpose of this chapter so far has been twofold. It began by examining Raz's account of the different types of reasons that an agent necessarily deliberates on when deciding how to act. It has shown that a hierarchy of reasons exists,

[64] Raz, *From Normativity to Responsibility* (n 21) 95.
[65] Raz *Practical Reason and Norms* (n 11) 50.
[66] ibid 58–59.
[67] ibid 65.
[68] ibid 72–73.

as it is necessarily true that – if reasons conflict – some must be stronger than others to allow action to ultimately take place. We have also demonstrated that, based on Raz's own conception of deliberative rationality, the PGC is capable of acting as an absolute and exclusionary second-order reason that limits the scope of permissible first-order reasons to those that are compatible with its requirements. This second section will pay closer attention to the hierarchy of reasons as conceptualised by Raz himself and will demonstrate that – on his own terms – the PGC necessarily sits at the top of any hierarchy of reasons for action.

The analysis will be constructed around what Raz refers to as the basic belief: that, when faced with competing reasons for action, an agent chooses which one to act upon by a rational process of elimination. Though it may not be irrational to prima facie reject any of these reasons, a process of deliberation can identify those that ought to be rejected as providing a reason that is defeated by a stronger reason, such as a mandatory second-order norm.[69] Raz suggests this process of evaluation takes place by considering the following propositions:

1. Φ is good simpliciter.
2. Φ is good for someone, thus a sufficient reason to Φ exists.
3. Someone has an appropriate reason to act in a certain way.
4. If an agent must do Φ and is acting irrationally if they do not, a conclusive reason to Φ exists.[70]

The first of these pertains when an end is prima facie good. Since the PGC holds that all GCAs are necessarily good due to their necessity for all agency itself, the first part of this section will focus on how Raz believes moral reasons fit into his deliberative hierarchy. As the PGC is identified through a process of rational deliberation, the first part of the section will also address evaluation based on the fourth evaluative proposition above. The second part of this section will deal with the second of his evaluative positions, deliberation based on perceived subjective good, and the final section will discuss the third evaluative position of reasons provided by an authority that provides an agent with appropriate reasons to act. The final part of this section will return briefly to the idea of incommensurability of reasons to demonstrate how these evaluative propositions show Raz's claims around this problem to be overstated.

3.1. Moral Rights as Reasons

As noted previously, Raz's belief that extant moral systems both prioritise individual action over the collective or presuppose common global standards mean that he is sceptical both as to whether a moral principle such as a categorical

[69] Raz, *Engaging Reason* (n 45) 100.
[70] ibid 106.

imperative could exist, and as to whether a moral system can be grounded in the idea of inalienable rights.[71] He instead endorses a humanistic principle: that goodness derives from the consequences of action and its contribution to the quality of human life.[72] Central to Gewirthian ethics, however, which we have shown Raz ought to accept, is the idea that all agents are rationally committed to seeing their GCAs as rights by dint of their agency; they are committed to respecting the rights of all other agents, thus creating the test for moral permissibility of all action of which Raz is sceptical. Fortunately, several of the justifications offered by Raz in support of his humanistic approach appear to operate in a way that is compatible with the logic underpinning the PGC. This analysis of the role of moral reasons in Raz's hierarchy of reasons will explore these similarities to show that Raz's scepticism should be set aside, and that he ought to accept – and integrate – the PGC into his approach to deliberative rationality.

Raz believes that that rights-based theories of morality should be rejected because their individualistic focus requires us to see collective goods as having only instrumental, contingent value to the extent that they support individual goods.[73] He believes this to be false as a matter of empirical reality, arguing that it is self-evident that collective rights can exist independently of independent rights if three criteria are met:

1. An aspect of the interest of human beings justifies holding some person(s) to a duty;
2. The interests in question are of individuals as members of a group in a public good and the public good serves their interest as members of group; and
3. The interest of no single member is good sufficient to create duty in itself.[74]

This appears to be a circular definition however, as Raz presupposes that criterion three is possible without attempting to justify how it might arise. Such a task may be difficult for him in light of our previous analysis, which has shown his own conception of deliberative rationality requires him to accept the PGC as valid. Raz may counter that it is safe to presuppose this assumption as 'It is difficult to imagine a successful argument imposing a duty to provide a collective good on the ground that it will serve the interests of one individual.'[75] This claim may be true – but it is not an accurate representation of the absolute and exclusionary reasons provided by the test for moral permissibility that derives from the PGC. This principle does not serve the interests of one individual; it serves the interests of all agents because their status as agents renders them moral

[71] J Raz, *The Morality of Freedom* (Oxford University Press 1986) 193.
[72] ibid 194.
[73] ibid 198.
[74] ibid 207.
[75] ibid 203.

patients. This is analogous to Raz's earlier commitment to viewing rationality as a criterion that sets us apart from other beings and endows us with a special status.[76] Raz must therefore accept that intrinsic value does exist at the level of the individual, or drop his commitment to the claim that individuals' rationality endows them with special moral status. Since dropping this commitment would render his broader theory of deliberative rationality incoherent, he ought instead to accept that moral patients are necessarily individual beings and that any collective rights must respect the rights of individuals to be valid. This is not to say that rights cannot better achieve good for the individual when operating at the level of the collective; this may be true. But we cannot ignore that the good necessarily exists prior to the collective, in that it is of fundamental importance to the individual.

This conclusion is in opposition, however, to his own stated position: that collective goods and rights are instead necessary for individual autonomy.[77] But this position does not sit easily with Raz's acceptance elsewhere that some collective goods are only desirable if we also accept that personal autonomy is intrinsically desirable, as this claim indicates his amenability to the idea that individual rights must be respected by collective rights.[78] We appear to have reached an impasse. Raz may claim that the collective should be prioritised as individualistic claims incorrectly conflate ought and duty, in that the claim that we ought to do what we have a duty to do is incorrectly interpreted as creating a duty to do what we ought to do.[79] If we have a duty to respect individual rights then we ought to do this, but it does not necessarily follow that because we ought to respect rights (as to do so is in the interest of the rights bearer) that we have a correlative duty to do so. This rebuttal does not, however, dismiss any rights claim arising from the PGC due to the self-reflexive ought upon which the rights claims are constructed. An agent ought to respect the rights of others as they are premised on the same foundation upon which an agent claims her own rights. This ought generates a correlative duty in the way that Raz says individualistic rights do not, thus circumventing his objection; given that Raz is committed to a theory of deliberative rationality that operates in the same way as that within the argument for the PGC, then this is a conclusion he ought to accept. He is thus required to drop his claim that collective rights must exist prior to those of the individual to maintain the coherence of his broader theories of both reasons and rationality. The fact that it is of fundamental importance to individual agents that their GCAs are protected by adherence to the PGC means that any and all collective rights must necessarily respect the GCAs of the individual in order to be valid.

[76] Raz, *Engaging Reason* (n 45) 67, 75; J Raz, *Value, Respect, and Attachment* (Cambridge University Press 2001) 153–57.

[77] Raz, *The Morality of Freedom* (n 71) 207.

[78] ibid 203.

[79] ibid 195.

As this conclusion relies heavily on Raz accepting that respect for individuals is necessary for the existence of community rights, this sub-section on moral rights as reasons will close by examining his own three-step account of respect for individuals to assess whether it is compatible with the PGC compliant account developed above. He begins with an observation that there is a mutual yet asymmetric dependence between things which are intrinsically good, in that they can be used for a given end, and those which are unconditionally good. Intrinsic good can only be enjoyed by those who are capable of reasoning, and therefore engaging with the object in the correct way;[80] if an object is capable of having value ascribed to it via a process of recognition, it follows that there are things that an agent must perceive as good. This leads to his second step: that this capacity to ascribe value actually creates the value in an object external to themselves, and this capacity shows that the agent themselves must possess unconditional value. This conclusion, according to his third step, is simply axiomatic: something must possess value to be able to relate to value and, because the agent can exist in the absence of another agent, that value must be unconditional. Our very ability to reason and perceive value therefore singles us out as being of special concern.[81]

A Gewirthian would claim that this argument for individual rights grounded in the unconditional value of the agents is not as fully grounded as that which emerges from the argument for the PGC, yet could still accept Raz's conclusion that individual agents possess a special status as moral patients. We can now turn to Raz's account of why this status is one other agents ought to respect: which is to state that unconditional value simply is worthy of respect.[82] He draws the analogy of a painting to support this claim. A painting, he claims, can be recognised as valuable even if an agent does not fully engage with it; it must thus possess unconditional value, and ought to be respected even if an agent does not fully engage with it.[83] This argument appears flawed. To continue the painting analogy, it is not inconsistent to envisage that an agent might recognise that a painting possesses unconditional value and still wish to destroy it; simply recognising unconditional value is not, in and of itself, a reason as to why that value ought to be respected. This is a problem for Raz, but his theory can be rescued by referring back to the Gewirthian foundation of his own observation: that deliberative rationality generates a self-reflexive ought in the agent, and that this makes acceptance of the argument for the PGC dialectically necessary. Gewirth's argument is not only capable of showing why agents possess unconditional value, but is also superior in that it also provides a strong moral reason as to why this value should be rejected. This moral reason is both absolute and exclusionary and, on a Razian account of conflict between reasons, it must sit at the top of any hierarchy of moral reasons for action.

[80] Raz provides the example of oranges, which are only perceived to be of value if they are eaten.
[81] Raz, *Value, Respect, and Attachment* (n 76) 153–57.
[82] ibid 158.
[83] Raz, *Value, Respect, and Attachment* (n 76) 164.

3.2. Reasons Based in Personal Interest

A second category of reasons present in Raz's hierarchy are those motivated by the subjective value an agent places on a given end – something Raz may describe as being of intrinsic value to the agent. This could be anything upon which the agent places value, but an example repeatedly highlighted by Raz as being of particular importance would be personal wellbeing. This concept will be discussed in depth.

Raz argues that personal wellbeing should be assessed by judging the success or failure of an agent's life, rather than the means by which that end is reached.[84] This means that the things that contribute to a person's wellbeing are relevant to the end but are fundamentally separable from the overall conclusion reached. Raz claims that '[A] person is better off when well fed, in moderate temperature, with sufficient sensory stimulation, in good health, etc., whether he adopts these as his goals or not.'[85] These wellbeing criteria are necessary for a life to be pursued at all and, if they are present to an adequate extent, can greatly increase an agent's ability to pursue whatever goals she wishes to attain. Raz is deliberately open about what he means by the term 'goal' here, defining it thus:

> In these initial clarifications, 'goals' is used so broadly that if a person wants something then it is his goal to get it. But the result of these clarifications is that the term is used more in keeping with its ordinary implication of a longer-term objective. Goals are not necessarily desirable or desired for themselves. But they are nested in larger goals, or are larger goals themselves. *At no point do I wish to suggest that the fact that a person wants something is in and by itself a reason for action either for him or for others.*[86]

The long quotation here is provided to establish a point on which Raz's theory again appears confused. The criteria Raz identifies as important for wellbeing are broadly analogous to those identified by Gewirth as being required for enjoyment of our GCAs. It therefore seems odd that Raz should claim that these goods are instrumentally valuable whilst at the same time claiming that agential desire is not itself a sufficient reason to motivate action. This is doubly the case given that, earlier in the same text, Raz holds that the only reason for a goal to be adopted is because they possess independent value that can be appreciated by the agent.[87] Reverting to Gewirthian terminology can show us the problem here: if certain conditions are either necessary or beneficial for an agent to undertake any action whatsoever then the principle of instrumental necessity means that they are necessarily of value to the agent. Such is the nature of agency, and something that Raz has elsewhere accepted through his endorsement of the principle of instrumental necessity or the potentially weaker facilitative principle as shown in section 2 above. It does not matter whether the end desired is

[84] Raz, *The Morality of Freedom* (n 71) 289.
[85] ibid 290.
[86] ibid fn 1; emphasis mine.
[87] ibid 308–09.

objectively of value; all that matters is that the agent perceives it as valuable. Raz is therefore incorrect to state that subjective desire is not a reason for action, as to make this claim is to misunderstand what it means to Φ.

This logical problem present in his conclusion is one that he attempts to reconcile in his later work without conceding the point, through the claim that different approaches to reasoning are being employed. He suggests the claim that 'valuable aspects of the world constitute reasons' is motivated by what he refers to as the 'Classical Approach' to reason – one he believes to be flawed in that the connection between perceived value and reason is not one that can be supported.[88] Yet in making this claim, Raz is, in effect, rejecting the standard view of what it means to be an agent: that if an agent perceives value in an end, instrumental necessity requires that she also values the circumstances necessary to obtain that end and thus has a reason to act. He instead invites us to distinguish between features that show an act to be a choice, and those that show it to be of value – with reasons being more connected to the idea of choice than to value. This point, he argues, can be demonstrated through the example of an agent undertaking an action whose purpose is to specifically harm another; this can be a reason for action, but it is incorrect to describe it as being of value. Thus, an act need not possess value in order for an agent to see a reason for action.[89] This claim can be rejected, however, insofar as it conflates the subjective value perceived by the agent with an objective, measurable value; the former is the value present in the classical approach to reason present in the standard view of what it means to be an agent, not the latter objective value upon which Raz relies in his attempt to separate value from reasons for action. In his own example, the agent who acts specifically to harm another must necessarily see value in undertaking that harm; were this not the case, they simply would not have begun to act. It is this perceived value on the part of the agent that provides a reason for them to act, rather than the objective value claimed by Raz. His attack against the standard view of agency fails, requiring him to default to his earlier endorsement of the processes of deliberative rationality that in turn requires him to accept the PGC. Subjective agential preferences can therefore provide sound reasons for action, provided they are permissible with reference to the PGC. Those that are would be located high in the hierarchy for reasons for action, and those that are impermissible are necessarily to be discarded given the status of the PGC as an absolute and exclusionary second order reason.

3.3. Reasons Based in Authority

The third type of reason that Raz locates in his hierarchy are those grounded in recognition of authority. He argues that deference to authority is frequently

[88] Raz, *Engaging Reason* (n 45) 22–23.
[89] ibid 25.

the best way to maximise individual interests, as a coordinating authority can minimise conflict between agents and, by extension, maximise the overall good that can be achieved.[90] The authority must be de facto authority in order to coordinate action and, if authority is de facto, then a duty exists to comply.[91] But de facto authority need not be legitimate; legitimate de facto authority is a special kind of authority that serves the needs of those living underneath it. Raz refers to this as the 'Service Conception' of authority, yet it is a characterisation of authority which, he concedes, is problematic. On the theoretical level Raz questions how a duty to obey an authority can exist if based entirely on the will of another,[92] and on a moral level he asks how submission to authority can be valid should it circumvent our own independent capacity for moral reasoning.[93] Helpfully for our purposes, he believes he has identified answers to these concerns. These will be examined in turn, firstly for their success and secondly for their compliance with the PGC that Raz is required to accept given his own conception of deliberative rationality. This will then allow us to see where in the hierarchy of reasons those based on authority are located.

Firstly, he believes the theoretical objection – that a duty to obey an authority cannot exist if grounded entirely in the will of another – can be addressed with a closer examination of the concept of reasons, suggesting that a duty to follow an authority can exist if there is sufficient reason to accept it.[94] This justification is at best circular. It is a restatement of the standard view of what it is to be an agent and does not provide an adequate explanation of why one ought to submit to the will of another. It is a problem that will be identified in section 3 of Chapter 3 with reference to Kelsen's Basic Norm, or Hart's Secondary Rule of Recognition; to say we have a reason to follow an authority merely shifts the question of justification one step upwards, rephrasing it as why this reason is one an agent should accept. Raz does not deal with this objection directly, which is a problem for any discussion of why one ought to submit to authority when our conception of authority includes that claimed by law. His attempt to overcome the theoretical objection does not succeed, and his solution to his moral objection fails for a similar reason. Raz suggests the moral problem identified, that we ought to ask why we should submit to authority when to do so would circumvent our own capacity for moral reasoning, can be circumvented if an agent would better comply with reasons that already apply to her by following the directive of an authority rather than by reasoning independently.[95] This solution again shifts the question one step upwards to a question of why an

[90] J Raz 'Facing Up: A Reply' (1989) 62 *Southern California Law Review* 1153, 1192.

[91] ibid 1194.

[92] J Raz, *Between Authority and Interpretation: On the Theory of Law and Practical Reason* (Oxford University Press 2009) 134–35.

[93] ibid 136–37.

[94] ibid 136.

[95] ibid 136–37.

agent ought to accept this substitution if to do so might be a derogation of one's responsibilities as a moral agent, and fails to justify deference to authority.

This failure appears to be founded in Raz's characterisation of reasons that stem from authority, which should be seen 'not as denial of people's capacity for rational action, but simply one device, one method, through the use of which people can achieve the goal (telos) of their capacity for rational action, albeit not through its direct use'.[96] This suggests that Raz does not believe that reasons from authority cannot be absolute reasons but are, at best, conclusive. This characterisation does not sit well with his claim that authority must be de facto in order to be valid, which goes some way to highlight the problems his account faces. For if Raz is correct in suggesting that authority must be de facto in that it makes a claim that it ought to be obeyed, this same *ought* is somewhat undermined if Raz concedes it is not an absolute reason but can potentially be overruled by a conflicting, stronger reason should one be identified. The best way to reconcile this paradox is to claim that authority can only be de facto if it is legitimate, insofar as it is compliant with an external test for its permissibility and can make a true claim to be a conclusive reason for action. For reasons outlined above, Raz must concede that this is possible only if the authority issues instructions that are permissible with reference to the PGC. Reasons stemming from authority that are PGC compliant are thus capable of acting as conclusive reasons that are capable of guiding action and are thus high in the hierarchy of reasons. Those that are not PGC compliant cannot make a claim to guide our action as they are necessarily overridden by the absolute and exclusionary second order reason from the PGC. They are thus low in the hierarchy of reasons and should be rejected as being incapable of providing a reason for compliance.

3.4. Incommensurability Revisited

The three previous subsections have each concluded that each type of reason anticipated by Raz within his hierarchy – whether based in morality, personal interest, authority or rationality – can only succeed in providing a reason for action at all if the action directed is compliant with the PGC. This raises a problem with the operation of his hierarchy; if all these reasons trace their permissibility back to the same source, how can they serve to overrule one another in the event of conflict?[97] This problem is made even more difficult given that the means by which the PGC suggests such incommensurability could be resolved is reason alone.[98] The inescapable fact of incommensurability has resurfaced[99] and must

[96] ibid 140.
[97] ibid 145.
[98] Raz, *Engaging Reason* (n 45) 46.
[99] ibid 46.

be again unpacked to show how a PGC-influenced Razian hierarchy of reasons would resolve conflicts arising from competing reasons for action.

The problem identified by Raz with regards to resolving incommensurability within reasons for action that are equally permissible can be traced to his beliefs concerning the connection between value and action. The standard view of what it means to be an agent is that action is undertaken because an individual perceives value in a given end. Value is therefore central to reasons and reasoning insofar as an agent only has reason to act if to act would allow her to attain an end in which she sees subjective value.[100] Yet, as was discussed in the previous section regarding reasons arising from personal interest, Raz rejects this 'classical approach' to reason as being just one of two competing conceptions of what it means to act. According to the rival rationalist conception, action takes place purely because, of all the options available to them, an agent believes they have the strongest reason to Φ regardless of whether they see value in Φ. Proponents of the classical approach might reply here that there is little difference between these positions, given an agent would necessarily see the strongest reason to Φ in their seeing value in undertaking Φ. Yet Raz proposes three key differences between the two positions:

1. Rationalism holds that a reason is needed in order to require an action; the classical approach holds a reason merely renders an option eligible to be chosen.
2. Rationalism holds agential desire to be a reason; the classical approach holds will to be an independent factor.
3. Rationalism is committed to the claim that incommensurability is very rare, if not impossible; the classical approach presupposes widespread incommensurable reasons.[101]

In order to assess which conception of reasons is the one we ought to accept, let us return to our previous example of a shopper confronted with a range of identical cans of soup. It was argued that, should a choice between these cans truly be incommensurable, then our supermarkets would be replete with shoppers trapped in a soup-based limbo. The fact this is not a regular feature of our shopping experience suggests that agents do have a reason to prefer one can over another, even it is only chosen because it is the closest can. This example shows that the dichotomy that Raz presents between these approaches to reasoning is false; far from being mutually exclusive, the two can be subsumed into a single approach. For if an agent adopts the rationalist approach and picks the closest can of soup just because they think that they have the strongest reason to choose that can, then they place value resolving the incommensurability with which they are presented so that they can move to the next item on their shopping list. What appears to be a reason grounded in the rationalist approach, choosing

[100] ibid 47.
[101] ibid 47–48.

the strongest reason regardless of whether they see value in attaining that end, is actually a form of the classical approach. Raz may contest that this conflation is incorrect; that the agent here is not choosing a particular can for a given reason upon which they place value but is simply choosing to give up the other cans in favour of the one they ultimately decide to purchase. This categorises the reason for acting as independent from the value present in my desire for a can of soup, in that my action is to discard whereas my intention is to acquire. By reversing this rationalisation, Raz suggests that action can still take place in light of incommensurable reasons, as reasons are separate from action.[102] This should be rejected as nothing more than a sleight of hand. It does not circumvent the fact that the agent values ending the incommensurability with which they were presented, and that this was the value that motivated the action. The rationalist account and classical account of agency are simply opposite sides of the same coin.

To overcome Raz's objection to this unified account of agency, we must first delve deeper into understanding his problem with its component parts. Firstly, he holds that – as reasons are multiple and competing – it is simply not enough to claim that the only reason to act that an agent has is to do what will satisfy her brute desires, as this explanation cannot account for conflicting desires where an agent may want several inconsistent outcomes.[103] Though this objection could be characterised as artificial, in that reasons to behave in inconsistent ways will already have been weighed against one another before an agent decides to act upon whichever they value the most, Raz would reject this dismissal through his claim that the idea of people deliberating what they would like the most out of several desirable outcomes is itself peculiar.[104] This view seems to be grounded in his belief that desire only possesses instrumental value as a means to an end, meaning that the value of any end is external to the desire to attain it.[105] It is at this point that Raz's argument demonstrates its weaknesses, for it presupposes that external and objective value is the motivating factor behind all action. This is not the case; as has been demonstrated earlier, subjective desire is enough to generate a value that motives action. This is apparent from the standard view of what it means to be an agent; the statement that *I do X for purpose E* does not contain any reference to external value, but rather the value that the agent places on the given end. The agent therefore only needs to perceive subjective value in the end they are choosing to pursue in order to see it as valuable enough to motivate action.

A second objection he might raise to this unified account of agency would be his view that a reason need only render a desire eligible to be chosen and need

[102] ibid 48.
[103] ibid 50.
[104] ibid 51.
[105] ibid 51–52.

not necessitate that the agent act to attain it. This may be true, but it does not undermine the unified account of agency above; for the account does not hold that all eligible reasons should be acted on, a view seemingly ascribed to it by Raz's objection, but that any reason that corresponds to agential desire provides that agent with a reason to act. This does not preclude the possibility of a hierarchy of desires; it merely holds that, once an agent has weighed their competing desires to ascertain which end they desire the most, this desire is necessarily the one upon which the agent places the greatest value and thus has the best reason to Φ to attain. Raz ought to accept this characterisation given his belief that, if desires are reasons, then a rational agent faced with incommensurate reasons should follow the desire which generates the strongest reason.[106] This, he suggests, must again lead us to the view that desires only possess contingent value connected to the end being pursued – and can again be rejected for mischaracterising the notion of value. Returning to our example of soup, when an agent chooses one from many similar cans, they must have a reason for doing so or they would be unable to act. The fact they do choose suggests that they have a reason for choosing one over the others; this is axiomatic in that all action is connected to a purpose that an agent necessarily desires. Desire is thus a prerequisite for all action and must possess at least a minimum content of independent value as without it an agent would be unable to act. This is a conclusion Raz rejects, but at the point he does so he claims there is not enough room in the volume to explain why this is the case.[107] As it is unsupported, his position should be rejected as unsound.

Having established that both rationalist and classical accounts of agency are mutually compatible; that reasons are necessarily linked to desire and that agential desire is itself sufficient reason for action, we can come back to our starting point of incommensurability. Should reasons compete with one another for primacy when an agent is deliberating action, we can accept that the weightiest reason is the one upon which the agent should act. This statement presupposes an external reference point upon which an agent can assess the weight of the reasons they initially perceive as valid.[108] The PGC, as an absolute and exclusionary reason, can provide this reference point against which non-compliant reasons for action can be rejected. Those permissible reasons that remain are prima facie of equal weight, and if all acts are equally permissible then – subject to issues such as coordination which will be discussed in the following section about PGC compatible legal rules – it does not matter which reason an agent prioritises. They possess equal weight and, like a can of soup, all are equally legitimate grounds for action. Raz may be correct to identify that incommensurability is possible, but if all outcomes are permissible then he is wrong to categorise this as a problem.

[106] ibid 58.
[107] ibid 65.
[108] ibid.

4. CONCLUSION

Part 1 of this book is now complete. Chapter 1 showed that the PGC is capable of serving as a supreme moral principle. This chapter has taken this conclusion and has demonstrated that, based on his own understanding of practical reason, Raz ought to accept that the PGC is valid. It has also shown that Raz's commitment to the process of deliberative rationality, by which reasons for action are weighed to ascertain whether they can provide an absolute or conclusive reason for action, has the same starting point as the argument for the PGC. As such, he is committed to either accepting the dialectically necessary progression of the remainder of the argument as valid or abandoning his own starting point. As the latter is undesirable in light of the fact his starting assumptions are reflective of the standard view of what it means to be an agent, the internal consistency of his own account of deliberative rationality requires him to accept the validity of the argument for the PGC.

This, in turn, requires him to view the PGC as an absolute and exclusionary second order reason that precludes all non-compliant behaviour; to breach its requirements would be prima facie irrational and, as agents are committed to acting in what they perceive to be their own interests (whether or not this is founded on a false belief), they have no valid reason to act in an irrational manner. As Raz's objections to this conclusion have all been shown to fail, we must accept that the PGC necessitates a unified conception of all practical reason governed by a single normative hierarchy over which it serves as the ultimate test for the permissibility of any and all action. This hierarchy necessarily includes legal directives, meaning that a Razian account of reasons has shown that the PGC must exclude non-compliant legal directives from the scope of successful conclusive or absolute reasons for action. A successful natural law claim must build on this conclusion and demonstrate why this means that non-compliant legal directives are not law at all. Only once this has been argued can we justify the claim that a rule's moral permissibility is a necessary condition of its legal validity. It is to this task that Part 2 of this book will now turn.

Part 2

Establishing Permissibility with Reference to the PGC as a Necessary Condition of a Rule's Legal Validity

3

Agency, Morality and Law

1. INTRODUCTION

THIS BOOK HAS so far demonstrated that the PGC is capable of serving as a supreme moral principle against whose requirements all actions can be assessed for their moral permissibility. It has also shown, with reference to Raz's account of reasons for action, why this moral obligation serves as an absolute and exclusionary second order moral reason that must necessarily sit at the top of a unified hierarchy of practical reason that includes legal directives. Reasons that are compliant with the PGC must therefore exclude any non-compliant legal rule from serving as an absolute or conclusive reason for action. But this does not mean that a non-PGC compliant rule is not legally valid; we could simply conclude that it requires a person to break the legal rule in question and accept the legal sanction that follows. The natural law claim, that a rule's moral permissibility is a necessary condition of its legal validity, requires engagement with a specifically legal enquiry: How do legal rules govern our conduct? In his 1998 Clarendon Lecture, Jules Coleman suggests that law does this by providing a reason *for* action. Such reasons are distinct from other reasons *to* act, in that they are motivational or otherwise causal, and provide a stronger, overriding normative reason on which I base my ultimate action.[1] In Razian terms, this means that legal rules necessarily claim to be conclusive or absolute in character.[2]

This chapter will argue that, if Coleman is correct and law must provide a reason for action, this requires us to accept the natural law claim that a rule's moral permissibility is a necessary condition of its legal validity. It will first be shown that Coleman's assumption is correct and one we ought to accept with regard to the normative claim made by law and that the natural law claim must be true as a matter of logic. This claim will then be defended against some preliminary objections that might be offered from the positions of Kantian orthodoxy and Brian Leiter. The chapter will close by accounting for how the PGC could function in the way required by a strong theory of natural law by demonstrating

[1] J Coleman, *The Practice of Principle: In Defence of a Pragmatist Approach to Legal Theory* (Oxford University Press 2001) 70–72.

[2] See section 2.2 of Chapter 2.

how it must be integrated into both Hart and Kelsen's account of the creation of legal norms in order for their theories to succeed.

2. THE PGC AND LEGAL NORMS

The first part of this chapter seeks to establish the truth of a claim that has been made several times in this work so far: that both natural lawyers and legal positivists necessarily accept that the purpose of law is to guide conduct, and thus that law is an essentially normative concept. It will do this in two parts. Firstly, it will be shown that any difference in the position taken by natural lawyers and legal positivists is more than a mere linguistic disagreement that has emerged from a problem with the translation and subsequent conflation of the Latin terms 'lex' and 'ius' into the single English word 'law,'[3] and that it is from this conflation of terminology that natural law theory mistakenly emerges. Secondly, it will be argued that, in order for any conclusions to be reached as to whether the moral permissibility of a legal rule is a necessary feature of its legal validity, both natural lawyers and legal positivists need to agree on a neutral starting point from which the enquiry can proceed. This will be referred to as an 'agreed referent' and is necessary to avoid the problem of linguistic indeterminacy. The remainder of the section will then move on to demonstrate why this starting point requires us to accept the truth of the natural law position.

2.1. The Need for an Agreed Referent

Many believe that the dispute between natural lawyers and legal positivists as to whether moral permissibility is a necessary criterion of a rule's legal validity arises from nothing more than a linguistic disagreement arising from a translation error and conflation of the Latin terms 'lex' and 'ius' into a single English word – law. Glanville Williams adhered to this view, suggesting that both schools of thought are speaking about normatively different concepts; 'lex' – positive law – is the proper focus of legal scholarship, whereas 'ius' as a term contains a conception of justice or fairness absent from 'lex', but upon which natural lawyers and legal idealists have improperly focused their work. As such, any disagreement is merely semantic and, by extension, not a disagreement that will ever be satisfactorily solved.[4] Some take this scepticism further and argue that successfully identifying a definition of the term 'law' is so difficult as to be impossible given that it appears to encompass so much, with regard to both

[3] GJ Postema, 'Law as Command: The Model of Command in Modern Jurisprudence' in E Sosa and E Villanueva (eds), *Social, Political and Legal Philosophy* (Blackwell 2001) 478–79.

[4] G Williams, 'The Controversy Concerning the Word "Law".' in P Laslett (ed), *Philosophy, Politics and Society*, (Basil Blackwell 1970) 134.

thought and action. This meaning-scepticism was clearly conveyed by Thurman Arnold, who said of 'law' that: 'Any attempt to define the word leads us into a maze of metaphysical literature, perhaps larger than has ever surrounded any other symbol in the history of the world.'[5] This linguistic confusion, according to Williams, can be said to arise from our tendency as human beings to attempt to objectify what are nothing more than conceptual abstractions:

> As soon as we realise that bird or law are simply mental abstractions from the raw material of the universe, and that they do not exist by themselves separately anywhere, we realize that the idea of a true definition is a superstition.[6]

If Williams is correct here, then no definition of law can ever be objectively true or untrue as there is no objective starting point from which the facts of law – or indeed, the existence of any concept – can be assessed.[7] Words cannot possess an 'intrinsically 'proper' or 'improper' meaning as they are merely a 'symbol for an idea [which] may vary with the person who uses the word'.[8] Williams' position appears close to Wittgenstein's paradox of meaning, as discussed in his *Philosophical Investigations*:

> [N]o course of action could be determined by a rule, because any course of action can be made out to accord with the rule. The answer was: if any action can be made out to accord with the rule, then it can also be made out to conflict with it. And so there would be neither accord nor conflict here.[9]

Wittgenstein is here suggesting that we can never be truly certain what we mean by a word used to express a given concept unless, when we use the word in question, we actively consider every possible meaning of the word and settle on one objective meaning. Since it is impossible to do this, it is impossible to ever state that we know the objective meaning of any word when we engage in any form of communication. If Wittgenstein is correct, then this book has a difficult task to overcome. Any use of the word 'law' would be entirely descriptive from the subjective viewpoint of the speaker; it would thus be impossible to successfully argue that the moral permissibility of a rule is a necessary criterion of its legal validity given that a single, objective definition of 'law' is itself impossible.

Saul Kripke can help us out of this paradox and demonstrates that concepts that are concerned with intentionality and future action are necessarily more than just descriptive.[10] This book has so far claimed that both positivists and natural lawyers ought to agree that law is essentially a normative concept so, if Kripke is correct, then our enterprise could perhaps be saved from Wittgenstein's and Williams' meaning-scepticism. We will begin with what Kripke has to say

[5] T Arnold, *The Symbols of Government*, (Yale University Press 1935) 216.
[6] Williams (n 4) 151.
[7] ibid 151.
[8] ibid 136.
[9] L Wittgenstein, *Philosophical Investigations* (GEM Anscombe tr, 3rd edn, Blackwell 1953) 69, §201.
[10] SA Kripke, *Wittgenstein on Rules and Private Language* (Harvard University Press 1982) 37.

about conceptual disciplines such as mathematics. He gives the example of addition, asking whether there is a correct answer to the question 'What is 68 plus 57?' Whilst we expect the answer to this question to be 125, this is dependent on both the questioner and respondent having a shared understanding as to the meaning of the word 'plus' as referring to the process of addition. He asks us to contemplate an individual who, instead of understanding 'plus' as meaning 'addition', instead understands it as referring to the process of 'quaddition'. Unlike addition, which adds both totals together, quaddition requires us to reject this conclusion if both values in our sum are 57 or above. If this is the case, then regardless of the value of each number, quaddition requires us to give the answer '5'. Would they be incorrect in answering thus upon hearing the word 'plus'?[11] If we were to answer 'yes' to this question, Kripke suggests we ought next to ask how we can be certain such an answer is indeed incorrect. Again, we must look to the shared understanding – or in this case, the lack of shared understanding – as to the meaning of the word 'plus'. To explain its absence in the above example, Kripke proposes two sources from which a shared understanding can arise; those resting on Brain Function (F_b) and those resting on a Community Function (F_c). To explain the difference, let us consider a situation in which we ask a speaker to present the statement '68 plus 57 = 125' to a community who accepts quaddition as described above. If any shared understanding of meaning rests on the interpretation of the concept by a given community, (F_c), then our community of quaddition would tell her they reject the statement as the correct answer would be five. If, however, our speaker was to insist that her initial statement was correct, she would be claiming that the validity of a claim does not rely on its acceptance by a community, even if that acceptance is unanimous, and would show herself to be relying on (F_b). In doing this, she therefore claims that any ascription of meaning contains an 'ought' in the form of a truth claim and is therefore normative in character.[12]

Applying this to our dispute around whether the moral permissibility of a rule is a necessary condition of its legal validity, then the quaddition vs addition dispute is analogous to the respective positions taken by legal positivists and natural lawyers. The lack of shared understanding as to the scope of the concept does not hide the fact that both natural lawyers and positivists, in believing their conception is correct, are adopting a position that prioritises (F_b) over (F_c) with regard to the meaning of the word 'law'. Were it not the case that both assume that the dispute is one that has a correct answer identifiable through (F_b), the dispute would not exist. Should a resolution be both possible and desirable, we must therefore work to identify a starting point for the enquiry that is equally acceptable to both schools of thought. This is necessary as, should either school begin their argumentation with a starting point that is not acceptable to the

[11] ibid 9.
[12] A Gibbard, *Meaning and Normativity* (Oxford University Press 2012) 45–46.

other, they would reach a conclusion resting on (F_c) that would be incapable of persuading the other side to reject their own conclusions that they contend rest on (F_b). This, Toddington acknowledges, may be easier said than done. It might be simple to reach a satisfactory definition for enquiries into natural phenomena such as mathematics, but in social phenomena such as law – founded in abstract and seemingly diverse theoretical suppositions – a single, acceptable starting point is more difficult to pin down.[13] It is not immediately obvious why this should be the case, however. Facts which concern states of affairs are as inherently natural as other facts; even if those situations are socially constructed, the controversy still revolves around determining a particular state of affairs. It therefore remains a normative question with regard to the validity of a truth claim that prioritises (F_b) over (F_c).[14] Any attempt to demonstrate the truth of a socially constructed state of affairs must thus focus on the social function of the phenomenon as its principle determinant, as without this it could not exist.[15] By prioritising social function, a plurality of conceptions can be permitted which can be legitimately debated for their truth whilst simultaneously ruling out conceptions that cannot be plausibly countenanced as possible.[16]

Applying this so far to our enquiry: both natural lawyers and positivists claim that their answer to the question of whether the moral permissibility of a rule is a necessary criterion of its legal validity is correct. Both therefore claim an understanding of law that prioritises (F_b) over (F_c). If we are to demonstrate the truth of one position over the other, then a starting point for the enquiry that is acceptable to both positions must be identified[17] – and given law is socially created, the only starting point that can be identified without presupposing a particular conception of the concept must place the function of legal rules at its core. Only from this starting point can a meaningful enquiry take place that allows a sound conceptional discussion of the social practice of law.[18] From here on, this starting point will be known as an *agreed referent*; the one that will be endorsed by this work is that contained in the work of Beyleveld and Brownsword:

> Law ... refers to '*the enterprise of subjecting human conduct to the governance of rules*', ... the choice of this referent is a stipulation and we can only have a genuine debate with those who are prepared to accept this starting point. Disagreement over the concept of law is to be viewed in terms of different ways of conceptualizing this referent.[19]

[13] S Toddington, *Rationality, Social Action and Moral Judgment* (Edinburgh University Press 1993) 28–29.

[14] Gibbard (n 12) 49.

[15] Toddington (n 13) 58; P Capps, *Human Dignity and the Foundations of International Law* (Hart 2009) 23, 43.

[16] Toddington (n 13) 65.

[17] D Beyleveld and R Brownsword, *Law as a Moral Judgment* (Sweet and Maxwell 1986) 119.

[18] Capps (n 15) 41.

[19] Beyleveld and Brownsword, (n 17) 120; emphasis added to denote referent.

The contention that law is 'the enterprise of subjecting human conduct to the governance of rules' is an appropriate referent in that it makes no reference to the moral permissibility of the rule posited as law, merely that law is an attempt to resolve disputes with reference to norms.[20] It is therefore neutral on the question of whether the moral permissibility of a rule is necessary for its legal validity, and should be equally acceptable to both legal positivists and natural lawyers.

At this point, some common objections to this choice of agreed referent ought to be addressed. Firstly, as I have noted in previous work,[21] some would disagree with the very idea that a functional definition of law is an acceptable starting point for jurisprudential enquiry. This objection is raised by Brian Tamanaha, who believes such definitions are over-inclusive as they can equally serve as the starting point of enquiries into social phenomena, such as etiquette or the rules of a club, that are not law. For this reason, he suggests such starting points should be rejected.[22] This conclusion is demonstrably false, as can be seen should we consider the example of a pen. It is axiomatically the purpose of a pen to allow its holder to make marks on a plane of some sort; the fact that this functional definition can equally be applied to a crayon, a pencil or a piece of chalk does not make it less true of the pen. Similarly, it remains possible to distinguish a pen from a crayon or a piece of chalk despite them sharing the same functional purpose. The same can be said of law; the fact that club rules or social etiquette also seek to guide human conduct does not make it any less true that legal rules also serve the exact same purpose whilst remaining a distinct social phenomena. A second, connected criticism of a referent that is functional is that such a limitation overlooks the structural component of law: that rules must necessarily emanate from a specific source, and it is this source alone that gives them binding, normative force. This criticism is also misplaced. Including a structural component that specifies a necessary source of the normative claim made by law is to take a side in the natural law or positivist debate, meaning any such account would be rejected by the opposing school as presupposing the thing it attempts to prove. Since an agreed referent is necessarily one upon which all sides to a debate must agree, including a structural element would preclude any such definition from the purpose it needs to fulfil; meaning the value of a purely functional account of law as an agreed referent is that it remains silent on the source of legal norms.[23]

In proposing this agreed referent, Beyleveld and Brownsword have identified an acceptable starting point for both schools of thought. In doing this, they have therefore arrived at a definition of 'law' which is properly grounded in (F_b) and

[20] ibid 120.

[21] J Jowitt, 'Legal Rights for Animals: Aspiration or Logical Necessity?' (2020) 11(2) *Journal of Human Rights and the Environment* 173, 187–88.

[22] B Tamanaha, *A Realistic Theory of Law* (Cambridge University Press 2017) 43. See also: J Austin, *The Province of Jurisprudence Determined* (first published 1832, WE Rumble ed. Cambridge University Press 1995) 123–25.

[23] Toddington (n 13) 65; Capps (n 15) 23, 43.

not (F_c). They have done this by prioritising the focal aspect of the referent, thus emphasising the non-semantic properties of the concept of law to explain its overall development as an idea.[24] This referent is thus capable of circumventing Wittgenstein and Williams' linguistic scepticism as to the possibility of a single, objective meaning behind a word such as 'law' as, by focusing on function instead of substance, our agreed referent allows for a plurality of conceptions and merely excludes those that are non-plausible candidates for consideration. (F_b) is therefore attained by consensus as to the core function of the term which is under dispute.

2.2. Law and Practical Reason

Having identified an agreed referent from which our enquiry can proceed, this work can begin to build towards advancing its main thesis by demonstrating the necessary link between law and practical reason. We will begin by noting that our agreed referent means that legal enquiry is axiomatically normative. Gibbard notes that, although this term 'has no single meaning in the academic fields that employ it', we are nonetheless able to state uncontroversially that 'normative judgements are "ought" judgements.'[25] By attempting to subject human conduct to the governance of rules, the very function of law is therefore to advance a normative claim – that the rule being advanced is one that ought to be followed by those to whom it is addressed. If our referent necessarily advances the view that law is a normative claim, it follows that legal directives rest firmly within the realm of practical reason in that an attempt is being made to guide our action. Law therefore necessarily claims to provide an absolute and overriding reason for us to follow its requirements.[26] Thus, any normative claim that is made by law, although it can be new and distinct from other normative claims, cannot be separated from the framework of deliberative rationality within which decisions on how we ought to act are formed. The point is made succinctly by Capps:

> [L]aw is autonomous in the sense of it being a set of distinctive general norms which are established to stabilise social relationships within a community, but it is not autonomous in the sense that it must be isolated from broader concerns of practical reasonableness if it is to fulfil this function.[27]

If it is true that the normative claim necessarily advanced by all legal rules cannot be separated from the broader framework of practical reason, then it follows that the concept of law also cannot be separated from the concept of agency. To unpack this claim fully, we must first ask what we mean by the term

[24] P Horwich, *Truth* (Oxford University Press 1990) 28.
[25] Gibbard (n 12) 10.
[26] S Bertea, *The Normative Claim of Law* (Hart 2009) 160–61.
[27] Capps (n 15) 129.

'practical reason'. Various conceptions exist of varying completeness, but Bertea identifies that a minimal core exists n each of them:

> [T]he minimally necessary self-conception is the outcome of the capacity for self-reflection that enables human agents to move about in the practical sphere in specific ways and makes each individual capable of recognising herself as such.[28]

This minimal conception of practical reason is, for Bertea, is what it means to be an agent:

> [H]uman agency is the capacity to act on models established by reflective, rational and autonomous choice; and human agents are subjects capable of acting on self-imposed reasons, reasons they have worked out for themselves exercising their capacity for reflection.[29]

Practical reason, on a minimal understanding of the concept, is inescapably connected with the ability of agents to respond to competing reasons for them to behave in different ways by assessing the strength of the reason they have to prioritise a given course of action over another.[30] As law necessarily contains a normative claim that it is capable of guiding our actions, then an agent must necessarily assess the validity of this claim when deciding whether to act according to the legal directive in question. A connection can therefore be seen to exist between the concepts of legal obligation, practical reason and agency.[31] A common counter to this necessary connection between agency and law is that any attempt to characterise agency in this way is meaningless. This minimal conception is simply too abstract; individuals in the real world do not see themselves as complying with such a definition. We do not exist as machines acting according to the demands placed upon us by practical reason. Instead, individuals necessarily see themselves as embedded within certain social and cultural practices; it is these practices which more often guide our actions than an appeal to the machine-like practical reason employed by minimal conceptions of agency. Therefore, to have any meaningful existence, definitions of agency must make reference to these social and cultural practices which, more often than not, are the true guides of our behaviour.[32] Such an observation may have its appeal, yet it appears to operate on a misunderstanding of what is *necessary* for agency and what may be considered as *contingent* influences on how an agent makes their decisions. It is thus analogous to the objection raised by Williams in section 3.1 of Chapter 1, and can be rejected for the same reasons.

A second objection to the connection between legal directives and individual agency could be the claim that law is systemic; that the validity of an individual

[28] Bertea (n 26) 208, emphasis original.
[29] ibid 202.
[30] ibid 197–202.
[31] ibid 224, 227–28.
[32] S Fish, *Doing What Comes Naturally: Change, Rhetoric, and the Practice of Theory in Literary and Legal Studies* (Duke University Press 1990) 13.

legal norm cannot be assessed independently of a broader judgement with regard to the validity of the bigger system of which it is a part.[33] Individual legal rules are merely a set of facts that describe, amongst other things, the action of a legislature and the power dynamics present within a particular legal system. By restating the claim of law in terms of socially contingent facts within a broader system, the claim of individual laws is recategorised away from a strict normative 'ought' and towards a socially constructed 'is'.[34] If this statement is true, then it might cause us to question whether individual legal norms themselves always possess normative content and, by extension, the acceptability of our agreed referent. This point will be addressed more fully in section 4 of Chapter 4, but for the time being we can offer a brief response: by claiming that a socially constructed fact is a valid legal rule without reference to any normative claim it may (or may not) possess, it adopts a starting point that presupposes a positivist conception of legal validity. It thus departs from our agreed referent and would be rejected by natural lawyers. Both arguments thus fail to disprove the claim that legal directives are necessarily normative and are thus located within the concept of agency and the broader hierarchy of practical reason.

2.3. Fitting the Pieces Together

Chapter 1 of this book summarised and defended Gewirth's argument for the PGC, showing it to be capable of operating as a test for the moral permissibility of all action through the dialectically necessary progression of its argument. The inescapable fact of agency requires all agents to make claim-rights to their GCAs, and this pragmatic, self-reflexive 'ought' is rendered a universal moral standard by becoming other regarding, insofar as agents must recognise that all other agents must also be capable of making the same claim rights by dint of their own agency. It thus follows that all agents must respect these rights or else undermine the foundation of their own rights claim, and any action that interferes with the GCAs of another agent without their consent is therefore morally impermissible. Chapter 2 then showed why this requires us to accept that the PGC operates as an absolute and exclusionary second order reason that sits at the top of all hierarchies of reasons to act, and therefore limits the scope of all permissible primary reasons to those that are compatible with its requirements. This chapter has, so far, provided the final piece in the jigsaw of a successful natural law argument – that we must proceed from a starting point that is acceptable to all schools of thought. This must be a functional account of law, as this is the only starting point that can successfully convey the normative claim made by legal rules whilst not taking a position on whether a rule's moral permissibility is a necessary condition of its legal validity. We have also

[33] Bertea (n 26) 30.
[34] ibid 140.

shown how this referent requires us to view legal directives as part of a unified conception of reasons for action grounded in practical rationality. This final section will demonstrate that, if we put these pieces together, we are required to conclude that a rule's moral permissibility with reference to the requirements of the PGC is a necessary condition of its legal validity.

Our starting point will be to return to a necessary feature of the agreed referent that was alluded to in the previous section; if the purpose of law is to subject human conduct to the governance of rules, then the nature of this normative claim requires the rule in question to be prima facie capable of serving as an absolute or conclusive reason for action. Legal rules are thus located at the level of practical rationality; they are therefore part of a unified hierarchy of norms, in which all normative claims compete to provide an absolute or conclusive reason to guide our behaviour. This hierarchy includes moral norms, thus locating the normative claim of law in the same hierarchy as the PGC.[35] Since the PGC acts as a test for moral permissibility of all action, and thus binds all agents to only act in a way that is compatible with its requirements, it axiomatically sits at the top of any normative hierarchy as an absolute and exclusionary reason to avoid behaving in a non-compliant manner. This means that only rules that are morally permissible, according to the test provided by the PGC, are capable of acting as an absolute or conclusive reason for action so as to be able to successfully make a claim that they should be followed. Since a rule must be capable of claiming this in order to meet the definition of law provided by our agreed referent, it follows that only PGC-compliant rules are capable of functioning as law. We can thus conclude, in agreement with Beyleveld and Brownsword, that all rules must be PGC compliant in order to be legally valid.[36]

If this conclusion is correct, and a rule's permissibility with reference to the PGC is a necessary condition of its legal validity, it follows that this test for moral permissibility necessarily forms part of what Hart might refer to as the rule of recognition; the test employed by legal officials operating in a legal system to identify which rules are legally valid.[37] Again, following Beyleveld and Brownsword, a PGC-compliant rule of recognition would take the following form:

(a) there is authority under the PGC to posit the rule for attempted enforcement; and
(b) the norm prescribed by the rule involves no substantive violation of the PGC's act morality.[38]

This rule of recognition contains two distinct components, both of which are necessary for the legal validity of a given norm. The first is procedural and is

[35] Beyleveld and Brownsword, *Law as a Moral Judgment* (n 17) 189.
[36] ibid 190.
[37] HLA Hart, *The Concept of Law* (3rd edn, Oxford University Press 2012) 94–95.
[38] Beyleveld and Brownsword, *Law as a Moral Judgment* (n 17) 328.

concerned with the legitimacy of the person(s) or body(/ies) tasked with creating legal rules. Beyleveld and Brownsword suggest that the lawmaker must have authority under the PGC to create legal rules, and such authority can be attained in two circumstances: where the act of the authorised agent is PGC compliant, and where the act of the authorised agent is based on a sincere attempt to successfully apply the PGC. These are referred to as theoretical and practical authority respectively, and are the only means by which a valid legal norm can be created.[39] If the act of the authorised agent is not based on a serious attempt to apply the PGC then this is an abuse of authority and cannot produce legally valid rules.[40] In this sense, the PGC acts as a limitation on the ability of officials to create legal norms. This is a claim that ought not to be controversial for legal scholars to accept, namely because such provisions already exist in many legal systems, in the form of constitutional provisions or Bills of Rights, that limit the ability of lawmakers to make law on similar, moral grounds. The PGC is therefore acting in a similar capacity to rules that already exist by requiring this first criterion within the PGC-compliant rule of recognition.[41]

We now turn to the second, substantive, criterion: that legal rules can only be valid if their content is morally permissible with reference to the requirements of the PGC. Two criticisms may be laid against this substantive criterion. Firstly, it could be argued – as a matter of legal realism – that morally impermissible laws simply have existed and will continue to exist. This objection is common but misplaced and can be dismissed because it presupposes a positivist conception of law. Unlike our agreed referent, which is silent as to why a rule can possess normative force, this objection assumes that a rule becomes law purely because it is posited by an authorised law-making body and that, by extension, its substantive requirements are not relevant to questions of its legal validity. Since it presupposes the point of view it seeks to demonstrate, it should be rejected. Should our critic persist, however, an analogy may help them understand why their criticism fails. Let us accept *arguendo* that a pie comprises of a filling encased in pastry, thus giving us a definition resting in (F_b) that is required for any dispute to be resolved. If one were to order a pie and be served a stew with a pastry lid balanced on top of it, then this is not a pie. The fact that the menu claims this is a pie; that the chef charged with making it is happy to serve it as a pie; or even the fact that other diners may have accepted it as a pie are all irrelevant (F_c) considerations. You may not even particularly care that this is not a pie at all, but this does not alter the central fact: if it does not meet the (F_b) definition of the thing it purports to be, then it is not a pie. It is something else. The same can be said of counterfeit money; fake banknotes are, for all intents and purposes, identical to real currency, and are widely accepted as such by the majority of the population. They may even fulfil the same function in certain

[39] ibid 297–98.
[40] ibid 292–93.
[41] ibid 302–03.

situations. However, they fail to meet the definition of what it means to be real currency. Mark Murphy makes the same claim with regard to diamonds, arguing that it is not inconsistent to insist that a fake diamond is not a diamond – even if it may otherwise pass as such.[42] The same, then, is true of law; the natural law claim is not that morally impermissible rules do not exist and are not enforced by legal systems, but that these rules are not law. What they are is not important for the present analysis; what matters is that it is not law per our necessary (F_b) agreed referent, but something else that is instead defined with reference to (F_c). This conclusion is necessary given our agreed referent is the only permissible, neutral starting point from which our enquiry can proceed; thus, by assuming the position it seeks to prove, the objection from legal realism simply cannot succeed in overcoming the natural law claim.

A second objection to the substantive claim that legal rules can only be valid if their requirements are compliant with the requirements of the PGC could be raised, in that this claim ignores the fact of legal pluralism; legal systems simply do differ as a matter of social fact, thus suggesting that any settled substantive content with regard to legal norms is misplaced. This argument is misplaced for two reasons. Firstly, it presupposes a positivist notion of legal validity in that it presupposes that legal validity arises when a rule is passed by the relevant law-making body; it is therefore incompatible with the agreed referent that necessarily must act as the starting point for our enquiry. Secondly, the critique mischaracterises the claim being made. A PGC-compliant rule of recognition need not result in a single set of rules that all legal systems must necessarily arrive at; it is, instead, a test for permissibility and the scope for the substantive content of the legal rules posited by a relevant authority remains extremely broad. Beyleveld and Brownsword address this point when they identify three types of rules which can allow for rational and not unreasonable disagreement, whilst retaining the force of law:

1. A choice of rule where the PGC allows multiple outcomes, but one must be chosen – such as a decision as to which side of the road to drive on.
2. A rule where the PGC gives different weight to different generic conditions of action and, by extension, the generic rights they generate, but where the extent to which these rights are affected is uncertain and disputed.
3. A rule which requires a complex application of the PGC which may give rise to reasonable doubt about the veracity of the PGC-compliance of the rule.[43]

It is only when a rule is clearly and unambiguously in breach of the requirements of the PGC that it is incapable of providing a reason why it ought to be followed, and thus cannot succeed as a valid legal rule. Thus, a community is still able to

[42] M Murphy, *Natural Law in Jurisprudence and Politics* (Cambridge University Press 2006) 20.

[43] D Beyleveld and R Brownsword, 'Principle, Proceduralism and Precaution in a Community of Rights' (2006) 19(2) *Ratio Juris* 141, 147–48.

legitimately propose diverse rules to co-ordinate the conduct of those to whom it is addressed, as a wide range of morally permissible rules are available to be posited as law. PGC-compliant legal rules can thus serve as a legitimate way to resolve disputes, and allow for legal pluralism rather than requiring a single set of legal rules in the form of a moral directive.[44] Another reason why legal pluralism is not just possible but unavoidable within a legal system in which the PGC operates as a test for the legal validity of posited rules is the fact that the application of the PGC is necessarily context specific, meaning that the permissibility of an action is dependent on the circumstances in which it takes place. The example is given of Society A, in which food is scarce, and Society B, where food is plentiful. A rule which allows citizens to retain crop production which is surplus to their requirements would be permissible in Society B, but not in Society A – where a result of the rule would be starving citizens who are unable to feed themselves.[45] This rule demonstrates that the PGC merely indicates whether a rule is permissible, and thus allows for reasonable legal pluralism.[46]

Any legal system must be supported by a functioning system of adjudication, and an account of what a PGC-compliant system of adjudication might look like will be briefly sketched here. Such a system must be capable of dealing not only with disputes in situations where the PGC permits multiple legal outcomes, but also in practical situations: such as where technological change may require rapid regulatory updates to ensure PGC compatibility of the relevant rules, or in otherwise complex situations where the PGC may not provide a clear answer about the permissibility of a given rule.[47] Our starting point must therefore be to acknowledge the procedural requirement necessary for compliance with PGC: that judges, in their capacity as legal officials, must act in a PGC compliant manner at all times in order for their judgments to be legally valid. They are thus required to make 'a sincere and serious attempt at reasonable justification' to ensure the PGC compatibility of the outcome of their deliberations.[48] The procedural soundness of this adjudicatory framework can be ensured by adopting legal maxims that are already widely upheld and accepted, such as *audi alteram partem* and *nemo iudex in causa sua*.[49] Yet substantive requirements must also be placed on the judicial role; assessing the moral permissibility of the application of an individual rule to a given situation is no longer a peripheral concern for a judge, but becomes, instead, an essential part of their deliberation.[50]

An objection to this account of the judicial role may be raised here as follows. If a judge, a single agent, must make a decision in which they are required to

[44] Capps (n 15) 161–62; 166–67.

[45] Beyleveld and Brownsword, *Law as a Moral Judgment* (n 17) 190.

[46] ibid 190–91.

[47] Beyleveld and Brownsword, 'Principle, Proceduralism and Precaution in a Community of Rights' (n 43) 148, 154.

[48] Beyleveld and Brownsword, *Law as a Moral Judgment* (n 17) 386 n 6; 402–03.

[49] ibid 393.

[50] ibid 401.

account for how a rule may affect all other agents, the PGC-compliant system above could collapse into a form of utilitarianism whereby a crude assessment as to the 'greater good' is reached rather than a sound and considered assessment of the permissibility of the rule.[51] This conclusion is not a given, however, as the following differences exist between the utilitarian approach and that required by an agent attempting to act in accordance with the PGC:

(a) The PGC prescribes an objective and identifiable end through a dialectically necessary method; there is no room for subjective value judgements on utility.
(b) The PGC is more limited; an objective limit exists to the duties which correlate with positive rights.
(c) The PGC imposes duties to help those who cannot help themselves, rather than legitimising action merely to maximise benefit to the community.
(d) Conflicts of rights legitimised by the PGC are not solved by appeal to utility maximisation, but by a cost–benefit analysis on which right best promotes the equal agency of all PPAs; those which are more essential to agency take priority.
(e) The purpose of the PGC is to ensure necessary conditions of agency are available to all PPAs rather than the majority; it is distributive, not aggregative.[52]

The PGC differs from utilitarian theories of morality in that it is self-justifying, insofar as a breach of its requirements creates a logical fallacy in which one argues it is permissible to violate the rights of others whilst relying on one's own rights to do so. The PGC, therefore, does not ask an agent to apply generic rights to recipients, but rather to render them in proportion with their own.[53]

It can be conceded, however, that the PGC-compliant account of legal adjudication outlined above is more easily applied to some spheres of law than others. For example, criminal law – including sanctions – can be seen as necessary to ensure the generic rights of agents are protected and upheld.[54] Equally, criminal defences can be justified – such as the permissibility of violence when used in self-defence, provided (a) no other course of action is available; and (b) the violence is not a retributive infliction of harm, but is a genuine attempt to restore the equilibrium of non-harm.[55] It would be more difficult to fully account for the scope of other legal rights given that, as well as precluding morally impermissible conduct, the PGC is capable of imposing positive legal obligations with regard to goods necessary to enjoy one's GCAs. To understand this, it is necessary to differentiate three kinds of goods:

(a) Basic Goods, which provide basic wellbeing required for action. These include life, physical integrity (including requisite food, shelter and the like), mental equilibrium and personal confidence that one's ends may be achieved.

[51] D Cumminsky, 'Gewirth's Kantian Consequentialism' in M Boylan (ed), *Gewirth: Critical Essays on Action, Rationality and Community* (Rowman & Littlefield 1998) 128.
[52] ibid 128–29.
[53] A Gewirth, *Reason and Morality* (University of Chicago Press 1978) 203–04.
[54] ibid 294, 298.
[55] ibid 213–15.

(b) Nonsubstantive Goods, which require that an agent's purpose fulfilment is not lowered by ensuring agents retain and do not lose what they already possess and see as a good.
(c) Additive Goods, whose aim is the amelioration of purpose fulfilment by allowing action whose aim is to increase the goods attained.[56]

It is conceivable that social conditions may mean that an individual lacks the basic goods that are necessary for them to enjoy their GCAs. If this is the case, and the PGC requires us to ensure our acts do not harm the GCAs of other agents, then the continued existence of the social conditions which deprive others of the basic goods necessary for their enjoyment of their GCAs is in breach of the PGC. A positive duty to assist is therefore created, provided this does not create a substantial loss to the assistor. The PGC may also serve to shift this burden predominantly upon the state itself, given it would be in a better position to undertake such legal obligations than a collection of individuals.[57] Although practically difficult to enforce, the concept of positive legal obligations stemming from the PGC is sound and ought to be accepted as valid. There is therefore no practical obstacle against our acceptance of the natural law claim advanced above.

2.4. Some Preliminary Objections

Having shown that the PGC must necessarily feature in any assessment as to the legal validity of a given rule, this section will close by considering two initial objections to the natural law claim that has been advanced. In light of the essentially Kantian conception of practical rationality and agency upon which the argument for the PGC rests, the first of these will proceed from Kant's own ideas on the nature of legal obligations. Our discussion will begin with the claim, grounded in a literal reading of the *Metaphysics of Morals*, that Kant firmly distinguishes between natural and juridical law. This has led some authors to characterise Kant as an early legal positivist;[58] yet this reading appears misplaced. Kant more subtly argues that juridical law itself contains content that is both positive and natural in origin.[59] He holds that knowledge of natural law is necessary for judicial science; only when moral knowledge is combined with empirical knowledge of the requirements of positive law can the subsequent enquiry appropriately be classed as jurisprudence.[60] Far from being a proto-positivist, Kant instead claims that a true knowledge and understanding

[56] ibid 53–56.
[57] A Gewirth, *The Community of Rights* (University of Chicago Press 1996) Ch. 2.
[58] M Willaschek, 'Which Imperatives for Right? On the Non-Prescriptive Character of Juridical Laws in Kant's *Metaphysics of Morals*' in M Timmons (ed) *Kant's Metaphysics of Morals: Interpretive Essays* (Oxford University Press 2002) 65–87.
[59] I Kant, *The Metaphysics of Morals* (M Gregor tr, Cambridge University Press 1996) 6:224.
[60] ibid 6:239.

of the nature and requirements of positive law can only be achieved if one sees it as being in isolation from morality and the broader realm of practical reason.

Law is necessarily part of this broader realm because all action itself rests on the axiom that certain practical principles are universally instrumentally necessary regardless of the end being pursued by the individual agent.[61] Such principles are thus intrinsically good, in that all agents must see them as necessary for all action.[62] Moral requirements that are designed to protect action can also be characterised as practical principles that are universally instrumentally necessary and are thus also intrinsically good, as action itself is intrinsically necessary for all ends and so should, itself, be seen as a good.[63] If moral laws thus act as if they are a categorical imperative,[64] then we must conclude that judicial laws that are morally impermissible are normatively inferior to a conflicting moral norm.[65] This briefly sketched position is remarkably similar to the argument that a rule's compliance with the PGC is a necessary condition of its legal validity. An accurate account of Kant's conception of positive law thus requires us to acknowledge that legal normativity is necessarily connected to moral permissibility.[66]

This conclusion again relies on the centrality of practical reason previously discussed; the 'function of [which] is to order concepts so as to give them the greatest possible unity combined with the widest possible application'.[67] Without reason, concepts claiming to guide our action would be unable to be applied to the world; they would exist '[I]solated and separated from one another (by an empty intervening space)'.[68] Agency, and the necessary grounds and limitations within which it operates, is therefore centrally important to the causality of concepts.[69] Since law itself is conceptual, rather than a physical object, it is not unreasonable to claim that 'the idea of [practical] reason runs through the whole length of law as a single fiber that connects each part with every other part'.[70] Practical reason requires us to see that any obligations that arise from the necessary conditions of agency are intrinsically obligatory and, by extension, cannot be excluded from any consideration of whether one is bound by a

[61] I Kant, *Groundwork of the Metaphysics of Morals* (M Gregor tr, Cambridge University Press 1998) 4:402.

[62] For our purposes, it is worth noting that Kant appears to be describing here what Gewirth would call our GCAs.

[63] Kant, *The Metaphysics of Morals* (n 59) 6:221.

[64] ibid 6:223.

[65] B Laurence, 'Juridical Laws as Moral Laws in Kant's *The Doctrine of Right*' in G Pavlakos and V Rodriguez-Blanco (eds), *Reasons and Intentions in Law and Practical Agency* (Cambridge University Press 2015) 208.

[66] EJ Weinrib, 'Law as a Kantian Idea of Reason' (1987) 87 *Columbia Law Review* 472, 472.

[67] I Kant, *Critique of Pure Reason* (P Guyer and A Wood tr, Cambridge University Press 1998) A644/B672.

[68] ibid A659/B687.

[69] Kant, *Groundwork of the Metaphysics of Morals* (n 61) 4:462.

[70] Weinrib (n 66) 481.

normative obligation.[71] It is, therefore, essential to see law as operating within a unified conception of normativity centred on practical reasoning, and thus necessary to see claims to legal validity as being true only to the extent that such claims are PGC compliant.

The second objection to be addressed in this section will proceed from the writing of Brian Leiter, who may make the following claim: that the PGC-compliant natural law argument presented so far raises the demarcation problem, insofar as it concerns extent to which legal and moral normative systems can be seen to be separable.[72] Leiter's starting point would be that the positive law is undeniably a human artefact, and could not exist were it not the product of human action.[73] The purpose and application of human constructs necessarily vary over time, meaning that essential attributes are difficult to identify – if they exist at all.[74] If this is true of all human constructs, Leiter asks why we should think it is not also true of law.[75] His scepticism therefore concerns the possibility of identifying an agreed referent upon which any claims about essential characteristics of law can be founded. That this scepticism is misplaced can be demonstrated by returning to his claim that all artefacts' purpose and application necessarily varies over time, suggesting that 'Because human ends and purposes shift, the concept of "chair" has no essential attributes.'[76] This claim is unfounded. Although the form the chair takes may vary over time – for example, the number of legs it possesses or the material from which it is constructed – its fundamental purpose is the same: to be capable of providing a raised surface upon which something can sit. If an item is incapable of fulfilling this function, it is simply not a chair. The function of an artefact can thus remain constant, despite the fact its substantive form varies throughout time. Thus, its form is only relevant if that form means that it becomes incapable of fulfilling its function. Leiter's scepticism overlooks this fact and is, instead, founded on a mistaken conflation of form and function. There is therefore no reason for him to be sceptical about the agreed referent identified earlier in this work, given that it is a purely functional account of law that is silent as to the form of individual legal rules. If Leiter has no reason to be sceptical as to the agreed referent, then he ought not to be sceptical of the argument built upon it. Secondly, implicit in Leiter's claim is that the difficulty in identifying an essential attribute of 'law', such as that claimed by our agreed referent, is itself a reason to abandon the enterprise. If correct, this claim would mean that a large part of human enquiry should be abandoned. Let us not forget that the scientific method is founded on

[71] ibid 486.

[72] B Leiter, 'The Demarcation Problem in Jurisprudence: A New Case for Scepticism' (2011) 31(4) *Oxford Journal of Legal Studies* 663, 633.

[73] ibid 666.

[74] ibid 666–67.

[75] ibid 669–70.

[76] ibid 666–67.

the understanding that the truth of a scientific claim is very difficult to establish, and that the nearest we can often come to a scientific truth claim is that a statement is sound based on the rational assessment of evidence that we have at the present time. It would be absurd to claim that vaccine research should be abandoned because, as vaccines are a human artefact, we can never be certain as to the reasons behind their efficacy; or to make the same claim for any other technology on which we presently rely. It is therefore unclear why the objection can legitimately be made against law.

3. THE OPERATION OF THE PGC WITHIN A LEGAL SYSTEM

This chapter has demonstrated that we are required to accept the natural law claim that has been defended so far, yet questions might be asked as to how exactly the PGC may fit into any process by which legal norms are judged to be valid or invalid. The second half of the chapter will therefore attempt to show how this could take place by locating it within existing literature on the topic. In doing so it takes inspiration from Beyleveld and Brownsword's claim, mentioned in passing in section 2.3 above, that the test for moral permissibility with reference to the PGC could function as part of what Hart would call a rule of recognition. This claim will be fully discussed, before moving on to consider an alternative means by which a rule's legal validity can be determined, as provided by Hans Kelsen's account of the operation of a basic norm. It should be noted at the outset that the purpose of the following section does not require it to fully engage with all secondary literature that has emerged concerning these concepts. It has the more limited aim of demonstrating why the internal logic underpinning both concepts as expressed in their primary form requires them to accept the natural law position as not only possible within an individual system, but conceptually necessary to every systemic order, in order for them to remain internally coherent.

3.1. Hart's 'Secondary Rule of Recognition'

The first concept to be addressed in this section will be HLA Hart's 'Secondary Rule of Recognition'. On an orthodox reading, Hart would contend that, although a moral principle such as the PGC could operate within such a rule, this would be contingent on its role being accepted by the system in question rather than forming a part of the concept of law itself. This section will demonstrate that Hart's attempted exclusion of morality fails, and that – if the PGC is valid – then a primary legal rule can only be legally valid if it permissible with reference to the PGC. An assessment of a rule's moral permissibility must therefore take place within any secondary rule of recognition for the concept to remain coherent.

3.1.1. *Primary and Secondary Rules*

Hart suggested that legal rules take two distinct forms and that most theoretical disagreements arise from the interplay between these rules and a failure to adequately distinguish between them. Only by clearly differentiating between them can we understand how they interact, and thus understand the operation and nature of legal obligations.[77] The two types of rule are:

(a) primary rules that impose a specific obligation and direct an agent to Φ; and
(b) secondary rules of recognition that establish the means by which valid primary rules are identified.[78]

Hart argued that it would be difficult for a legal system to be comprised exclusively of primary rules as they would remain static and irresponsive unless a means of adjudicating, amending and updating them were possible. Secondary rules are thus required to provide a means by which we can amend, identify and adjudicate upon primary rules by ascertaining their validity.

Hart accepts that a valid primary legal rule is normative in that, through law, 'human conduct is made in some sense non-optional or obligatory.'[79] He goes to great lengths to distinguish the word 'obligatory' from the related notion of 'being obliged'; the latter could describe a bank robbery in which a member of staff was forced to hand over the contents of the safe, and Hart believed that a legal obligation was more than merely an order backed by threat of sanction in this way.[80] Primary legal rules must be internalised by the agent as exerting a valid claim to authority, and a secondary rule of recognition exists to provide a benchmark against which the validity of any claim to authority can be assessed.[81] This benchmark must be grounded in reasons that an agent must see as objective and intelligible, rather than somehow subjective or grounded purely in self-interest.[82] He could, then, endorse our agreed referent at this point – and be led to a sound conclusion that a rule's moral permissibility is a necessary condition of its legal validity. Yet he does not, arguing instead that a rule of recognition can produce primary rules that are able to create a valid obligation even if the primary rule is morally impermissible. It is difficult to see how this can be true if a primary rule must be internalised as valid by the agent to whom it is addressed; if a primary rule is morally impermissible, section two of this chapter has demonstrated that it cannot claim to be capable of providing a successful reason as to why it ought to be followed. This reason could be provided by a desire to avoid a given sanction but, as Hart agrees that law must necessarily be more than sovereign command backed by threat of sanction, the

[77] Hart, *The Concept of Law* (n 37) 81.
[78] ibid 91–94.
[79] ibid 1, 82.
[80] ibid 82; HLA Hart, 'Positivism and the Separation of Law and Morals' (1958) 71(4) *Harvard Law Review* 593, 603.
[81] Hart, *The Concept of Law* (n 37) 100.
[82] ibid xliii.

only way to rescue Hart's claim is for him to abandon his commitment to a positivist theory of legal authority. The following section will demonstrate that, for his theory to remain internally coherent, he must recognise that the legal validity of a primary rule is contingent on its moral permissibility. It follows that a test for the moral permissibility of primary rules must necessarily be part of any successful secondary rule of recognition.

3.1.2. *The PGC as a Necessary Component of a Rule of Recognition*

Hart's attempt to exclude the necessity of recognising a test for a rule's moral permissibility within any successful rule of recognition is connected to his belief that identifying an objective moral standard which can survive rational criticism is impossible in a pluralistic world; if such a test cannot be identified, then it cannot be a necessary condition for the legal validity of a primary rule.[83] In making this claim, Hart shows that his definition of morality is one which is collective, rather than critical in nature; he holds that a rule's observance is the key to its moral status, as opposed to its philosophical validity. His objection does not apply to the critical moral standard present within the argument for the PGC, meaning no coherent reason has thus far been provided as to why Hart believes that a rule's moral permissibility is not a necessary condition of its legal validity. He may at this point attempt a common rebuttal of the natural law position: that the claim is simply not reflective of legal reality whereby morally impermissible rules are regularly accepted and upheld as valid law.[84] This claim can be rejected for reasons previously given[85] but, even were we to grant this *arguendo*, his positivist assumption remains untenable based on his own characterisation of the two necessary and sufficient conditions that are required for the existence of a legal system:

> On the one hand, those rules of behaviour which are valid according to the system's ultimate criteria of validity must be generally obeyed, and, on the other hand, its rules of recognition specifying the criteria of legal validity and its rules of change and adjudication must be effectively accepted as common public standards of official behaviour by its officials.[86]

Hart's acceptance of the claim that the function of law is to guide human conduct requires him to accept that the following assumptions are necessarily part of these conditions. If the purpose of a secondary rule of recognition is to provide a reason as to why a primary rule should be seen as valid, and Hart is correct that a primary rule must be capable of guiding human conduct to be legally valid, then it follows that all primary rules identified by a secondary rule

[83] ibid 181.
[84] ibid 209.
[85] See our discussion of the necessity of a (F_b) rather than an (F_c) conception of law demonstrated through the example of pie in section 2.3 of this chapter.
[86] Hart, *The Concept of Law* (n 37) 116.

of recognition as legally valid must be morally permissible. A means of assessing the moral permissibility of primary rules must therefore be a necessary part of any successful secondary rule of recognition. The PGC, if valid, must therefore necessarily be incorporated into any secondary rule of recognition if it is to be capable of generating valid primary legal rules. An example of what form such a rule of recognition might take may help clarify this claim. Leslie Green summarises Hart's own position with regard to the rule of recognition operating within the United Kingdom: that whatever the Queen in Parliament enacts is law. Rules of recognition will vary between jurisdictions, but may themselves be accepted as valid for a number of reasons such as historical convention, a belief that the rule is culturally significant or that it serves a higher purpose.[87] Hart might accept that this *could* form part of a rule of recognition if expressly required by the rule itself – but his commitment to legal positivism requires him to reject the claim that it is necessary.[88] This limiting claim is incompatible with Hart's earlier endorsement of a functional account of law for the reasons given above;[89] meaning that Green's summary of Hart's position on rules of recognition is at best partial. Any and all rules of recognition must also contain a test for moral permissibility to produce valid primary legal rules that can claim to be capable of guiding our actions.

If Hart does not accept this conclusion, he is required to drop one or both of the following claims: that the purpose of law is to guide human conduct; or that law must create an obligation when internalised by an agent and cannot merely take the form of a sovereign command enforced by threat of sanction. Yet his own writing on adjudication makes it difficult for him to abandon these positions. He claims that, where conflict may arise as to which primary rule ought to apply, a rule of recognition resolves this conflict by ranking primary rules 'in an order of relative subordination and primacy.'[90] In acknowledging that a normative hierarchy of primary rules must exist for conflict to be resolved, Hart presupposes that criteria must exist by which such a hierarchy may be established. He reinforces this assumption by claiming that, in using such criteria, legal officials must internalise competing claims to resolve any dispute.[91] Thus, by introducing a requirement that a secondary rule of recognition must be internalised by those to whom it is addressed, Hart doubles down on his commitment to the claim that the function of all legal rules is to guide our conduct. Since, on his own terms, this commitment to a functional account of law that makes claims on those to whom its directives are addressed is necessary for the successful functioning of any and all legal systems, they are positions that Hart cannot abandon. He must, therefore, abandon his commitment to the positivist position

[87] ibid xx, xxiii.
[88] ibid 103.
[89] See development of the natural law claim advanced in section 2 above.
[90] Hart, *The Concept of Law* (n 37) 101.
[91] ibid 101–02.

that a rule's moral permissibility can only be a condition of its legal validity on a contingent basis. Instead, his theory can only successfully account for the existence of valid legal rules if he accepts that the test for moral permissibility provided by the PGC is necessarily part of any and all rules of recognition.

3.2. Hans Kelsen

Kelsen's contribution begins with an observation that legal theory is frequently incapable of clearly and coherently explaining the normative claim necessarily made by law. He argued that jurisprudence in the nineteenth century had become overly concerned with elements of political ideology and both natural and social science, and that a new 'pure' theory of law was required to avoid the reductionism encouraged by these non-legal enquiries. Kelsen sees the scope of legal obligations as broad, noting that '[t]here is no kind of human behaviour that, because of its nature, could not be made into a legal duty corresponding to a legal right.'[92] We ought to note here that Kelsen could accept our agreed referent, that law is the enterprise of subjecting human conduct to the governance of rules. But he does not, and instead offers the following explanation as to how a valid legal norm can arise:

> An "order" is a system of norms whose unity is constituted by the fact that they all have the same reason for their validity; and the reason for the validity of a normative order is a basic norm – as we shall see – from which the validity of all norms of the order are derived. A single norm is a valid legal norm, if it corresponds to the concept of "law" and is part of a legal order; and it is part of a legal order, if its validity is based on the basic norm of that order.[93]

A legal rule is therefore valid iff it is in compliance with the basic norm of the legal system of which it is a part. The following analysis will address the extent to which a basic norm must necessarily require that all legal rules are morally permissible with reference to the PGC. It will be shown that a basic norm is incapable of producing rules that can function as law without this requirement. Kelsen's theory can thus not adequately explain the normative claim made by legal rules unless we see a rule's moral permissibility as a necessary condition of its legal validity.

3.2.1. *A Pure Theory*

Before we can address Kelsen's own conception of a basic norm, we must first present an initial outline of his theory to shine a light on assumptions he makes in its construction, including the limits that he places on the scope of his enquiry.

[92] H Kelsen, *General Theory of Law and State* (Transaction Publishers 2005) 113.
[93] H Kelsen, *Pure Theory of Law* (2nd edn, M Knight tr, University of California Press 1970) 31.

He begins his *Pure Theory of Law* with a statement of intent: that his theory is not specific to a particular legal system but is a theory as to the general nature of law itself. Its purpose is 'to answer the question of what and how the law is, not how it ought to be.'[94] By introducing this distinction, Kelsen is endorsing a common categorisation of natural law theories and showing that he believes his theory to be one of legal positivism. This is worth acknowledging from the outset of this analysis, as it shows us that Kelsen is question begging in assuming a position whose truth he seeks to demonstrate; even though he could accept our agreed referent, he instead limits his enquiry from the outset to exclude the possibility that the moral permissibility of a rule is a necessary criterion for its legal validity. Kelsen attempts to justify this exclusion in several ways. Firstly, he characterises law as a normative enterprise,[95] though one in which norms can be generated by sanctions rather than a sense of obligation by those to whom the rules are addressed:[96]

> The law is not a coercive order in the sense that it exerts a psychic coercion; but in the sense that it prescribes coercive acts, namely the forcible deprivation of life, freedom, economic and other values as a consequence of certain conditions.[97]

He believes this is true as it is the only way by which legal norms can be clearly distinguished from other normative claims.[98] This differentiation is necessary so that a legal obligation can be clearly identified and differentiated from other normative claims such as those of morality.[99] This separation is itself influenced by his belief that moral norms are only identifiable with reference to a particular religious creed, meaning they are necessarily contingent; they are thus incompatible with the objective legal norm whose existence can be demonstrated by a readily identifiable legal coercive sanction.[100]

A second way in which he attempts to justify the exclusion of morality from assessments of a rule's legal validity can be found in the issue of factual causation. Kelsen argues that it does not make sense to speak of factual causation between action A and sanction B within a purely legal setting, as causation has no fixed end point: further things may flow from it. He argues that the connection between action and sanction in law must therefore be one of imputation. He suggests this term is superior insofar as it is more closed than claims to causation; it allows a sanction to serve as a fixed end point for the enforcement of a particular legal norm.[101] Moral interactions are not imputational in this way, as categorical moral norms necessarily impose obligations beyond

[94] ibid 1.
[95] ibid 4.
[96] ibid 33.
[97] ibid 35.
[98] ibid 35, 115.
[99] ibid 59.
[100] ibid 62–63.
[101] ibid 76, 91.

the initial interaction.[102] The causation that is necessary in moral interaction is therefore incompatible with the imputation necessary in legal interactions, meaning that tests for moral permissibility are conceptually incapable of serving as part of the test for the legal validity of a given rule.

Kelsen thus identifies a clear object of his theory, a set of norms governing human interaction which are enforced through coercive sanctions justified through a relationship of imputation between Action A and Sanction B. A natural lawyer may point out at this stage that Kelsen has not succeeded in identifying why these legal rules possess normative force; he has merely described that they do. Kelsen suggests that this is not a problem; he would accept that this account is descriptive of a 'Static Theory of Law' – law as a system of valid norms. Questions as to how law comes to attain this normative force are instead addressed by a 'Dynamic Theory of Law' that is concerned with the process by which law is created and applied.[103] It is at this stage that Kelsen introduces his Basic Norm, according to which legal norms are necessarily created.

3.2.2. *The PGC and the Basic Norm*

An immediate problem with the dynamic aspect of Kelsen's theory is that, just as he did with questions about how we can assess the validity of an existing legal rule, he again immediately excludes moral considerations from the scope of his enquiry as to how valid legal rules are created:

> [T]he Pure Theory of Law asks: 'How is it possible to interpret without recourse to meta-legal authorities, like God or nature, the subjective meaning of certain facts as a system of objectively valid legal norms describable in rules of law?'[104]

He instead claims that this assessment should be made with reference to a 'Basic Norm.' A basic norm exists with every legal system, and legal rules that are created in accordance with this norm gain their own normative force purely by the fact that they are made in accordance with its requirements.[105] The fact that morality is essentially subjective and that moral interactions operate causally, whereas legal interactions operate imputationally, led Kelsen to believe that a basic norm can never contain a condition that requires a rule to be morally permissible in order to be legally valid. Its conditions must be identifiable via a purely legal chain of authority: 'The norm which confers upon an act the meaning of legality or illegality is itself created by an act, which, in turn receives its legal character from yet another norm.'[106]

An attempt to identify the basic norm operating within the Scottish legal system may look like this. An Act of the Scottish Parliament such as the

[102] ibid 100.
[103] ibid 70–71.
[104] ibid 202.
[105] ibid 193–95; 198.
[106] ibid 4.

Licensing (Scotland) Act 2005, attains its legal character as it was enacted via the legislative process required for the creation of an Act of the Scottish Parliament. The Scottish Parliament derives its authority to create such legislation from a higher norm, namely the Scotland Act 1998. This Act is valid because it was created in accordance with the procedure required for the creation of an Act of the Westminster Parliament. The Westminster Parliament derives its authority to create such legislation from a yet higher norm, that of Parliamentary Sovereignty – the legal (if politically constrained) ability of Parliament to pass any legislation it sees fit. Kelsen would thus accept that this social fact of parliamentary sovereignty is the basic norm from which the Licensing (Scotland) Act 2005 attains its status as valid law. Its own existence and validity as a basic norm is presupposed by the existence of the legal system, and no further justification beyond this is required.[107] To ask why this basic norm is valid is to confuse 'is' and 'ought' and introduces moral questions that are inappropriate for legal enquiry for the reasons outlined above.[108]

The claim that a basic norm ought simply to be accepted as a matter of social fact is one that a natural lawyer would not find satisfactory. As has been noted above, excluding moral norms from the scope of the enquiry presupposes the position that it seeks to demonstrate; the question of where a basic norm gains its own normative validity therefore remains open. For example, given his claim that such a norm can be identified as a matter of social fact, could we envisage a situation where the majority of a population rejected a basic norm on the basis that it allowed for the creation of unjust law that they did not feel bound to follow? Would the basic norm remain valid in light of this countervailing social fact? Kelsen does anticipate this objection, and claims that 'minimum effectiveness is a condition of validity'.[109] Yet, in conceding this point, Kelsen invites a more difficult question – if efficacy is required for the validity of a legal system, by what standard ought individuals or legal officials assess legal rules to ask whether they feel bound to follow or enforce them?

This question demonstrates a key flaw in Kelsen's argument; if efficacy is part of a test for legal validity, then a test by which a rule's efficacy can be assessed is also required. It follows that, if only rules that are morally permissible are able to make claims to direct our behaviour and thus be capable of efficacy, the test for moral permissibility provided by the PGC must necessarily form part of all basic norms if they are to be seen as valid. Kelsen would, of course, reject this conclusion, arguing that to ask *why* a basic norm should be obeyed is to ignore that it simply operates as a matter of social fact and is a moral, rather than a legal, question.[110] Yet, as suggested above, in conceding that a minimum level efficacy is a prerequisite for the basic norm's validity, Kelsen invites the question

[107] ibid 8.
[108] ibid 10.
[109] ibid 11.
[110] Kelsen, *General Theory of Law and State* (n 92) 116–17.

'By what standard should a basic norm be judged as effective?' It makes no sense to judge it according to its own standards, as this would yield no result. Yet to use external considerations such as morality or religion would, in Kelsen's view, go against the positivist account which his theory is intended to produce. Doing neither is not an option, as Kelsen maintains that the efficacy of a Basic Norm is the means by which law is differentiated from a pure threat.[111] The only means by which this dilemma can be overcome is if Kelsen were either to drop his claim that a basic norm must possess efficacy, or his commitment to positivism. He is precluded from the former given his insistence that a basic norm must be observable as a social fact, meaning it must possess efficacy in order for it to be identifiable as a basic norm at all. He must therefore abandon his positivism and accept that the test for a rule's permissibility with reference to the PGC is a necessary condition of a rule's legal validity.

This conclusion would be rejected by Kelsen because it introduces a non-positivist aspect to his theory. Yet this rejection is founded on Kelsen's original question-begging assumption that tests for the moral permissibility of rules cannot form part of enquiries as to their legal validity. Kelsen assumes this in part because of his own belief, discussed earlier, that moral norms are only identifiable with reference to a particular theistic source and are thus subjective. He claims that theories of natural law, such as that proposed by St Augustine in *Civitas Dei*, exclude all obligations of positive law that are not compliant with their own particular conception of morality; and that 'a concept of law with such consequences is unacceptable by a positivist legal science.'[112] Morality must thus necessarily be excluded from tests for legal validity as it does not permit the empirically observable fact of legal pluralism, meaning that theories of natural law ought to be rejected in favour of a positivist account of legal obligations. Whilst this might be true of a natural law claim as characterised by Kelsen, this is not an accurate representation of a natural law claim such as that endorsed here. The PGC is grounded in a critical, normative conception of morality which serves as a test for the moral permissibility of all action regardless of the subjective beliefs of the agent, meaning it is conceptually capable of serving as an objective test for legal validity that Kelsen believes is essential for such enquiries. If Kelsen is forced to concede the conceptual possibility that a moral norm is *capable* of forming part of a basic norm, then he must withdraw his initial commitment to exclude moral considerations from questions of legal validity. By doing this his objection to accepting our initial agreed referent is also removed, and he is bound to accept the theory endorsed by this thesis: that incorporation of the PGC into a basic norm is not just possible, but conceptually necessary. For rules that emerge from its procedural requirements to be legally valid, a basic norm must require that they are morally permissible with reference to the PGC

[111] Kelsen, *Pure Theory of Law* (n 93) 44–47.
[112] ibid 48–49.

4. CONCLUSION

The purpose of this chapter has been twofold. The first was to bring together the disparate pieces of the argument in favour of the strong natural law position, which itself began by demonstrating the importance of a single starting point to our enquiry that is acceptable to all theoretical positions. Only a functional account of law can meet this requirement, as all substantive definitions as to the nature of legal norms necessarily assume the validity of a particular position. In assuming this position, they attempt to prove they should be rejected as non-neutral starting points. As such, our enquiry needs to begin with the simple claim that law is a normative enterprise. This requires us to accept that the PGC, given its status as an absolute and exclusionary second-order reason, must sit at the top of any unified hierarchy of norms. Any legal rule that is not PGC compliant cannot claim that it ought to be followed; and, as it is axiomatic of legal rules that they must be capable of claiming that they ought to be followed, then we are required to endorse the conclusion that a rule must be morally permissible with reference to the PGC to be legally valid. The section closed by considering objections to this conclusion from the Kantian legal positivist position and, from Leiter's scepticism to the possibility of a successful natural law claim, have been shown to be equally flawed.

The second part of this chapter sought to locate this conclusion in existing, positivist accounts of how legal systems recognise the validity of legal rules. Not only have we seen that the PGC-compliant natural law thesis advanced above is capable of serving as part of what Hart may call a 'secondary rule of recognition' or within Kelsen's account of the operation of a basic norm, we have shown that both of these theoretical constructs can only remain internally coherent if both authors accept that a test for a rule's moral permissibility with reference to the PGC is a necessary, rather than merely contingent condition of its legal validity. The strong natural law claim endorsed by this work must be accepted as a logical necessity.

4

Raz and Legitimate Legal Authority

1. INTRODUCTION

HAVING LAID OUT and justified the natural law claim necessitated by the PGC in the previous chapter, we can now turn to addressing the work of specific contemporary theorists in light of this conclusion. We will firstly return to the work of Joseph Raz and ask whether his writings on the nature of the claim made by legal rules remain sound in light of the PGC-compliant conception of natural law thus established. Given that Raz's earlier work has already been subjected to a Gewirthian critique by Beyleveld and Brownsword, the main focus here will be Raz's work published after their *Law as a Moral Judgment*.[1] The chapter will open by considering Raz's account of how legal norms interact with moral norms, and the importance of what Raz calls 'the legal point of view' in any coherent theory of the nature of law. It is this point in particular that will be critiqued, as a consequence of having established a PGC-compliant account of reasons for action in the Razian tradition in Chapter 2 is the creation of a unified conception of practical reasoning, meaning that the distinct legal and moral normative spheres presupposed by Raz are no longer tenable. An overview of Raz's conception of legal authority will follow, which will show that his conception of the normative claim of law is only internally coherent if modified so as to be compatible with the requirements of the PGC. The chapter will close by discussing the importance placed by Raz on the systemic nature of law, and whether this shift in focus away from individual norms can overcome the Gewirthian position, before assessing whether any PGC-compliant Razian theory would require him to reassess his views on whether a prima facie obligation exists that requires us to follow legal rules.

2. RAZ, LEGAL AUTHORITY AND THE CONTINGENCY THESIS

We have previously shown that Raz's own conception of deliberative rationality is founded on the same starting premise as the PGC; this means that he is required to accept the PGC as valid due to the dialectically necessary progression of the argument whose starting point he accepts. Failure to do this would

[1] D Beyleveld and R Brownsword, *Law as a Moral Judgment* (Sheffield Academic Press 1986).

either show that Raz misunderstands what it means to be an agent or require him to abandon his own account of deliberative rationality. Given both of these are implausible, we can conclude that Raz's account of reasons can only be successfully maintained if he accepts that the PGC acts as an absolute and exclusionary second order normative reason that limits the scope of permissible first-order reasons to those that are in compliance with its requirements. The fact that it applies to all action equally means that we are required to locate it at the top of any hierarchy of reasons upon which an agent might deliberate, requiring us to see practical reason as a unified concept. This includes deliberation on the validity of legal norms, as has been shown in Chapter 3, where it was established that a rule's moral permissibility with reference to the PGC is a necessary criterion of its legal validity. However, this claim is clearly incompatible with Raz's commitment to the legal positivist position that: '[D]etermining what the law is does not necessarily, or conceptually, depend on moral or other evaluative considerations about what the law ought to be in the relevant circumstances.'[2] As such, he is committed to the claim that legal rules are higher order absolute and exclusionary reasons and, that when a moral norm conflicts with a legal norm, the legal norm remains valid. He goes on to suggest that natural lawyer can disprove this position if they can demonstrate that the contingency thesis, the claim that a connection between morality and law conceptually exists but that is merely contingent as opposed to necessary, is false.[3]

This section accepts Raz's challenge and will argue that his own account of reasons and rationality, coupled with the agreed referrent from which any enquiry into the question of whether a rule's moral permissibility is a necessary condition of its legal validity must begin, requires him to accept that non-PGC-compliant rules cannot make a claim to guide our behaviour and, as such, cannot function as valid legal rules. This will be argued following a structure provided by Raz himself in his account of the necessary features of any legal system:

> The three most general features of the law are that it is normative, institutionalized, and coercive. It is normative in that it serves, and is meant to serve, as a guide for human behaviour. It is institutionalized in that its application and modification are to a large extent performed or regulated by institutions. And it is coercive in that obedience to it, and its application, are internally guaranteed, ultimately, by the use of force … Naturally, ever theory of legal system [sic] must be compatible with an explanation of these features.[4]

We will firstly examine Raz's beliefs around why law appears distinct from other normative systems and how, if at all, legal reasoning is sui generis and distinct from other forms of reasoning. Central to this will be his arguments concerning

[2] A Marmor, *Positive Law and Objective Values* (Oxford University Press 2001) 71.

[3] J Raz, *The Authority of Law* (2nd edn, Oxford University Press 2009) 318.

[4] J Raz, *The Concept of a Legal System: An Introduction to the Theory of a Legal System* (2nd edn, Oxford University Press 1980) 3.

the 'legal point of view'. Drawing on Raz's account of reasons and deliberative rationality, his account of legal normativity and its interaction with other normative claims will be shown to question beg by assuming the positivist position that they attempt to prove. The chapter will conclude by addressing Raz's claims as to how the systemic nature of law means that it should be seen as different to other normative systems, before finally addressing his belief that there is no prima facie obligation to follow a valid legal norm. This analysis will show that Raz's position must be amended to endorse the PGC to remain internally coherent, meaning that he is forced to abandon his commitment to legal positivism.

Raz would, of course, reject this conclusion on the grounds that the Gewirthian method attempts to disprove the contingency thesis via a general theory of intentional action that denies that there is anything particularly special about the law and legal norms.[5] This prima facie rejection of the Gewirthian approach betrays, however, his prior commitment to a positivist account of legal norms; in assuming that legal norms are sui generis he departs from the agreed referent that any serious engagement with the debate between natural lawyers and positivists must begin from, and thus begs the question. We are therefore able to use the Gewirthian approach to accept Raz's challenge and demonstrate the falseness of the contingency thesis.

2.1. The Nature of Legal Authority and Legal Reasoning

Before our analysis can begin, it is worth acknowledging that Raz might reject our categorisation of him as a legal positivist because, despite being committed to many positivist concepts, he maintains that the traditional dichotomy between natural law and positivism is unhelpful and overblown. He agrees, for example, that three clear and obvious overlaps between legal and moral norms necessarily exist:

1. No legal system can be stable without attempting to adequately protect life and/or property.
2. Acts contrary to bodily integrity (such as rape) cannot be committed by law or by legal institutions.
3. The fact of value pluralism renders it impossible for a state to manifest either virtue or vice to the highest possible degree.[6]

Despite this observation, he remains committed to the positivist belief that the natural law position – that an individual rule's moral permissibility is a necessary criterion of its legal validity – is to conflate the issue of what law is with

[5] Raz, *The Authority of Law* (n 3) 325.

[6] J Raz, 'About Morality and the Nature of Law' (2003) 48 *American Journal of Jurisprudence* 1, 2–3.

what it ought to be.[7] At best, the primary connection between morality and legal validity is the claim that the purpose of law is one of coordination of good maximisation; to '[S]ecure a situation whereby moral goals which, given the current social situation in the country whose law it is, would be unlikely to be achieved without it, and whose achievement by the law is not counter-productive, are realised.'[8] It is this claim that will be examined first, drawing on Raz's own account of the nature of legal authority and legal reasoning.

2.1.1. The Sources Thesis and the Nature of Legal Authority

Raz is of the belief that theories of law can never be purely semantic but must be focused on explaining the nature of legal institutions and practices.[9] It is for this reason that the claim was made in Chapter 3, that an agreed referent is important to agree upon the subject of our enquiry. One might expect Raz to agree with this position, given that it is an attempt to delineate a concept that is in accordance with his own idea of what a good explanation of a concept would look like: '[A good explanation is one that c]onsists of true propositions that meet the concerns and the puzzles that led to it, and that are within the grasp of the people to whom it is (implicitly or explicitly) addressed.'[10] Yet Raz is sceptical that such an agreed referent is ever possible for law, instead suggesting that there could be a large number of equally correct yet alternative explanations for the concept of law.[11] A single, unified conception of law ignores the fact of legal and jurisdictional pluralism and would therefore be of little use to legal institutions whose job it is to apply the law, meaning it ought to be rejected as irreflective of legal reality.[12] Yet in objecting in this way, Raz adopts the positivist account of legal validity that he seeks to prove; in assuming that all systems within this plurality are *valid* legal systems, he commits himself to the sources thesis – that a rule's legal validity arises from being passed according to correct legal procedure – rather than being open to the possibility that a rule's substantive directive may also be a relevant criterion. Were he to instead begin from the agreed referent, it would be obvious that some of these systems might be made up of rules that are not legally valid. As such, his scepticism as to the possibility of an agreed referent can be rejected for presupposing a position he seeks to prove. He should, therefore, be open to the possibility of arriving at a sound definition of the concept of law, and suggests three approaches that could be used to achieve this: linguistic; by adopting the lawyer's perspective and asking what it is appropriate for the

[7] ibid 13.
[8] ibid 12.
[9] J Raz, 'Two Views on the Nature of the Theory of Law: A Partial Comparison.' (1998) 4(3) *Legal Theory* 249, 251.
[10] ibid 256.
[11] ibid 257.
[12] ibid 278.

courts to rely on in reaching their decisions; or, lastly, through the 'institutional approach' of accepting that the law is what legal professionals believe it to be when they apply it.[13]

The latter two will be considered first in light of their institutional focus, before we return to the linguistic approach towards the end of this section. Both are in conformity with the agreed referent we are required to adopt: they acknowledge that the purpose of law is to guide human conduct, whilst not taking an exclusive position on how these rules claim their normative force. But if they are as yet silent on how the positive rules of law attain their status as valid legal rules, then Raz is required to provide this explanation. To do this, we should remind ourselves of his account of reasons grounded in authority from section 3.3 of Chapter 2 and locate them within the broader context of his belief that a hierarchy of reasons is necessary to resolve conflicts between reasons. This established that Raz's commitment to the process of deliberative rationality proceeds from the same starting point as the PGC, thus requiring him to accept the dialectically necessary argument that shows it to be a supreme moral principle. Such a principle must necessarily override all other non-compliant reasons for action – including those issued from authority. In light of Raz's belief that legal rules must provide a successful reason for action to be valid law,[14] and the only reason a directive can do so is by being compliant with the requirements of the PGC, then he must accept that a rule's permissibility with reference to the PGC must be a necessary condition of that rule's legal validity. He may attempt to circumvent this ascription by proposing one of three alternative means by which a rule can attain legal authority, and thus save his commitment to the sources thesis.[15] These are the dependence thesis, the normal justification thesis and the pre-emption thesis, and each will now be addressed in turn to see whether they can successfully grant authority to a non-PGC compliant legal rule.

The dependence thesis simply holds that directives should be based on reasons which apply to those to whom they are addressed with regard to the circumstances covered by the directive in question. Given we have shown that Raz's commitment to deliberative rationality requires him to accept that the PGC serves as an absolute and exclusionary reason that overrules all non-compliant reasons for action, any directive must be PGC compliant to successfully guide action. It is at the top of any hierarchy of reasons for action, and thus highly relevant in a subject's deliberations as to what reasons apply to them when considering the applicability of a given directive. Thus, if law necessarily claims to make a legitimate claim, and any directive must be PGC compliant for an agent to accept that it makes a legitimate claim, the dependence thesis must

[13] J Raz, *Ethics in the Public Domain: Essays in the Morality of Law and Politics* (Rev. ed. Oxford University Press 1994) 195, 199, 204–205.

[14] Raz, 'About Morality and the Nature of Law' (n 6) 15.

[15] Raz, *Ethics in the Public Domain* (n 13) 214.

hold that all legal rules must be in compliance with the PGC if they are to claim legitimacy if it is to succeed.

If the dependence thesis is incapable of granting valid legal authority to non-PGC-compliant legal rules, we can turn to the normal justification thesis. This holds that an authority can be viewed as legitimate iff to accept it would mean an agent to whom its directives are addressed would be more likely to comply with reasons they already have. Yet, as with the dependence thesis, we must return to the fact that the PGC necessarily serves as an absolute and exclusionary reason within Raz's hierarchy of norms. A non-compliant directive would be incapable of acting as a conclusive or absolute reason, and thus would be incapable of serving as a reason for action at all. Thus, if it would be impossible for an agent to have a reason to follow such a directive, it would be impossible for their likelihood of compliance to increase just because they are directed to do so by a claimed authority. Any authority that attempted to do so could not claim to be legitimate, thus any directive issued by them to undertake non-PGC compliant action could not be seen as valid law.

Raz's final suggestion as to how a posited rule can attain the legitimacy required to be categorised as law is through the pre-emption thesis: that directives of an authority must be accepted as legitimate because they necessarily replace and override all other reasons for action. Again, this cannot overcome the absolute and exclusionary reason provided by the PGC. Both the normal justification thesis and pre-emption thesis can also overcome the problem of potential incommensurability; both can explain why an agent ought to accept a PGC-compliant rule as a valid legal directive rather than any other PGC-compliant course of action. The sources thesis can thus adequately account for why a particular directive ought to be seen as law – but only if it is seen alongside the claim that all rules must also be permissible with reference to the PGC in order to be legally valid. If he wishes to engage in an institutional approach to resolving the question of legal authority, Raz's commitment to the sources thesis would thus require him to accept the natural law claim advanced by this work: that a rule must be both passed by legitimate authority and be morally permissible in order to make a valid normative claim.

Having dismissed these institutional approaches, we can address Raz's final approach to questions of legal authority – that of linguistics, through which we are invited to consider and justify the shared terminology present in both legal and moral directives.[16] Raz notes that this suggests that any connection between legal and moral norms is aspirational rather than axiomatic, in that it seems to indicate that the natural law claim is directed at what the law ought to be as opposed to what it is.[17] This characterisation is misguided insofar as it does not engage with the argument for the PGC that Raz is required to accept given his

[16] J Raz, *Between Authority and Interpretation: On the Theory of Law and Practical Reason* (Oxford University Press 2009) 111.

[17] ibid 111, 115.

own characterisation of the process of deliberative reasoning. If legal authority requires legal directives to be capable of claiming legitimacy, the only way that a legal rule can claim to be legitimate is if its directive is PGC compliant. The moral permissibility of a rule with reference to the PGC is thus not aspirational, but necessary for its legal validity.

Raz may here claim that if legal rules must be morally permissible then this would require us to accept that a single, correct range of permissible legal rules must exist. This means that there is no longer a discernible difference between legal and moral requirements; but the fact that we do appear to view law and morality as distinct, coupled with the fact of widespread legal pluralism, means that this position is irreflective of legal reality. Thus, the sources thesis cannot refer to the moral permissibility of a legal rule as a condition of its legal validity. This objection can also be rejected for two reasons. Firstly, the PGC does not dictate the content of the law; it merely provides a test for the moral permissibility of legal rules and is thus perfectly compatible with legal pluralism. For example, let us imagine a rule that requires drivers in a given jurisdiction to drive on a particular side of the road. It does not matter which side of the road the rule requires as both are morally permissible, meaning that either directive would be equally legally valid. This norm is thus distinct from an independent moral assessment of the problem at hand, and accommodates legal pluralism. Secondly, it again ignores that the PGC is necessarily at the top of Raz's hierarchy of reasons for action due to its status as an absolute and exclusionary reason. A linguistic approach to identifying the concept of law thus leads us to the same conclusion as the institutional approach: that the sources thesis can only succeed if we also accept that a posited rule's moral permissibility with reference to the PGC is a necessary condition of its legal validity.

A final attempt to rebut this conclusion may take the following form: that the fluctuation of moral standards over time suggests that moral pluralism is an incontrovertible fact, meaning that moral standards are definitionally unpredictable. Given that people need to be able to plan their lives according to fixed and objective legal rules, to make a legal rule's validity contingent on such a flexible and unpredictable reference point is fundamentally unworkable.[18] This objection fails, however, in that it relies on a characterisation of morality that is not representative of the claim made by the PGC. Raz's objection characterises morality as a collective enterprise that is empirically observable in a given community; yet, as we discussed with reference to Bernard Williams in section 3 of Chapter 1, the PGC instead makes a claim based on normative, critical morality. Its requirements are therefore not variable and unpredictable, but rationally identifiable and applicable to all agents regardless of their subjective beliefs. The PGC is equally compatible with a wide range of collective moral pluralism that Raz identifies; if a given community decides that it wishes to adopt a particular directive as a collective moral standard then this is perfectly legitimate provided

[18] ibid 118.

that the directive is itself PGC compliant. The collective moral pluralism observed by Raz is thus perfectly legitimate but is not the same moral standard against which rules are assessed for their legal validity. This test is necessarily provided by the PGC, and Raz's objection does not overcome the argument in favour of the claim that the sources thesis can only succeed if we accept that a rule's moral permissibility is a necessary condition of its legal validity.

2.1.2. Legal Reasoning and the Legal Point of View

This section has so far demonstrated that if Raz wishes to commit to the sources thesis then a rule must be morally permissible with reference to the PGC in order to claim to possess the legitimate authority that he believes all legal rules must necessarily claim. We now move on to discuss the implications of this conclusion on Raz's account of legal reasoning, and will begin by returning to Raz's belief that the practical impossibility of identifying an acceptable test for moral permissibility means that it is equally impossible to integrate such a theory into an account of legal reasoning. As such, any resultant system of legal reasoning would be unworkably complex.[19] This scepticism can be rejected insofar as it does not engage with the argument for the PGC; even were we to concede that the test would be complicated in its application in certain cases, complexity is not a good reason to reject a valid argument. We would question Raz's seriousness were he to suggest that the complexity of a scientific theorem was a valid reason for us to reject it, and we ought to reject the claim here for the same reason. If we can demonstrate that the PGC's status as an absolute and exclusionary second order reason necessarily limits the scope of valid legal rules to those that are morally permissible with regards to its requirements, then to reject this claim simply because it is complicated does not engage with the issue at all. Given that this claim has been shown to be sound on Raz's own account of deliberative rationality, we can continue to apply it to his account of legal reasoning unless we receive a legitimate reason to reject it.

Raz ought to accept this given his belief that legal reasoning is ultimately concerned with either discerning what the law is or the resolution of legal disputes, and is therefore subject to the same rules of reasoning as other disputes and enquiries.[20] Yet he maintains that this is not directly analogous to the claim that legal reasoning can be reduced to a purely moral consideration of how one ought to act in a given circumstance.[21] He argues this point by using the example of civil disobedience, where he suggests that the question '[H]ow should a case be decided according to the law?' could have a different outcome to the question '[H]ow should be [sic] case be decided, all things considered?'[22] He concludes that this requires us to accept that legal reasoning must begin from

[19] ibid.
[20] Raz, *Ethics in the Public Domain* (n 13) 327.
[21] ibid.
[22] ibid 328, fn 1.

a distinct starting point that he calls the 'legal point of view'. This is the view taken by legal practitioners as to what weight they would ascribe to competing reasons for action when faced with a conflict between moral and legal directives. Because legal actors would generally claim that the legal rule should prevail, Raz concludes that the legal point of view requires us to accept that the absolute and exclusionary claim made by law must override that made by morality.[23]

This claim is partially true and returning to Raz's example of how to act in a situation of civil disobedience will show why this is the case. He is correct that the question of how we ought to act according to the legal point of view may require a different answer to a question asked all things considered, but not for the reason implicit in his conclusion – which appears to rely on an account of the legal point of view that presupposes a positivist account of legal authority. The real reason why these two questions may require divergent answers is instead connected to the breadth of legitimate courses of action available to the agent in each situation. For, as has been demonstrated in the previous section, Raz's account of legal authority can only succeed if legal rules are themselves permissible with reference to the PGC. Through the normal justification or pre-emptive theses, a legal system may thus legitimately identify one of multiple PGC-compliant actions as one that is legally required, and this should be accepted from the legal point of view. To choose a non-PGC-compliant rule claiming to possess legal validity would be to depart from the legal point of view, as the sources thesis cannot ascribe legal validity to such a legal directive; should a legal actor choose to do this, they would be simply mistaken in their belief that they are applying a valid law. By contrast, reasoning all things considered would lead to an agent having to choose between multiple equally permissible courses of action. Thus, Raz is correct that reasoning from the legal point of view is different from reasoning all things considered; but is wrong to conclude that this requires us to accept that any rule claiming to be law must necessarily override contradictory moral claims. To do so would rest on the positivist assumption that the sources thesis is distinguishable from moral reasoning,[24] a point that the preceding section has shown to be incoherent. Any successful account of legal reasoning must, therefore, take account of the fact that the PGC serves as an absolute and exclusionary second order reason and that only rules that are morally permissible according to its requirements are capable of claiming legal authority. Moral reasoning is thus necessarily fully integrated into legal reasoning.

3. AUTHORITY TO MAKE LAW AND THE SOURCES THESIS

Raz endorses the position that a legal rule's success in directing our action is contingent on it being able to claim that it possesses the legitimate authority

[23] ibid 329.
[24] ibid 332–333.

necessary for it to do so. He thus accepts that the claim made by law is one that must be normatively valid. The second part of this chapter will demonstrate that this claim again requires Raz to endorse the natural law position; that a rule's legal validity is necessarily dependent on its moral permissibility with reference to the PGC. It will demonstrate this by applying our PGC compliant account of legal authority to Raz's account of how legal norms are created, before moving on to highlight how the sources thesis must be amended to reflect the natural law position in order for his theory of legal authority to remain internally coherent.

3.1. Recognition of Authority to Create Law

In order to create law, a body must claim that it possesses the authority to do so. Yet Raz is of the belief that the idea of authority appears to create a paradox:

> To be subjected to authority, it is argued, is incompatible with reason, for reason requires that one should always act on the balance of reasons of which one is aware. It is of the nature of authority that it requires submission even when one thinks that what is required is against reason. Therefore, submission to autonomy is irrational. Similarly, the principle of autonomy entails action on one's own judgment on all moral questions. Since authority sometimes requires action against one's own judgment, it requires abandoning one's moral autonomy. Since all practical questions may involve moral considerations, all practical authority denies moral autonomy and is consequently immoral.[25]

On this account, we can infer that any authority that always acts in a way that is morally permissible cannot be a true authority, for in limiting the scope of its directives it concedes that it is itself subject to external requirements. This would mean that if a law maker were to subscribe to our account of PGC-compliant legal authority outlined to this point, it would be no authority at all. This raises problems for a Gewirthian theory of natural law, but this subsection will reject this characterisation of authority as inconsistent with Raz's broader writing on the nature of reasons.

He rejects four common concepts of authority as largely descriptive[26] before endorsing that offered by John Lucas; that 'A man, or body of men, *has authority* if it follows from his saying "Let *X* happen", that *X* ought to happen'.[27] In order to clarify that authority must necessarily be over others, he modifies the statement is to become '*X* has authority over *Y* if his saying 'Let *Y* Φ', is a reason for *Y* to Φ'.[28] Raz accepts, however, that this statement remains descriptive; for though it is correct in its claim that to possess authority is to have the power to

[25] Raz, *The Authority of Law* (n 3) 3.
[26] ibid 5–9.
[27] J Lucas, *The Principles of Politics* (Oxford University Press 1966) 16.
[28] Raz, *The Authority of Law* (n 3) 12.

change reasons for action, it does not provide a normative explanation as to how this change can occur.[29] Such normative claims must arise from special types of reasons known as 'protected reasons for action' that combine a reason for action with an exclusionary reason to disregard all conflicting reasons. Normative claims thus possess two characteristics:

(a) there is reason for regarding them as a protected reason or as cancelling a protected reason; AND
(b) the reason is that that it is desirable to enable people to change protected reasons by such acts, if they wish to do so.[30]

As reasons issued from positions of authority claim both these characteristics, they possess normative character. Raz is therefore able to define *X has authority to Φ* as implying the following is true:

(a) *Y* permitted *X* to Φ or gave him power to do so;
(b) *Y* has power to do so; and
(c) *X*'s Φ-ing will affect the interests of *Z* and *Y* has authority over.[31]

To apply this to legal authority:

(a) *Y* permits a law maker to make law or gives him power to do so;
(b) *Y* has power to do so; and
(c) a law-maker's making of a law will affect the interests of a subject of the law, and *Y* has authority over the subject of the law.

Our enquiry as to the question of valid authority to make law must therefore be directed to the nature of *Y* in Raz's account above; namely, what can simultaneously enable a lawmaker to make law whilst also possessing an authority over the subjects of law prior to the law-making taking place. An orthodox response from positivism may be to suggest that *Y* is a norm-generator that allows a designated body to create legal rules, such as the basic norm proposed by Kelsen or the secondary rule of recognition outlined by Hart. As was shown in section 3 of Chapter 3, however, these concepts do not have absolute discretion to generate norms that require any action at all; the argument for the PGC necessarily requires that any resulting legal rule must be PGC compliant if it is to function as law. We are therefore able frame our enquiry thus: if a law maker makes the normative claim that their authority is legitimate, how can this claim be verified?

Raz does acknowledge that morality can play a role here.[32] This does not seem a controversial statement; given his own observation that normative reasons for action frequently conflict, a positivist account of law has to recognise that

[29] ibid 16.
[30] Raz, *The Authority of Law* (n 3) 18.
[31] ibid 20.
[32] Raz, *The Concept of a Legal System* (n 4) 44.

legal and moral norms may conflict and that a way of resolving the conflict is required. This is because, like morality, law makes a direct normative claim against those to whom it is addressed in the following form: '*p* ought to be the case, and that it is true if, and only if, there is, in a certain normative system, a norm to the effect that *p* ought to be the case.'[33] Yet to be capable of making this claim, a justificatory norm is required that explains why the statement is true, and the claim made by this work is that this justificatory norm must necessarily be compliant with the PGC to be capable of generating any normative requirements.

A positivist reply to this claim may take the form of the practical difference thesis: that, on this account, the law merely re-states reasons for action that individuals already have in the form of moral directives, meaning that the law becomes a tautology that makes no difference to how people would otherwise act. Our reasons for rejecting this approach will be covered more fully in the following chapter, meaning that, for now, we can limit our dismissal of this point to one Raz himself should uncontroversially accept. This will be achieved through the use of his normal justification thesis as discussed in section 2.1.1 of this chapter, which holds that authority is legitimate if its subjects are more likely to comply with reasons that already ought to justify their behaviour if they follow the authority, than if they were to act independently.[34] In order to demonstrate why this is compatible with the PGC-compliant conception of legal authority, we considered the example of a legislator faced with the task of establishing which side of the road the law will require drivers to drive on. Both are morally permissible, meaning that the PGC does not provide a definitive answer to the question. Thus, by choosing one of them, the legislator acts in a way that is compliant with the normal justification thesis; the need for social coordination can motivate the legislator to legislate for either left or right;[35] this law would provide a driver with a stronger reason to choose the mandated side than they already had under the PGC. It does not, as Raz would perhaps characterise the approach, merely restate an obligation that the agent is '[r]equired to observe and endorse' prior to it becoming law.[36] It instead allows for legal pluralism, in that it would not matter which side of the road the legislator mandated, whilst providing the driver a stronger reason to act than they had before. In this sense, the theory conforms entirely with Raz's description of a valid legal rule as being '[O]ne which has the normative effects (in law) which it claims to have.'[37] Objections from the practical difference thesis thus fail; the fact that it can overcome the problem of social coordination means that the

[33] ibid 47.

[34] JE Penner, 'Legal Reasoning and the Authority of Law' in LH Meyer et al. (eds), *Rights, Culture, and the Law: Themes from the Legal and Political Philosophy of Joseph Raz* (Oxford University Press 2003) 72.

[35] J Raz 'Facing Up: A Reply' (1989) 62 *Southern California Law Review* 1153, 1190–94.

[36] Raz, *The Authority of Law* (n 3) 149.

[37] ibid 149.

normal justification thesis is capable of providing the PGC-compliant account of legal authority with the de facto and de jure legitimacy required for it to be capable of issuing legal rules.[38]

Before we move on to the next section, some final comments must be made on what might take place were a judge to be confronted with a rule claiming to be law that is not PGC compliant. Raz argues that, if this rule is valid law, then it must necessarily claim exclusionary force over all other considerations – including conflicting moral norms. He suggests this is self-evidently true as a matter of legal reality, as we can easily envisage a situation in which neither a citizen nor a judge want to conform to such a rule, but must do so because that is what the law requires.[39] This claim operates on the common positivist observation discussed in our analogy of the nature of a pie in section 2.3 of Chapter 2: that immoral legal rules simply do exist, thus showing the natural law claim to be false. As it is constructed on a foundation grounded in (F_c) rather than the (F_b) foundation constructed from our agreed referent, we can reject the claim for the reasons previously discussed. The argument presented shows that, on Raz's own terms, that the PGC-compliant account of legal authority is one we must accept if we are committed to the claim that law must be capable of claiming legitimate authority. If a rule is not PGC compliant, it is simply not law – and if a judge or other legal official were to apply it as if it were, then they would err. What the rule is is beyond the scope of the present argument; all that matters is that it is simply not a valid legal rule. A judge or legal official faced with the rule would thus be obliged to disregard it if they take the application of legal rules as the central component of their role.

This conclusion is simply necessary given Raz's conception of the legal point of view, and the role of judges in upholding this perspective. He has this to say on how judges must necessarily view a rule that grants law-making authority to a given person or body:

> [R]ules telling other people what they *ought* to do can only be justified by *their* self-interest or by moral considerations. My self-interest cannot explain why they ought to do one thing or another except if one assumes that they have a *moral* duty to protect my interest, or that it is in *their* interest to do so. While a person's self-interest can justify saying that he ought to act in a certain way, it cannot justify a duty to act in any way except if one assumes that he has a *moral* reason to protect this interest of his. Therefore, it seems to follow that I cannot accept rules imposing duties on other people except, if I am sincere, for moral reasons. Judges who accept the rule of recognition accept a rule which requires them to accept other rules imposing obligations on other people. They, therefore, accept a rule that can only be accepted in good faith for moral reasons. They, therefore, either accept it for moral reasons or at least pretend to do so.[40]

[38] ibid 29; 146, fn 2.

[39] ibid 30.

[40] J Raz, 'Hart on Moral Rights and Legal Duties' (1984) 4 *Oxford Journal of Legal Studies* 123, 130.

It is therefore not only optional, but necessary for a judge to factor the moral permissibility of upholding a given legal rule as part of the adjudicatory process. This is a claim that Mark McBride sees difficulty in, a difficulty he conveys by breaking the argument down as follows:

1. Judges accept their legal system's rule of recognition.
2. If judges accept a rule of recognition, those judges accept rules imposing obligations on other people.
3. If one accepts rules imposing obligations on other people, some or all of one's reasons for doing so are moral.
4. Therefore [from (1), (2), and (3)]: judges accept rules imposing obligations on other people, and some or all of their reasons for doing so are moral.
5. Therefore: judges accept the rule of recognition, and some or all of their reasons for doing so are moral.[41]

McBride sees the two key steps here as being steps two and five. He accepts that the second step, what he labels 'acceptance closure' is valid as a general statement of logic,[42] but rejects that step five, or 'reverse closure', in that it requires the following to be true: 'If one accepts [a legal rule] for [a moral reason], and one accepts [a rule of recognition], and [rule of recognition] validates [a legal rule], then one accepts [a rule of recognition] for [a moral reason].'[43] McBride states that this cannot be true, as it presupposes that all decisions are influenced by a single reason; he claims this is irreflective of legal reality, as judges often balance conflicting moral and doctrinal reasons in reaching a decision.[44]

McBride's objection, however, question begs in that it presupposes that a doctrinal reason that is not morally permissible is a valid reason legal reason capable of being upheld. It has been shown repeatedly throughout this chapter that, if Raz is correct that a legal rule must be capable of claiming authority in order to be valid, then his own conception of deliberative rationality requires him to accept that the only way that a legal rule can be valid is if it is compatible with the requirements of the PGC. The objection therefore fails which, in turn, necessitates the following conclusion; if Raz is open to the possibility that judges *may* use moral reasoning, then the PGC's status as an absolute and exclusionary reason requires him to accept that judges *must* factor a calculation as to the PGC compatibility of all legal rules into their deliberations. The legal point of view is therefore committed to holding that legal directives are only valid insofar as they are PGC compatible, requiring him to reject his characterisation of legal and moral systems as requiring differing viewpoints; only if a legal rule is morally permissible can it make the exclusionary claim that Raz believes it must if it is to be seen as valid law.[45] His account of law creating authority is

[41] M McBride, 'Raz on the Internal Point of View' (2011) 17 *Legal Theory* 227, 228–29.
[42] ibid 229.
[43] ibid 230.
[44] ibid 230–231.
[45] J Raz *Practical Reason and Norms* (2nd edn, Oxford 1999) 143–44.

thus committed to the natural law position; that any justificatory norm granting power to create legal rules must necessarily contain a provision that requires the legal rules that are created to be morally permissible with reference to the PGC as, without this, they are incapable of claiming the legitimate authority necessary to guide our actions.

3.2. Reconceptualising the Sources Thesis

We now return to Raz's conception of the sources thesis and will attempt to more fully demonstrate that it must be reconceptualised to respect this natural law claim for Raz's theory of legal authority to remain internally coherent. This may prove difficult given that his sources thesis characterises law as no more than a social fact that is distinct from morality or metaphysics; a point he believes necessary given that legal rules can be both created and repealed.[46] This means that they must be capable of tracing their authority back to a particular social source that is itself capable of creating legal obligations. As the same cannot be said to be true of moral rules, any connection between moral and legal authority may only be contingent rather than necessary.[47] It thus follows for Raz that:

> A jurisprudential theory is acceptable only if its test for identifying the content of the law and determining its existence depend exclusively on facts of human behaviour capable of being described in value-neutral terms, and applied without reason to moral argument.[48]

This statement begs the question it seeks to prove, in that by being closed off to the possibility of a necessary connection between the moral permissibility of a rule and its legal validity it assumes a positivist account of legal authority that departs from the agreed referent shown to be necessary in Chapter 3. We will, however, still grant the statement *arguendo* to more fully demonstrate the flaws in Raz's position. This must begin with a restatement of Raz's belief that law is inescapably a social phenomenon and must be explained solely as such, with references to ideas of efficacy, its institutional character and its sources as follows. A legal system exists if it possesses efficacy, in that a population accepts its validity on a systemic level as opposed to at the level of individual legal rules. To be accepted by a population, such a system must be comprised of standards that are connected to adjudicative bodies whose purpose it is to resolve disputes between standards; as such, standards being upheld must have a relevant institutional connection to a source that is capable of producing them.[49] As this source is necessarily a social institution, any incorporation of moral standards into the creation of legal rules can only be contingent as opposed to necessary. It is thus

[46] Raz, *The Authority of Law* (n 3) 151.
[47] ibid 38.
[48] ibid 39–40.
[49] ibid 42–45.

the final step of this logical chain that demonstrates, for Raz, that the legal positivist account of legal validity is correct: unless a legal rule is created by a body charged with its creation, it cannot possess the legal character necessary for its efficacy or capacity to be adjudicated upon. As such, it must be at the centre of any account of why norms possess legal character. This is a simple statement of the sources thesis, a principle that Raz conveys as follows: 'A law has a source if its contents and existence can be determined without using moral arguments … The sources of law are those facts by virtue of which it is valid and which identify its content.'[50]

This is a definition Raz believes we should accept because it adequately reflects our real-life experience of how legal rules are identified, and that this accuracy is sufficient reason for us to accept that the law must:

> mark the point at which a private view of members of the society, or of influential sections or powerful groups within it, ceases to be their private view and becomes … a view binding on all members notwithstanding their disagreement with it. It does so and can only do so by providing publicly ascertainable ways of guiding behaviour and regulating aspects of social life.[51]

A natural lawyer would, of course, again note the problem with Raz's sources thesis is that it begs the question; by stating that a law can only have a source if its contents and existence can be determined without recourse to moral reasoning, his thesis relies on the position that it attempts to prove. He would defend this assumption by observing that legal rules are enforced in a way that suggests they possess their own exclusionary character, thus meaning that reference to moral reasons when assessing the validity of a legal rule may only be contingent and not necessary.[52] If Raz is correct, however, then legal rules are reducible to nothing more than an expression of power and the will of a certain sector of society; doubly so when the courts are required to fill a lacuna by ruling on a dispute where existing legal rules do not provide a clear solution. This must be true if its emanating from a particular source is a sufficient reason to view a rule as legally valid.

On these terms, the sources thesis, as described, thus appears incompatible with Raz's view that legal rules must be legitimate to be valid; for, as has been shown, his account of deliberative rationality requires him to accept that the substantive content of the legal directive must be permissible with reference to the PGC for it to claim legitimate authority, and thus to be legally valid. Central to the sources thesis is the claim that only procedural considerations must be considered when assessing a rule's legal validity, whereas his account of legitimate authority requires the substance of the rule to be considered alongside its procedural pedigree. Raz may claim here that these are two separate questions;

[50] ibid 47–48.
[51] ibid 48–51.
[52] ibid 52.

that the moral content is not legal until it is declared as such by the source of the legal rule. Yet this is a restatement of the natural law claim that a rule's moral permissibility is a necessary condition of its legal validity, thus requiring him to drop his commitment to the purely procedural focus of the sources thesis.

Raz would reject this conclusion by inviting us to consider a situation where two laws are seen to be equally valid according to his purely procedural account of the sources thesis, creating a legal issue that must be addressed. Both laws cannot be equally valid, as two exclusionary reasons cannot operate in contradiction with one another. Raz expresses this using the following formula: $\vdash -(R_c\ x, \Phi\ \&\ R_c\ x, -\Phi)$.[53] Neither can it be true that $(R_c\ x, \Phi)$ v $(R_c\ x, -\Phi)$ and that the two reasons can exist in perpetual opposition, otherwise the paradoxical claim that two conflicting exclusionary reasons are equally valid is maintained.[54] It is unclear how a purely procedural account of the sources thesis can resolve this paradox, particularly in light of Raz's belief that judges are necessarily committed to the use of moral reasoning in such situations.[55] This belief requires us to question Raz's claim that the sources thesis necessarily excludes all moral considerations from the determination of whether a legal rule is valid, insofar as it necessitates that the adjudicative process operates in the broader realm of practical reason. Given that his commitment to deliberative rationality requires him to accept the starting point of the PGC, the dialectically necessary progression of the argument requires him to accept its status as an absolute and exclusionary reason that overrules all non-compliant directives. Thus, if legal rules must claim legitimate authority to be valid, and the only way a rule can claim legitimate authority is through compliance with the PGC, its compliance with the PGC is a necessary condition of a rule's legal validity. The sources thesis thus cannot operate purely procedurally, as Raz's own conception of deliberative rationality requires him to accept that any justificatory norm that identifies a source as a legitimate source of law must require that the legal rules it creates are themselves morally permissible.

The fact that Raz accepts that conflicts between legal and moral norms are possible means that he is bound to accept this conclusion to maintain the internal coherence of his own conceptualisation of both the legitimate authority necessarily claimed by legal rules and reasons for action more broadly. This can be demonstrated by using the following reasoning. If a rule must claim legitimate authority to be law, and the only way a law can claim legitimate authority is by being morally permissible with reference to the PGC, then it cannot be true that a legal reason x requiring Φ can exist if a PGC compliant reason x requires us to not Φ. Thus the statement $\vdash -(R_L\ x, \Phi\ \&\ R_M\ x, -\Phi)$[56] is true. The absolute exclusionary reason present in the PGC requires statement $R_M\ x, -\Phi$ to take primacy. It is therefore necessary that $(R_M\ x, -\Phi) > (R_L\ x, \Phi)$. Raz ought

[53] ibid 62–64. R_c in this formula refers to a conclusive reason for action.

[54] ibid 64.

[55] See discussion of McBride in section 3.1 above.

[56] R_M in this formula refers to a moral rule; R_L refers to a directive claiming to be a valid legal rule.

to accept this conclusion given he accepts that moral requirements *may* apply to legal institutions and practitioners;[57] for in allowing for a contingent connection, he should accept that this connection could become necessary should the moral principle in question act as an absolute and exclusionary reason as is the case for the PGC. He may attempt to rebut this by raising the practical difference thesis,[58] yet – as demonstrated above in section 3.1 – this objection mischaracterises the nature of the natural law claim. The thesis advanced by this work is perfectly compatible with Raz's own normal justification thesis, thus overcoming the problem he himself raises with regard to the practical difference made by a PGC-compliant legal rule. Thus, if it is true that legal rules necessarily claim to possess legitimate exclusionary force and it is also true that $(R_M\ x, -\Phi) > (R_L\ x, \Phi)$, then the sources thesis must account for the fact that only morally permissible rules emanating from the identified source are capable of functioning as law.

4. SYSTEMIC FUNCTIONALITY

This section will address the truth of the claim that questions of legal normativity, and thus validity, are better asked of legal systems as a whole rather than with regard to individual norms. Given the shift in focus of this enquiry to the institution as a whole, the validity of any individual norms arising from that system must equally be traceable to processes of creation, adjudication, enforcement and appeal operating as a systemic whole:

> [T]he law is normative because its function is to guide human behaviour, and that it guides human behaviour in two ways: either by affecting the consequences of a certain course of conduct in a way which constitutes a standard reason for avoiding that course of conduct, or by affecting the consequences of a certain course of conduct in a way which constitutes a reason for pursuing or avoiding it, depending upon one's wishes.[59]

This observation follows from the axiomatic fact that the applicability of legal rules to a given situation is decided by the officials whose job it is to adjudicate upon and enforce them. Since the ultimate arbiters of legal validity are operating at a systemic level rather than adjudicating the validity of individual norms, claims to legal validity must also be systemic.[60] This view is supported by Raz's belief that law necessarily must possess efficacy and be supported by institutions capable of adjudication and enforcing sanctions to ensure compliance.[61] These features will be examined in turn to ascertain whether it is true to believe that

[57] J Raz, 'Incorporation by Law' (2004) 10 *Legal Theory* 1, 2, 6.
[58] ibid 6, 10.
[59] Raz, *The Concept of a Legal System* (n 4) 168–69.
[60] ibid 199; Raz *Practical Reason and Norms* (n 45) 155.
[61] Raz, *The Concept of a Legal System* (n 4) 232.

they provide support to the claim that legal normativity can only be understood when viewed as operating at a systemic level.

Firstly, we will address the idea of efficacy. Before this can take place in full, we ought to remind ourself that Raz's commitment to a positivist conception of the sources thesis that holds that legal norms and reasons are social facts that do not depend on external moral validation for their validity.[62] This means that two different types of reasons operate to direct an individual as to how the law requires them to act: primary reasons to either Φ or not Φ, and secondary reasons that allow them to identify which primary reason is the one upon which they ought to ultimately act. Moral reasons are a type of secondary reason in that they are deliberative, whereas legal reasons claim exclusionary character that preclude deliberation. They are therefore reasons that operate at the executive stage of action as opposed to being deliberative in character. It follows that, if a rule does not attain legal character until a legislator or court acknowledges this, questions as to the efficacy of a legal rule must take place on a systemic level.[63]

Though internally consistent, this series of claims must be rejected as it is incompatible with Raz's own account of reasons for action. This can be shown if we remind ourselves of his view expressed at the outset of this section: that legal philosophy is a branch of practical philosophy akin to any other.[64] If this is true, then his characterisation of the interplay between primary and secondary rules is incomplete. Action is, by definition, aimed at specific goals and objectives, meaning that the legal reason under deliberation fits into a unified hierarchy of reasons. Should this be the case, then we can hypothesise a situation where a reason which claims to be law, and therefore claims to possess exclusionary force, might conflict with a moral reason which also claims the same exclusionary force. Such a conflict re-introduces the paradoxical formulation raised in section 3.2, that $\vdash -(R_L\ x, \Phi\ \&\ R_M\ x, -\Phi)$. Since the PGC is an absolute and exclusionary reason that excludes all non-compliant directives, a legal rule cannot claim legitimate exclusionary force unless its directives are PGC compliant. This necessitates that $(R_M\ x, -\Phi) > (R_L\ x, \Phi)$ is true. Systemic actors are bound by this conclusion as much as the individual agent, meaning they are required to reject non-PGC-compliant rules. Thus, considerations as to efficacy at the systemic level can only reach sound conclusions if sufficient account is paid to the validity of individual legal rules.

Having shown that assessments of systemic efficacy are impossible without an assessment of the legal validity of individual norms, we may now consider the second phenomenon that Raz suggests indicates that efficacy operates at a systemic level: the fact that disputes are adjudicated upon by social institutions. We will begin by outlining four general characteristics of interpretation

[62] ibid 212.
[63] ibid 213–15.
[64] Raz *Practical Reason and Norms* (n 45) 149.

before applying them to Raz's account of how the courts interpret legal norms. These are: that an original object must be the subject of the interpretation; that the interpretation must demonstrate the meaning of the original object; that the interpretation itself is subject to an assessment as to its correctness; and that interpretation must be a deliberate enterprise.[65] It is the third of these features – that any interpretation must be capable of being assessed for its correctness – that is of particular interest here. Raz labels this feature the 'intention thesis'; that any interpretation can only be viewed as valid iff it correctly captures the intention of the creator of the original artefact.[66] He notes that it is not immediately apparent that judicial practices and legal doctrine which develop over the years can be attributed to a single author in the way that this account requires and proposes a modification that makes the feature more appropriate for legal norms. He refers to this as the 'radical intention thesis': 'An interpretation [of a legal principle] is correct in law if and only if it reflects the author's intention.'[67] This, for Raz, is a key feature of the operation of legal interpretation – though one to which he anticipates three objections. The first two are similar in scope: that there is no reason to base an interpretation on an author's intention; and that, even if there were, it is often impossible to establish authorial intent for a legal doctrine which been developed by several different institutions.[68] He dismisses both objections as nonsensical based on his sources thesis; as law is necessarily created, an author must exist and, since creation requires intention, intention must also exist. The third objection he anticipates is, however, built on this dismissal: that legal institutions do not always seek to establish the authorial intent of the principles which they establish or apply; they instead generally apply legal rules as they exist.[69] Yet Raz claims that this can be dismissed for the same reasons; that principles necessarily contain authorial intent as they are applied, in that the authors intend them to possess binding authority.

This final rebuttal is an expression of what Raz calls the 'authoritative intention thesis;' that the law must be intelligible in the authoritative claim that it makes on its subjects.[70] He proposes that this must be the authorial intention underpinning all legal interpretation and, by extension, adjudication. Crucially, he holds that this authorial intention allows the rule to be upheld even if it is normatively defective – provided that the system as a whole possesses efficacy.[71] This claim is curious in light of his own commitment to the processes of deliberative rationality. For given our earlier observation that $(R_M\, x, -\Phi) > (R_L\, x, \Phi)$, we can see that the absolute and exclusionary reason provided by the PGC to

[65] J Raz, 'Intention in Interpretation' in RP George (ed) *The Autonomy of Law: Essays on Legal Positivism* (Oxford University Press 1996) 249, 252.

[66] ibid 256.

[67] ibid 257.

[68] ibid 257.

[69] ibid 258.

[70] ibid 260–61.

[71] ibid 261.

disregard non-compliant norms means that, if a legal actor were to do as Raz suggests, they would be acting prima facie irrationally. Raz could, of course, mean that the legal agent in question could happily enforce the rule in question whilst acknowledging that it is not valid law and ought not to place a legitimate demand upon them – but this conclusion is clearly absurd. Raz's observation thus only holds if he is happy to accept that a legal actor upholding the defective norm is acting in an irrational manner. Since this conclusion is one that he would be unlikely to endorse, we are unable to accept his conclusion that adjudication is a process that necessarily operates on the systemic level as opposed to at the level of individual legal norms.

Having shown that two of the three features of legal systems that Raz believes indicates that legal normativity operates at the systemic level do not necessitate this conclusion, we can now turn to the third: that social institutions are able to ensure compliance through the imposition of sanctions. He begins with an attempt to distinguish legal sanctions from bare force: sanctions, he claims, need not be forceful in themselves – although force can be used to ensure that a sanction is carried out. All legal systems necessarily claim to legitimately regulate this force, by at least prohibiting attempts to prevent legal officials from undertaking their legitimate duties or permitting force to be used to ensure sanctions are complied with. Force should therefore be seen as a tool necessarily adopted by at a systemic level to ensure that sanctions are upheld.[72] Such sanctions are, however, characterised by Raz as auxiliary, second-order reasons for compliance with a valid legal rule.[73] As such, they operate at the level of deliberative rationality – which, again, subsumes the secondary reason provided by the threat of sanction to considerations as to the validity of individual legal norms with reference to the absolute and exclusionary reason provided by the PGC. It is again incorrect to categorise sanctions as operating primarily on a systemic level when they cannot be legitimately enforced without a consideration of the moral permissibility, and thus legal validity, of individual legal norms. We must therefore conclude that assessments of systemic efficacy or the legitimacy of adjudicatory bodies and sanctions cannot be reached without considering the validity of individual legal norms, as valid legal norms are themselves necessary for a system to be seen as legitimate.

5. OBLIGATIONS TO OBEY THE LAW

The final part of Raz's work to be addressed will be his claim that there is no prima facie moral obligation to obey legal rules.[74] Given he reached this conclusion on a positivist understanding of legal validity, we ought to ask whether it

[72] Raz *Practical Reason and Norms* (n 45) 157–58.
[73] ibid 161.
[74] Raz, *The Authority of Law* (n 3) 233.

remains valid in light of our conclusion that his views on practical reason and rationality require him to accept that a rule's moral permissibility with reference to the PGC is a necessary condition of its legal validity. He defines an obligation to obey the law as follows:

> An obligation to obey the law] includes admission that the reasons to obey have the weight and implications which the law determines for them. In other words, it entails a reason to obey in all circumstances defeated only by the considerations which are legally recognised as excusing from prosecution or conviction.[75]

His claim that no prima facie moral obligation to obey legal rules exists may seem surprising in light of claims made elsewhere that the law's recourse to normative language itself implies that the validity and bindingness of legal rules is something that should be accepted.[76] He explains the contradiction away, however, by stating that the claim conflates exclusionary and absolute reasons.[77] To say that an obligation to follow the law exists is to say that the rule in question is itself justified by reference to a higher principle; if this is the case, then it is this higher reason which one has a reason to obey rather than the law itself.[78] In order to demonstrate this objection, Raz hypothesises an obligation to keep rivers clean. He says such an obligation exists iff the obligation is one which is already accepted by the majority of the population, and that if '[M]ost people pollute them and they are badly polluted there is normally no reason why I should refrain from polluting them myself.'[79]

In providing this example, Raz appears to suggest that his rejection of an obligation to follow the law rests on the efficacy of the norm in question; if the rule is one which the population rejects then an agent has no reason to follow it himself. As has been the case so often with Raz's work, however, this conclusion is incompatible with his own account of deliberative rationality and his commitment to the claim that legal rules must necessarily claim legitimate authority. Both these claims require him to accept that a test for moral permissibility with reference to the PGC is a necessary condition of the validity of a legal rule and, given the PGC serves as both an absolute and exclusionary second order reason, non-compliant behaviour is necessarily both illegitimate and irrational. It is this factor that an agent must consider above all others when ascertaining whether a rule makes a valid legal claim to direct their behaviour; the general efficacy of the rule is irrelevant.

Raz might here claim that this requires us to accept that the law is merely a tautology, insofar as it can only provide us with a reason to do something we already have reason to do; and that since this is irreflective of legal reality,

[75] ibid 236.
[76] Raz, *The Concept of a Legal System* (n 4) 235.
[77] Raz, *The Authority of Law* (n 3) 236.
[78] ibid 245.
[79] ibid 248.

it should be rejected.[80] Yet, as has been noted previously in section 2.1.1 above – this objection mischaracterises the nature of the natural law claim advanced by this work. The PGC-compliant natural law thesis is entirely capable of generating a distinct legal requirement as shown through the operation of the normal justification thesis, meaning Raz's objection fails. Thus, provided that the legal rule in question is permissible with respect to the PGC and can be seen to possess authority under the normal justification thesis, it is capable of making a legitimate claim that it ought to be obeyed. Raz does concede that in certain situations the law does create an obligation to be obeyed, but that any general obligation to obey would vary from person to person. He demonstrates this point with three hypothetical scenarios:

1. A duty exists to comply with Health and Safety Regulations. These possess legitimate authority in that they are designed by experts who possess more knowledge than the layman as to how to work safely. Submission to this authority would therefore better enable an agent to pursue his goal of working safely than he may do were he to reason independently.
2. A regulation designed to reduce specific examples of pollution. The example given would ban barbecues from being used in the countryside in all but a few designated areas. Since this would reduce overall environmental degradation more effectively than individuals' own reasoning, a reason exits to obey the rule.
3. Should the government have a policy to construct nuclear power stations that an agent disagrees with, the agent should still not engage in Civil Disobedience. To do so would encourage others to do the same when they disagree with another government policy, meaning that it would be impossible for the government to function effectively. It is therefore in my interests to obey this rule in order for social institutions generally to continue to function.[81]

All three examples, however, appear to rely on the normal justification thesis as the means by which an obligation to obey is created. If the normal justification thesis applies to legal norms more generally, as has been held to be the case by this work, then we can conclude that the general obligation to obey that Raz seeks to deny does, in fact, exist.

This conclusion fits well with Raz's claim, made elsewhere, that the Rule of Law necessitates the claim that people should obey the law and consent to be ruled by it by virtue of its status as law.[82] He supports this claim by contrasting the Rule of Law with the exercise of arbitrary power, which he defines as: '[Power which is exercised] with indifference as to whether it will serve the purposes which alone can justify use of that power or with belief that it will

[80] Raz, *Ethics in the Public Domain* (n 13) 342.
[81] ibid 347.
[82] Raz, *The Authority of Law* (n 3) 212.

not serve them.'[83] Though Raz claims that this obligation is merely pragmatic as opposed to moral, insofar as it allows for stable social relations and allow individuals to plan their lives,[84] he makes this claim of his own conception of legal validity rather than the PGC compliant theory of natural law that we have argued he ought to accept in light of his commitment to the principles of deliberative rationality. This would hold that, if we accept Raz's earlier idea that law necessarily is a legitimate authority, and legitimate authority is that which does not contradict the requirements of the PGC, then arbitrary power is analogous to the imposition of rules that are not PGC compliant and, thus, not valid law. If such rules are not law then it is a nonsense to see them as within the remit of the broader concept of the Rule of Law. We can thus accept that the Rule of Law would not endorse an obligation to obey such rules, but to disregard them, based entirely on moral considerations. If this is the case, then we cannot prima facie disregard the claim that any obligation to obey PGC compliant legal rules is moral in character.

6. CONCLUSION

This chapter has examined Raz's writings on the nature of law in light of our conclusions reached as to his broader conception of reasons for action and deliberative rationality in Chapter 2. This commitment, when seen alongside his view that the law must necessarily make a claim to legitimate authority, requires Raz to accept the natural law position that a rule's moral permissibility with reference to the PGC is a necessary condition of its legal validity. This has been shown via four steps. The first two sections demonstrated that Raz's 'sources thesis' misrepresents the natural law claim advanced in this work and presupposes the positivist conception of legal validity that it attempts to prove. Once these problems are addressed, it can only remain coherent if modified to account for the absolute and exclusionary reason provided by the PGC. This has implications for his conceptions of the legal point of view, which in turn affect his conception of legal authority, the authority to make law and legal reasoning. If Raz wishes to remain committed to the claim that law necessarily makes a claim to legitimate authority, and it is true that $(R_M\, x, -\Phi) > (R_L\, x, \Phi)$, we must accept that all legal rules must be compliant with the PGC to be valid. Having demonstrated this, the chapter went on to demonstrate that Raz's claim that law can only be understood at the systemic level equally mischaracterises the nature of the authority claimed by the PGC-compliant theory of natural law, and that his own conception of the 'normal justification thesis' means that he ought to accept the conclusion that ascertaining systemic validity cannot take place without an assessment of the validity of the individual legal norms that make up the

[83] ibid 219.
[84] ibid 220.

system. We concluded with the observation that Raz's justification for his claim that no prima facie moral obligation to obey the law can also not withstand the argument from the PGC. His commitment to the concept of deliberative reason thus requires him to accept that his entire conception of the nature of law is only coherent if it incorporates the natural law claim that a rule can only be legally valid if it is morally permissible with reference to the PGC.

5

Contemporary Inclusive Positivism

1. INTRODUCTION

THE THREE FINAL theorists to be considered as part of this work each propose theories grounded specifically in inclusive legal positivism, and are thus considered together in one chapter. They have been deliberately chosen because their conceptions differ significantly, and thus demonstrate the plurality of viewpoints that exist within this school of thought. Each will be scrutinised in turn to assess their coherence in light of the natural law position necessitated by the validity of the PGC as demonstrated in Chapter 3. We will firstly consider the normative justification for the formalist position adopted by David Lyons, before moving on to consider his commitment to inclusive positivism demonstrated through his 'minimal separation thesis'. The second theorist to be considered will be Jules Coleman, who rejects the label of 'inclusive positivism' in favour of 'incorporationism'. His differentiation between negative and positive positivism and his conceptualisation of law as a primarily economic theory will be considered, before the discussion closes with a critique of the importance he places on the 'practical difference thesis'. The final theorist to be considered will be Matthew Kramer, who views himself as a moderate incorporationist and rejects moral-political approaches to legal theory in favour of his preferred theoretical-explanatory approach.[1] Kramer is the only of the three theorists who will be considered in this chapter who addresses the Gewirthian position directly and concludes that it is lacking. The coherence of this claim will be ascertained based on an analysis of Kramer's own conception of the nature of morality before a critique is undertaken of his claim that any connection between moral permissibility and legal validity can only be contingent in nature.

2. DAVID LYONS AND FORMALISM

Lyons' formalism is grounded on his own particular conception of legal authority: that the law is not morally infallible, and that the law must earn the respect that it claims through a process of fair and impartial adjudication. If

[1] M Kramer, *Where Law and Morality Meet* (Oxford University Press 2008) 156–57.

the adjudication results in an outcome that is unjust, even though the outcome is legally valid, this does not mean that the directive that follows is one that ought to be respected and complied with.[2] Rather, such an outcome is a clear indication that the law is deficient and ought to be reformed to generate an obligation. The natural lawyer's desire to assess the moral permissibility of individual legal rules is therefore of use to Lyons' project insofar as it is the means by which we can assess the legitimacy of legal rules,[3] though he would reject the natural lawyers' conclusion that an illegitimate law is not law at all. It is from this claim that our analysis of Lyons' position will begin, with an initial focus on how this opposition is informed by his formalist approach to legal reasoning. From this we will assess his conception of the 'minimal separation thesis' for the extent to which it can remain coherent in light of the PGC-compatible natural law claim.

2.1. Formalism and Legal Positivism

A full account of formalist approaches to legal reasoning is beyond the scope of this work, but a few words will be said here about some central claims of the position in order for Lyons' view to be fully contextualised. These theories proceed from the empirically observable starting point that legal systems do exist, as do disputes as to what course of action that system may require in a given situation. It is pragmatically desirable that disputes should be adjudicated upon in a way that enforces rules consistently, and that the application of a rule in a given situation should thus create a precedent whereby it is applied the same way in analogous situations that arise at a later time. This requires us to accept that legal directives have a verifiable meaning that indicates whether they apply to any and all situations. Lyons holds that this account of formalism is necessary for any workable conception of law, as the outcome of adjudication is always either that a rule applies or that it does not. This could be through a restatement of the existing law in a given area, a declaration of a new legal directive to be applied, a combination of both of these outcomes or a rejection that the rule applies at all. Legal declarations are thus necessarily located in the statements of legal officials issued as part of the deliberative process operating within adjudication. If true, then Lyons concludes that 'an injustice is done whenever an official fails to act within the law, regardless of the circumstances.'[4]

This conclusion presupposes that the legal directive being applied must claim authority to direct the behaviour of those to whom it is addressed, and that the existence of the legal system is itself enough for it to claim that the directives

[2] D Lyons, *Moral Aspects of Legal Theory: Essays on Law, Justice, and Political Responsibility* (Cambridge University Press 1993) 1.

[3] ibid 2. A parallel can be drawn here between Lyon's work and Coleman's claim, discussed below in section 3, that the term 'law' should be seen as a term of success.

[4] Lyons, *Essays on Law, Justice, and Political Responsibility* (n 2) 13.

it issues are de facto legitimate. Deviation from these requirements is therefore a prima facie injustice, a claim that Lyons argues would be the case even if the substantive content of the legal rule being considered was morally impermissible. Formalism is therefore content neutral, insofar as value is placed on the consistent application of existing legal rules regardless of the moral status of those same rules.[5] Lyons' formalism is thus grounded in legal positivism as an injustice can be triggered by the application of a rule independently of its moral permissibility. Formal justice thus requires us to ensure that legal officials adjudicate consistently, and moral judgment can be levied against them if they fail to do so. By extension, natural lawyers are incorrect to focus on the substance of individual rules, as true injustice can only arise in connection with their application. Departure from the substantive requirements of a given rule may be morally justifiable, but remains a legal injustice if to do so would breach the formalist principle of consistency.[6] Legal officials would therefore legally err if they decided to depart from a clear legal rule for moral reasons. Although the strength of their commitment to this principle of formal justice is something that Lyons believes can vary between legal systems, he maintains that a bare minimum commitment remains a necessary function of their operation. He believes this is evident from the familiar claim that law should be assessed impartially, and that this minimum commitment is indicative that the positivist claim that a rule's moral permissibility is not a necessary condition of its legal validity is true.[7]

The claim that the primary nexus of injustice in legal systems is in the inconsistent application of rules appears to be incompatible with the core claim advanced throughout this work: that a rule's moral permissibility with reference to the PGC is a necessary condition of its legal validity. This is because, as per our agreed referent, the purpose of law is to guide our action, and since non-PGC-compliant law is incapable of claiming to be capable of guiding action, it cannot be law. This position requires us to reconsider Lyons' claim that a legal official would err if they refuse to apply a morally impermissible rule; for if the duty of a legal official is to apply legal rules, and non-PGC-compliant rules cannot be law, then if an official were to apply them they would be applying rules that were not legal in character. They also have a direct obligation to act in ways that are compliant with the PGC given their own status as agents; thus, if to apply a non-PGC-compliant rule would itself breach the PGC, they have an absolute and exclusionary reason to refrain from doing so. Their primary legal obligation would therefore be to depart from the morally impermissible rule, rather than apply it because of a commitment to consistency.

It may come as a surprise, then, that Lyons might partially accept this conclusion. Though he would reject the claim that morally impermissible rules

[5] ibid.
[6] ibid 20.
[7] ibid 16.

were not law, he would have no objection to a legal official rejecting a rule that they saw as morally impermissible given he believes that 'other moral factors which have a bearing upon official conduct maintain that those [reasons] favouring deviation may outweigh those favouring adherence … in specific cases.'[8] Legal officials' departure from a morally impermissible rule would therefore be warranted where this would result in less injustice than to enforce it, although he caveats this with the claim that this would still be a prima facie injustice.[9] It is difficult to accept this categorisation of injustice if our natural law claim is sound however, as it is equivalent to the claim that formal justice would require a legal official to consistently enforce rules that are not law. As hypothesised by Lyons, the legal official who departs from a substantively morally impermissible rule would therefore be committing a justified injustice.This statement gives rise to a paradox, suggesting that there is a logical flaw in Lyons' claim which requires us to reconsider its validity; a problem that can be resolved if we endorse the PGC-compliant natural law position. Non-PGC-compliant rules can claim no authority to guide our actions and, since it cannot be the case that $(R_L\ x, \Phi\ \&\ R_M\ x, -\Phi)$, it must be true that $(R_M\ x, -\Phi) > (R_L\ x, \Phi)$. Our legal official is precluded from applying the non-PGC-compliant rule; their decision to depart from it is thus necessarily just, as opposed to being prima facie unjust as Lyons suggests. This is not to totally dismiss Lyons' statement that an element of injustice may be committed in the departure from the unjust rule in question; but that any injustice is both morally and legally necessary, thus not the problem he believes it to be. Formalism as a doctrine is only internally coherent if the substantive rules being applied are themselves PGC compliant, requiring us to reject Lyons' transferral of the moral nexus away from substance to adjudication as irrational.

2.2. The Minimal Separation Thesis

Having shown that the formalist approach to legal reasoning can only coherently operate on a natural law understanding of the validity of legal rules, the second part of this section will consider what Lyons believes to be a less controversial component of his conceptualisation of law: what he calls the 'minimal separation thesis'.[10] To understand this concept we must see it as deriving from the separation thesis as normally understood: that there is no necessary connection between a rule's moral permissibility and its legal validity. Lyons rejects this statement as vague and potentially acceptable to both natural lawyers and positivists.[11] This led him to develop a new, minimal formulation of the thesis:

[8] ibid 20.
[9] ibid 26.
[10] ibid 64–65.
[11] D Lyons, 'Moral Aspects of Legal Theory' (1982) 7 *Midwest Studies in Philosophy* 223, 223.

'Law is subject to moral appraisal and does not automatically satisfy whatever standards may properly be used in its appraisal.'[12] He contends that reformulating the separation thesis along these lines can demonstrate the truth in the inclusive positivist position: that any connection between a rule's moral permissibility and its legal validity is only contingent, rather than necessary.

The problem with this statement is not that it is contentious, but that the attempt to reformulate the separation thesis has rendered it incapable of achieving what Lyons believes it does. Firstly, the way in which he uses the word 'law' in the formulation suggests it is intended to be read on a positivist understanding of legal validity insofar as it does not claim the legal rule would not possess legal character should it fail the moral appraisal to which it is subjected. A more generous reading may grant that Lyons is here referring to 'the law' of a specific jurisdiction, but even with this concession the statement remains problematic; even if this narrower focus was intended, the principle still does not indicate whether the rules under consideration can be considered legally valid if they are found to be morally impermissible. It certainly implies that such a rule would be somehow deficient, but that it would be improper to argue that this deficiency means it cannot be recognised as valid law. It seems odd to argue that something which is necessarily deficient should be seen as operative in the same way as a perfect example of the artefact – but on this the thesis is silent. Its inability to indicate the outcome of the moral appraisal it allows renders it of minimal utility in attempting to answer the question about whether a rule's moral permissibility is a necessary feature of its legal validity. The thesis could be saved, however, should we consider that Lyons does attempt to guide us as to what standard of assessment the thesis would endorse when appraising the law. He believes that outcome of any adjudication by legal officials cannot be morally neutral, requiring the standard of assessment to be one that appraises the justice or injustice of the decision in light of the moral standard being applied.[13] Given that Lyons endorses a formalist conception of legal reasoning that the previous subsection has demonstrated can only remain internally coherent after having accepted that a rule's moral permissibility with reference to the PGC is a necessary criterion of its legal validity; he must accept that the appraisal referred to in the minimal separation thesis must be one as to the PGC compliance of the rule in question. This would render the minimal separation thesis a restatement of the natural law position, which is the opposite conclusion anticipated by Lyons. It has, however, been shown to be one that is required given his commitment to formalism in legal reasoning, meaning that he is required to abandon his commitment to inclusive positivism.

The minimal separation thesis thus requires Lyons to accept one of two things: that he ought to abandon his commitment to positivism, or accept that

[12] ibid 226; Lyons, *Essays on Law, Justice, and Political Responsibility* (n 2) 68.
[13] Lyons, *Essays on Law, Justice, and Political Responsibility* (n 2) 74.

the principle is too vague to be capable of performing the function it exists to serve. Despite this conclusion, we ought to recognise that Lyons does see value in the principle – and his justifications for it will be considered in turn. This will begin with a restatement of his claim that our PGC-compliant natural law account locates justice exclusively within the substantive content of individual rules, rather than being open to this value being located in other aspects. He is happy to concede that a rule's substantive content is a relevant consideration, and his belief that Raz's sources thesis ignores this possibility is the main reason he rejects that account of legal validity in favour of one he sees as more plausible.[14] His account identifies three loci around which appraisal as to a rule's legal validity can take place: the substantive moral permissibility of a rule, the procedural quality by which it was created and whether an agent would freely obey the rule in question.[15] It is this tripartite locus that Lyons believes can justify the vagueness of the minimal separation thesis.[16] This justification of his position does not, however, succeed. The first and third loci are both concerned with the normative claim that is made by the rule in question and operate on the assumption that the rule in question is deficient if it is incapable of making a claim that it ought to be freely followed. Both are therefore analogous with the PGC-compliant theory of natural law that has been advanced here. Our previous account of the operation of justificatory norms and law creation in section 3 of Chapter 3 necessitates that the second, concerned with procedure, must also necessarily be PGC compliant if the rule that emerges is to be capable of claiming legal validity. As all three loci presuppose the validity of the PGC-compliant conception of natural law endorsed by this thesis, Lyons' attempt to circumvent it has failed. Lyons' commitment to a formalist approach to legal reasoning and his formulation of the minimum of the separation thesis both require him to abandon his approach to legal positivism and accept the claim that a rule's moral permissibility with reference to the PGC is a necessary condition of its legal validity.

3. INCORPORATIONISM AND JULES COLEMAN

Having established that both Lyons' formalism and his proposed 'minimum separation thesis' are only capable of functioning coherently if our PGC-compliant theory of natural law is itself endorsed, we can now turn to our second inclusive legal positivist. As was noted in the introduction to this chapter, Coleman prefers to refer to the doctrine as 'incorporationism' in the belief that this term more accurately depicts the core claim of his position: that moral permissibility can only be a condition of a rule's legal validity if this

[14] ibid 79.
[15] ibid 96.
[16] ibid 100.

criterion is properly incorporated into a legal system through the appropriate law-creating mechanism. Our engagement with this position first requires us to return to a claim alluded to in our previous discussion of Lyons;[17] namely Coleman's discussion of the claim that law can only be fully understood if viewed as a 'success-term'. By this, Coleman means that because law is created via a social process with the aim of guiding action, a rule it must be successful in making those to whom it is addressed submit to its authority in order to be worthy of the label at all.[18] Coleman thus addresses the key natural law claim endorsed by this work: that if the purpose of law is to subject human conduct to the governance of rules, a rule must be prima facie capable of doing so to be valid law. Yet he dismisses this position as one deliberately deployed by natural lawyers to avoid what he believes to be the ordinary and settled meaning of the word 'law':

> However we disambiguate the expression, restricting law to norms that bind the conscience involves departing from the ordinary concept of law … [I]t is neither essential to the concept nor is it entailed by anything that is.[19]

Coleman's claim is that it is a matter of historical fact that morally impermissible rules have been recognised as legally valid; thus, an ordinary understanding of 'law' cannot see a rule's moral permissibility as a criterion of its legal validity.[20]

It is peculiar that Coleman would endorse this claim. The 'ordinary concept of law' is clearly disputed both in jurisprudence and legal practice, as can be demonstrated by extra-judicial writing in which judges confront the extent to which they have felt bound to recognise a rule as legally valid despite the moral impermissibility of its directives.[21] The fact that Coleman feels compelled to dismiss such views through a defence of his own position belies a simple fact; his 'ordinary concept of law' is not as apodictic as he suggests, thus legitimising the present scrutiny of his position. This will begin with an examination of the importance he places on the 'conventionality thesis' in the positivist position, before considering how the concept of wrongfulness developed through his characterisation of law as an economic doctrine may contribute to the dispute between the positivist and natural law positions. The section will then apply the conclusions reached in these discussions to his commitment to the 'practical difference thesis' to demonstrate that Coleman must abandon his commitment to legal positivism in order for the remainder of his beliefs on the nature of law to remain internally coherent.

[17] See n 3.

[18] J Coleman, 'The Architecture of Jurisprudence' in J Ferrer Beltrán et al (eds), *Neutrality and Theory of Law* (Springer 2013) 70, 71 n 14.

[19] ibid 75.

[20] ibid.

[21] See, inter alia, S Haffner, *Defying Hitler: A Memoir* (Phoenix 2003).

3.1. 'Positive Positivism' and the Conventionality Thesis

One of Coleman's most valuable insights into the nature of legal positivism is his observation that the doctrine contains two distinct claims. He refers to the first of these as 'negative positivism', which he characterises as the commitment to the separation thesis – the claim that a rule's moral permissibility need not be a condition of its legal validity, and that any rule of recognition is limited in its content in that it must be committed to this core claim.[22] Yet Coleman concedes that the existence of just one legal system that holds a rule's moral permissibility to be a necessary condition of its legal validity would completely undermine this claim, thus justifying his preference for what he calls 'positive positivism'.[23] Instead of focusing on the negative point of what criteria for legal validity a rule of recognition cannot contain, positive positivism instead asks what features are universally necessary in any legal system. He identifies what he calls the 'conventionality thesis' as such a necessary feature: that 'law is ultimately conventional: that the authority of law is a matter of its acceptance by officials.'[24] He proposes that this necessitates a clear and objective test by which officials can identify valid legal rules and that because no such test is possible for the identification of valid moral norms, conformity with moral criteria cannot be a prima facie necessary condition of a rule's legal validity.[25] This is not to say that Coleman does not believe such a connection is never possible; merely that moral rules would not attain the status of legal rules unless recognised as such by a rule of recognition. This requires us to differentiate between the content of a rule of recognition, which can require that a rule's moral permissibility is a necessary condition of its legal validity, and the grounds upon which a rule is constructed, which cannot. This is because the conventionality thesis demonstrates a rule of recognition is valid if it is accepted by officials, regardless of its content.[26] Because a rule of recognition's acceptance is an empirically observable social fact that leaves open the possibility that a rule of recognition might be accepted despite failing to require that moral permissibility is a necessary condition of a rule's legal validity, we must endorse the inclusive positivist position: 'that *whether or not morality is a condition of legality in a particular legal system depends on a social or conventional rule, namely the Rule of Recognition*.'[27]

Coleman anticipates that a sceptic may question this conclusion based on his previous claim that the test used by legal officials tasked with ascertaining the

[22] J Coleman, *Markets, Morals and the Law* (Cambridge University Press 1988) 4.

[23] ibid 7.

[24] ibid 12. This starting point should be rejected as it departs from our agreed referent but will be accepted *arguendo* to demonstrate that Coleman's attempt to justify his positivist position fails on its own terms.

[25] ibid 9.

[26] J Coleman, *The Practice of Principle: In Defence of a Pragmatist Approach to Legal Theory* (Oxford University Press 2001) 107.

[27] ibid 108; emphasis in the original.

validity of legal rules must be clear, and that morality is too vague a concept to be used for this purpose. If this is true with regard to the grounding of a rule of recognition, it must equally be true for their content within individual systems. If the purpose of a rule of recognition is to resolve dissensus around the validity of a given rule – and any test for moral permissibility necessarily introduces vagueness – then allowing for a such a test within a rule of recognition, even on a contingent basis, must still undermine its purpose.[28] Coleman rejects the criticism on two grounds. Firstly, he contends that it ignores the fact that allowing such a criterion to form part of the content of a rule of recognition would allow dissensus to be arbitrated within legal institutions; this would provide an avenue through which dissensus could be resolved, rendering the objection moot.[29] Secondly, he contends that the criticism is grounded on a mischaracterisation of a rule of recognition's role with regard to dispute resolution. He invites us to consider a society that benefits from complete moral consensus and contends that individuals in such a society may still wish for these principles to be incorporated into a formal legal structure. As such, a rule of recognition could incorporate a test for the moral permissibility of legal rules even in the absence of dissensus around these rules.[30]

This second justification from Coleman is one that requires analysis. Let us imagine the society he envisages, one in which all moral precepts are universally accepted by all citizens with no dissensus as to either their applicability or bindingness in any and all situations. Two questions arise. Firstly, we ought to ask why a citizen in the society he anticipates would, as he claims, wish for a formal adjudicatory structure to be put in place. The only reason one might desire an adjudicatory system would be to resolve disputes that might arise as to the applicability of a given rule. But in Coleman's society, where there is universal consensus that legal rules are made in accordance with universally accepted moral directives, it follows that the possibility that these directives would not be followed would be zero. Establishing such a system would only be desirable to the citizens of such a system were they to concede that, either now or at some point in the future, the moral principles they all accept as universally binding may no longer hold. This is analogous to the claim that deviation from an accepted moral principle is permissible, in which case the society can no longer be said to benefit from complete moral consensus in the way Coleman wishes us to believe. It is therefore impossible for us to conceptualise this society in the way Coleman asks of us.

Secondly, and perhaps more damagingly for Coleman's broader position, is that this society ought to be impossible based on his own commitment to the claim that it is impossible to identify a test for moral permissibility upon which we could all agree. We ought to recall that it is because of the impossibility

[28] ibid 111.
[29] ibid 112.
[30] ibid 112–13.

of such a test that he rejects the possibility that the moral permissibility of a rule could ever be a necessary condition of its legal validity. Thus, the fact that he considers it legitimate to conceptualise a society that has identified such a universally applicable moral test requires us to doubt his commitment to the claim that such a test is impossible and, by extension, doubt his conclusion that such tests can never be part of a test for the legal validity of an individual rule. The very fact he acknowledges that such a society could reasonably exist requires him to do one of two things. He could first acknowledge he is incorrect to believe such a society can exist, which weakens his defence of the inclusive positivist position that a test for the moral permissibility of a rule can form part of a rule of recognition on a contingent basis. Alternatively, he could continue to use the example to defend the inclusive positivist position and maintain that such a society is possible. This claim requires that this society has identified a test for the moral permissibility of all action that is located prior to its incorporation into law through any rule of recognition, thus requiring him to abandon the reason behind his prima facie rejection of the strong natural law position: that the identification of such a universally acceptable test for moral permissibility is impossible. If Coleman is open to the possibility of such a principle, then the dialectically necessary argument for the PGC requires him to accept that it must necessarily function as the absolute and exclusionary reason required.

Even if he were to accept this step, he may still reject the core of the natural law claim: that the operation of such a principle requires him to accept that a rule's moral permissibility must be a criterion of its legal validity, rather than such a connection being contingent on its recognition as such by a rule of recognition as per the incorporationist position. This, he argues, is required by the fact that the conventionality thesis can explain the exclusionary force necessarily claimed by law without recourse to moral reasoning.[31] This would, of course, require him to provide a reason as to why convention can ground an exclusionary normative claim made by legal rules that successfully overrides the absolute and exclusionary reason against non-compliant behaviour that is present in the argument for the PGC. He argues this reason can be located in the following formulation of the conventionality thesis:

> [T]he possibility of legal authority is to be explained in terms of a *conventional* social practice, namely, the adherence by officials to a rule of recognition that imposes a duty on them to apply all and only those rules valid under it.[32]

Coleman believes this formulation is justified given the fact that a rule of recognition that identifies which rules are legally valid can only truly exist if it is

[31] ibid 123, 126–29.

[32] ibid 74, 77; emphasis in the original. Implicit in this claim is a commitment to the practical difference thesis. The merits of this thesis will be considered in detail in section 3.3 of this chapter, but for the moment this assumption – and the location of normative reasons within practical reasons that it necessitates – will be granted *arguendo* to allow the remainder of Coleman's defence of the conventionality thesis to be addressed together to ensure its accuracy.

followed by legal officials; adherence to it is therefore a necessary condition of the existence of such a rule. If a primary legal rule can only be legally valid if an official recognises it is valid with reference to a secondary rule of recognition, then a primary rule must achieve its normative exclusionary force because of its conformity with the requirements of the secondary rule. The distinct and exclusionary normative claim made by law can therefore be explained with reference to the internal viewpoint adopted by legal officials when they collectively act in a way that endorses the validity of such a secondary rule of recognition, something that Coleman believes legal officials have a duty to do for no other reason than their status as legal officials.[33] This duty, however, cannot be a moral duty because moral rules, if they can be identified, are practice independent. It follows that, if a rule of recognition is a social fact whose existence depends on its being accepted, they cannot be grounded in an authority that comes prior to their existence otherwise they would be a mere tautology – and incapable of making a practical difference in how we ought to act.[34] Coleman instead grounds the duty because of their status as a social fact; that the internal point of view adopted by officials in accepting a rule of recognition as valid creates a shared intention to create an obligation to recognise that rule as valid and binding. Thus, a secondary rule of recognition possesses normative content – and can pass this to primary rules that comply with its requirements – for no other reason than legal officials have decided that the rule ought to be accepted.[35] The argument that this agreement generates a normative claim is founded, for the most part, on the theory of shared intention proposed by Michael Bratman:

> [S]hared intention, as I understand it, is not an attitude in any mind. It is not an attitude in the mind of some fused agent, for there is no such mind; and it is not an attitude in the mind or minds of either or both participants. Rather, it is a state of affairs that consists primarily in attitudes (none of which are themselves shared intentions) of the participants and interrelations between those attitudes.[36]

A shared intention can form the foundation of shared cooperative agency, which itself consists of three tenets:

1. Mutual Responsiveness: Agents must be aware of the intentions and actions of other agents with whom they cooperate.
2. Commitment to the joint activity.
3. Commitment to mutual support through joint pursuance of shared activity.[37]

Coleman characterises the actions of legal officials, particularly the judicial office, as conforming to this conception of shared cooperative agency. The social

[33] ibid 83–85.
[34] ibid 86.
[35] ibid 90.
[36] ME Bratman 'Shared Intentions' (1993) 104 *Ethics* 97, 107.
[37] ME Bratman 'Shared Cooperative Activity' (1992) 101(2) *Philosophical Review* 327, 328.

fact that a rule of recognition is accepted as operative by multiple independent actors gives rise to a 'system of interdependent and reciprocal expectations'[38] which takes the form of a normative claim to act according to the requirements of the accepted rule. The fact a primary rule has been created in accordance with this normative requirement is enough to allow it to claim its directives possess an exclusionary normative force which overrides all other conflicting claims on our actions.

Three objections can be made to this account of how rules gain the status of valid legal norm, the first of which is anticipated by Coleman. He concedes that this argument may be somewhat circular, in that the creation of a rule of recognition through shared cooperative agency presupposes that legal officials already exist who are able to create a rule of recognition because of their status as such. Law is therefore being explained on the understanding that a certain class of legal officialdom exists prior to the creation of the legal system. Coleman argues that this is a straw man argument, and that the creators of a rule of recognition only become legal officials when they use their shared cooperative agency to recognise a rule of recognition. The fact that a rule of recognition is accepted by the legal officials who follow them suggests that, even though at some point in history a group of individuals decided to see themselves as officials without being able to legitimise their claim as such, the rule of recognition remains legitimate because it is accepted as such. Officialdom is therefore itself explained by conventionality.[39] This can be granted *arguendo*, as the remaining objections can more clearly show the reasons why Coleman's account cannot succeed.

The second objection examines the validity of the claim that the officialdom necessary for a group of individuals to create a rule of recognition can be retroactively legitimised by the continued acceptance of that rule of recognition by subsequent generations of legal officials. Coleman's claim that this is a social fact overlooks the simple observation that subsequent legal officials would not see the rule of recognition as valid, and thus retroactively legitimise its creation, unless they saw a good reason to accept it as such. To demonstrate this point, let us imagine a situation where my colleagues and I declare ourselves to be officials in a new legal system, and that it is our shared intention that our new legal system will replace that under which we currently live. It seems likely that our endeavour would fail on two grounds. Firstly, we would be unlikely to persuade the majority of our fellow citizens that we are, in fact, legitimate in our claim to authority and that our claim to officialdom ought to be accepted; and secondly, we would be likely to face resistance from those who currently claim the status of legal officials and whose authority we seek to supplant. Our endeavour could thus only succeed if we were to impose our will through force, or by convincing the majority of our claimed subjects and the present body of legal officials that our own claim possesses greater legitimacy than that which is currently in

[38] Coleman, *The Practice of Principle* (n 26) 94.
[39] ibid 100–01.

place. Should we adopt the former and impose our will by force, then it would be incorrect to claim that it would be adopted voluntarily by a free exercise of the shared cooperative agency of subsequent generations of officials and, by extension, could not generate a normative claim as Coleman requires. Indeed, if a legal system is no more than sovereign will imposed by threat of sanction then no independent normative claim need ever be established.[40] This leaves us with the task of persuading both officials and non-officials that the present rule of recognition ought to be rejected in favour of our new legal system which, in turn, requires us to provide them with a reason why they should see our system as prima facie more legitimate than that which currently exists.

It is this observation that allows us to raise our third objection to the argument that the conventionality thesis can ground the exclusionary normative claim made by legal rules. If a proto-legal system must provide a reason as to why it ought to be accepted as more able to claim legitimate de facto authority over whatever system of dispute resolution existed before, then we are required to accept that a standard must exist by which this legitimacy can be assessed. Coleman accepts that morality can play a role in assessing the legitimacy of normative claims, which is highly relevant to an observation already made: that in locating the source of the normative claim made by law in the shared cooperative agency of legal officials, he locates the source of the normative claim within their practical reasoning *prior* to the existence of the new legal system whose legitimacy is being assessed. This means that these ur-officials are acting according to a hierarchy of practical reasons in which any moral absolute and exclusionary reason cannot be overridden by a legal claim, as no legal claims yet exist. Thus, given that the PGC serves as an absolute and exclusionary reason against non-compliant action for all agents, the ur-officials charged with exercising their agency by creating a rule of recognition are bound to act in a way that is PGC compliant. This requires that they create a rule of recognition that is incapable of issuing directives that breach the PGC. We are required to conclude that, in order for a rule of recognition to be accepted as legitimate at the genesis of a legal system, it must hold that moral permissibility with reference to the PGC is a necessary condition of the legal validity of all subsequent legal rules. In order for his thesis to remain coherent, Coleman must either reject the conventionality thesis, or accept that it can only succeed if he abandons his commitment to inclusive positivism.

3.2. Law as Economic Rights

Having demonstrated that his conventionality thesis can only succeed in explaining the normative claim of law if any rule of recognition is PGC compliant, we can move on to address a second contribution he makes to the legal

[40] ibid 71.

theory: his characterisation of law as a primarily economic undertaking. This recharacterisation will be assessed for the extent to which it can contribute to the debate around whether a rule's moral permissibility is a necessary condition of its legal validity, before moving on to address the place of wrongfulness in this economically grounded framework. This analysis assumes the correctness of our previous claim that the conventionality thesis can only succeed if any resultant rule of recognition limits the scope of valid legal norms to those that are permissible with reference to the PGC.

Central to Coleman's claim that law is an economic undertaking is his view that legal-rights claims must be made with reference to a correlative duty, and that this reciprocity renders them akin to an economic dispute. He believes that this characterisation of the interplay between legal rights and duties presupposes the existence of two overarching rules:

1. Rights are allocated 'under conditions of rational cooperation, full information and zero transaction costs' that create conditions under which mutually advantageous bargaining can take place.
2. Procedures must be in place to remedy outcomes when these conditions are not satisfied.[41]

It is the reciprocity inherent in correlative rights and duties that motivates Coleman to see them as being similar in their operation to bargaining in the marketplace; this similarity means that rules that govern rights and duties can look to the marketplace for guidance as to their scope and content, one of which must be that the conditions under which bargaining can take place must be established in advance. If this does not occur, then it falls to the courts to imagine what would have been achieved in a hypothetical 'perfect market' and work from there.[42] At this point we see an interaction between the PGC and Coleman's characterisation, as he accepts that bargaining would require a minimum level of freedom and wellbeing on the part of the agent to allow the market to function at optimum efficiency. Thus, an explanation of the foundation of these rights is necessary for any broader system of institutional rights to exist.[43]

This claim requires Coleman to accept that a rule which breaches the PGC by interfering with an agent's freedom or wellbeing cannot be legally valid. His belief that this could only be true within a legal system if expressly provided for, rather than it being necessarily true of all legal systems, would lead him to disagree[44] – but he ought to accept instead that the content of all legal rights must be constrained by the requirements of the PGC. The first of these is his characterisation of rights as 'conceptual markers' or 'place holders' that demonstrate

[41] Coleman, *Markets, Morals and the Law* (n 22) 28.
[42] ibid 29.
[43] ibid 33–35.
[44] ibid 34.

that an interest is something that *should* be protected by law.[45] Coleman suggests that concepts such as property, liability and inalienability interact to form the substantive content of such rights – but gives no account as to how this interaction would occur or why we should accept that a right emerges from it. The PGC-compliant conventionality thesis previously established is capable of filling this theoretical gap, but this natural law conception of the validity of legal norms establishes a minimum threshold of permissibility that requires Coleman to abandon his claim to the absolute contingency of the content of legal rights.

Far from rejecting this conclusion, it is one that Coleman appears to inadvertently condone twice in his closing analysis of the purpose of any adjudicatory system. Firstly, he argues: 'For ease of exposition, let us assume that the purpose of a system of institutional rights is to maximize net welfare.'[46] It is not immediately clear whether Coleman here means the maximisation of individual welfare or that of society as a whole but, given his commitment to viewing individual wellbeing as essential for any bargaining to occur, we can presume that a minimum threshold of individual welfare must be of some concern to him in making this claim. This conclusion is also implicit in the operation of the market generally, as the market interaction is undertaken between individuals who must feel that they get some kind of subjective benefit from agreements made within it; were this not the case, the individual would have no reason to participate in the bargaining exercise nor to agree to the conclusions reached. This claim is analogous to that made by the PGC; that wellbeing is a necessary pre-condition of any action, and its status as a GCA is something that an agent must claim as a right that ought not to be interfered with without their consent. As bargaining would require the agent to use their agency, they are committed to acting in a PGC-compliant manner throughout the process. A similar claim is made when Coleman suggests that there would be no rational reason for an agent to participate in a bargaining exercise if the outcome of the transaction would leave them worse off.[47] As this deliberation about net-benefit takes place within the realm of practical reason, then the PGC must also feature in the agent's deliberations for their conclusion to be sound. Maximisation of net welfare for either individual or community cannot take place in a way that is not compliant with the requirements of the PGC.

This conclusion leads us to Coleman's second inadvertent acceptance of the PGC, present in his acceptance of the claim that a minimum threshold amount of freedom is required to bargain in the marketplace. He argues that this claim requires us to accept that rules concerning individual liberty are thus necessarily normative in their content as, if this freedom to bargain is essential for the existence of any sound agreement, then our default position is that it is something that ought to be protected by the officials overseeing the transactions

[45] ibid 35.
[46] ibid 36.
[47] J Coleman, *Risks and Wrongs* (Cambridge University Press 1992) 19.

in question.[48] This claim is analogous to that made by the PGC; that freedom is a necessary pre-condition of any action so its status as a GCA is something that an agent must claim as a right that ought not to be interfered with without their consent. Thus, Coleman can be shown to accept the Gewirthian position that both freedom and wellbeing are GCAs that an agent must claim rights to; so if he must accept this, he must also accept the remainder of the argument for the PGC. He must also accept the connection established between the PGC and legal normativity; this is necessary given his commitment to the claim that political morality and attempts at coercion by the state can only be legitimate if it provides both systemic pareto efficiency and is rationally acceptable on an individual level.[49] As respect for individual freedom and wellbeing are necessary for both of these conditions to be satisfied, any legitimate political structures must limit the substantive scope of their legal directives to those that are compatible with the requirements of the PGC.

Coleman's recharacterisation of law as grounded in an economic model of reciprocal bargaining thus requires him to accept our natural law claim, that only rules that are morally permissible with reference to the PGC are capable of being legally valid. Having reached this conclusion, we are now able to consider whether this claim is compatible with his conception of 'wrongness' in such a system. He believes that this cannot exist without in the absence of a specific act of 'wrongdoing', itself defined as 'the unjustifiable or otherwise impermissible injuring of others' legitimate interests',[50] with legitimate interests being those that are protected by legitimate rights claims. Wrongs are therefore defined in opposition to a right, meaning that both rights and wrongs are to be viewed as being components of a unified normative framework of obligations, meaning that a legally remediable wrong is one that breaches a protected right that has been recognised as legal in character according to the characterisation of law as an economic model.[51] Coleman would prima facie reject, however, our claim that this characterisation requires him to commit to a PGC-compliant natural law claim due to his differentiation between the form and content of rights – analogous to his differentiation between the grounding and content of a rule of recognition discussed above. This rejection relies on the claim that the form of rights must be capable of demonstrating that their content is analytically true; this can be distinguished from their content insofar as a particular substantive content can never be *a priori* necessary in the same way.[52] Using an economic model of law as a case study to illustrate this point, he claims that the rules' content is contingent on particular models of liability and property ownership: if somebody possesses a property right, then they have a valid claim that those who seek their resources must seek their consent; this, then necessitates

[48] Coleman, *Markets, Morals and the Law* (n 22) 38.
[49] Coleman, *Risks and Wrongs* (n 47) 21, 29–30.
[50] ibid 331.
[51] ibid 332, 335.
[52] ibid 338.

a corresponding liability right, which holds that a valid claim to compensation arises if another secures their resources without having secured their consent. The content of rights is thus highly contingent on the specific model adopted by each system; a remediable wrong is only committed when these specific and contingent rights are interfered with.[53]

Yet this explanation is circular, in that it holds a given right to be valid purely by dint of its existence within a system. Coleman would likely invoke the conventionality thesis to argue that this is not a problematic statement. However – as has been shown previously – the conventionality thesis can only remain coherent if it is reconceptualised in a way that ensures that the substantive content of all emergent rules is permissible with reference to the PGC. Coleman's claim that the content of rights and, by extension, the concept of wrongfulness, is always contingent on the requirements of a given system is thus only partially true; in order to be a valid legal rule at all, its substantive content must be morally permissible. Contingency of content is therefore only possible beyond the necessary constraints imposed by the PGC.

3.3. Legal Authority and the Practical Difference Thesis

This section has so far demonstrated that both Coleman's conventionality thesis and his reconceptualisation of law as an economic model require him to accept that the substantive content of legal rules be limited to those that are compatible with the requirements of the PGC. Our third and final subsection can now turn to a final element of his approach to legal validity, his commitment to the practical difference thesis. We ask whether this approach is capable of holding that legal rules can be valid even if their directives are morally impermissible. Our starting point ought to be that Coleman's positivism is inclusive in character; he accepts the existence of several legal rules that expressly reference moral permissibility as a requirement of legal validity, but notes that these are only legally valid because this permissibility is expressly required by the legal rule in question. He therefore refers to his form of inclusive positivism as 'incorporationism', to highlight that substantive moral principles are capable of acting as law – but only if these are deliberately incorporated by the correct law-making procedure in a given jurisdiction.[54] This thesis requires us to accept that any directive can have two separate components: an analytic component, which is concerned with the different types of reasons that may make claims on an agent, and a normative component, which is concerned with the legitimacy of these claims.[55] Yet, as has been shown on multiple occasions, this neat distinction is

[53] ibid 339–40.

[54] J Coleman, 'Authority and Reason' in RP George (ed), *The Autonomy of Law: Essays on Legal Positivism* (Clarendon Press 1996) 287–88.

[55] ibid 296.

somewhat blurred insofar as it does not fully account for the absolute and exclusionary reason that the PGC provides for compliance with its requirements. Thus, if Coleman characterises the primary purpose of law as being concerned with social coordination,[56] we must assume that the legal positivist position is impossible and that the PGC must necessarily constrain the scope of valid rules of coordination to those that conform with its requirements.

Coleman is aware of this common argument from the natural law position and might attempt to rely on the practical difference thesis as a way to reject it. This thesis holds that the natural law account of legal authority endorsed by this work – that legal validity can only be possessed by rules that are morally permissible – requires us to accept that legal directives are otiose insofar as they merely restate reasons for action that we already possess.[57] It follows that, if the law is incapable of generating its own exclusionary reasons for compliance that override pre-existing moral reasons, then the law is no longer an authority;[58] it is a tautology that does not make any difference to how people would act. Since law necessarily must make a difference to how people act, a test for the moral permissibility of legal rules cannot form part of any justificatory norm.[59] This strong version of the practical difference thesis is, however, rejected by Coleman as being incompatible with his incorporationist claim that moral norms *can* be incorporated into a legal system if this is expressly allowed for.[60] He thus prefers a softer version of the thesis: that law must be a distinct normative regime *capable* of overriding all non-compliant directives – including those grounded in morality.[61]

Coleman anticipates that a natural lawyer would reject this conclusion on the following grounds: that if the purpose of law is to guide our action, and only directives that are morally permissible are rationally capable of guiding our action, then legal directives must be morally permissible in order to be valid.[62] He thus anticipates precisely why we ought to reject the practical difference thesis: that Raz's normal justification thesis demonstrates that legal authority stems from a place beyond human reasoning, meaning legal reasons need not form part of the same hierarchy of practical reason as other competing reasons for action.[63] This claim can be rejected for two reasons. Firstly, it does explain away the fact that his independent commitment to the conventionality thesis can also only explain legal authority if we accept that a rule's moral permissibility

[56] ibid; Coleman, *The Practice of Principle* (n 26) 70–71.

[57] Coleman, 'Authority and Reason' (n 54) 304.

[58] JE Penner, 'Legal Reasoning and the Authority of Law' in LH Meyer et al. (eds), *Rights, Culture, and the Law: Themes from the Legal and Political Philosophy of Joseph Raz* (Oxford University Press 2003) 71.

[59] ibid.

[60] Jules Coleman, 'Incorporationism, Conventionality, and the Practical Difference Thesis' (1998) 4(4) *Legal Theory* 381, 387, 396.

[61] ibid 424–25.

[62] Coleman, 'Authority and Reason' (n 54) 309.

[63] ibid 309–10.

with reference to the PGC is a necessary condition of its legal validity. Secondly, his objection rests on a mischaracterisation of the normal justification thesis; as demonstrated by our previous discussion of Raz in section 2.1.1 of Chapter 4, this thesis actually holds that an authority is legitimate iff accepting it would mean that an agent would be more likely to comply with its directives than they would be otherwise. Far from locating legal authority outside of our standard hierarchy of practical reason, the normal difference thesis locates legal authority firmly within this hierarchy. Thus, if the PGC is a valid absolute and exclusionary reason against non-compliant behaviour, a non-compliant directive claiming the status of law could not claim to be an exclusionary reason for action as it is necessarily overridden by the requirements of the PGC and could not function as law. Given that Coleman is committed to endorsing the natural law claim endorsed by this thesis on two counts, we ought to briefly turn to his contention that this renders the law either irrational or otiose. This claim can be rejected as it mischaracterises the moral claim present in the theory; rather than specifying a correct set of universal legal rules, it instead holds that a legal rule must be morally permissible to be valid. It therefore allows for legal pluralism insofar as multiple legal directives would be equally morally permissible and thus does not issue a directive that is otiose. It rather acts in full accordance with Raz's normal justification thesis, in that by coordinating our behaviour by requiring one of many permissible outcomes, it provides a reason as to why an agent would be more likely to comply with its directives than they would be otherwise.

We can thus conclude that the practical difference thesis does not provide the sound rejection of the natural law claim that Coleman believes it does. Two final routes are therefore open to Coleman if he wishes to reject our PGC-compliant natural law position, the first of which would be to attempt an alternative means of demonstrating that the legal reasoning is sui generis and separable from the moral reasoning required by the PGC. He attempts to show in his claim that there is an important difference between something being a reason to act and something being a reason on which a subject acts.[64] Coleman hypothesises a situation in which person A promises to meet person B at noon. A forgets that the promise was made, but still meets B at noon as a new reason emerged for them to do so. Coleman suggests that the promise remains a reason for action, despite not being a reason that actually led to the action taking place. Reasons for action therefore need not be causal, but merely create a reason to act, a fact that applies to legal reasons as much as any other.[65] It is not immediately obvious, however, that this characterisation aids Coleman in his attempt to dismiss the connection between legal validity and moral permissibility that this work argues is necessary. His argument implies that moral directives, by their claim to provide an absolute and exclusionary reason for compliant behaviour, offer

[64] Coleman, *The Practice of Principle* (n 26) 71.
[65] ibid 72.

a stronger reason than that offered by legal directives. This, however, is not the case; as observed by Beyleveld, the 'ought' present in a moral directive is prescriptive rather than obligatory insofar as it claims it ought to be followed, rather than it would be impossible for an agent to choose to disregard it.[66] The very fact that an agent could choose to disregard a moral norm and act immorally shows that, like legal directives, moral norms remain reasons to act even if they are not ultimately acted upon. By showing this similarity between the nature of moral and legal directives, Coleman inadvertently locates law and morality within the same nexus of practical reasoning and opens up the paradox we encountered in our previous discussion of Raz in section 3.2 of Chapter 4: that it is impossible for ($R_L\ x, \Phi$ & $R_M\ x, -\Phi$). As the only means by which this paradox can be overcome is via endorsement of the PGC-compliant natural law claim advanced in Chapter 3, Coleman's attempt to distinguish reasons for action from reasons upon which a subject acts actually requires him to accept the natural law claim that a rule's moral permissibility is a necessary condition of its legal validity.

The second way in which we might attempt to avoid this conclusion would be to characterise the methodology of the argument for the PGC as being incompatible with legal theory. Coleman attempts to do this by recognising Hart's claim that the scope of his own descriptive account of law is methodologically distinct from the normative account provided by the natural law tradition. He suggests the latter is problematic in that it would invalidate all positivist accounts of legal validity, and thus cannot account for the plurality of theories that are a necessary feature of jurisprudential enquiry.[67] This conclusion is undoubtedly true, but it is not immediately clear why its ability to demonstrate that other theories are false means that a theory ought not to be accepted; indeed, this claim would be viewed as absurd if made in other areas of enquiry. It is axiomatic of theoretical claims that they are exclusive in nature, as their claim to truth necessarily comes at the expense of other claims that have been shown to be unsupportable. Yet, given that Coleman seriously contends that a plurality of incommensurate theories is not only necessary but also valuable, we are required to examine it for its validity. His claim progresses from the conventionality thesis: that a legal system exists as a matter of social fact if it is accepted by legal officials operating within it.[68] As such, law makes a claim to prima facie legitimacy that requires a minimum level of moral argument that can justify this legitimacy, but does not require a connection between moral permissibility and legal validity unless expressly required by the system.[69] Such a connection can be present in what he calls the 'predicate of commendation'; that any legal system is morally

[66] D Beyleveld, 'The Principle of Generic Consistency as the Supreme Principle of Human Rights' (2012) 13(1) *Human Rights Review* 1, 4 n 7.

[67] Coleman, *The Practice of Principle* (n 26) 186.

[68] ibid 186–87.

[69] ibid 188.

preferable to alternative means of government for the pragmatic reason that even a legal system comprised of entirely immoral directives would at least allow an agent to plan their lives and better attain their goals. Legal authority can thus be normatively legitimate because it is 'pragmatic, theoretical, epistemic, and most importantly, discursive'.[70]

This claim can be quickly rejected, however, in that it presupposes the starting point that it wishes to demonstrate: that a rule can be legally valid even if its directive is morally impermissible. Such rules would, for a natural lawyer, simply not be law – they could be enforced systemically, but in the same way as our stew with a pastry lid in section 2.3 of Chapter 3 is not a pie, such rules could not be legitimately described as legal despite appearing similar in character. Coleman's argument thus does not overcome the argument for a PGC-compliant natural law for the simple reason that it does not engage with it; in the absence of a serious engagement with the claim being made, it cannot succeed in demonstrating it to be false. We therefore have no reason to reject our conclusion that Coleman's theoretical positions, whether the conventionality thesis, the practical difference thesis or his reconceptualisation of law as an economic enterprise, can only succeed if they endorse the claim that a rule's moral permissibility with reference to the PGC is a necessary condition of its legal validity.

4. THE MODERATE INCORPORATIONISM OF MATTHEW KRAMER

The final author to be addressed in this chapter will be Matthew Kramer, who endorses the positivist claim that a rule's moral permissibility must be separable from any assessment as to its legal validity. His positivism is inclusive in nature as he accepts that such a criterion for legal validity is conceptually possible, but its existence is purely contingent on it being expressly allowed for by the legal system in question.[71] The section will form two parts. The first will outline Kramer's reasons for rejecting the PGC, before addressing whether this rejection should be questioned in light of his own conceptualisation of the nature of morality and moral norms. We will then move on to consider his commitment to the separation thesis.

4.1. Kramer on the Nature of Moral Claims

Kramer is the only one of the three authors covered in the present chapter who directly engages with the Gewirthian project, which he claims fails in its stated objective of creating a supreme moral principle against which the permissibility

[70] ibid 196.

[71] M Kramer, *In Defense of Legal Positivism: Law Without Trimmings* (Oxford University Press 1999) 1.

of action can be assessed.[72] This scepticism must therefore be addressed and overcome for any connection between the PGC and legal validity to be conceptually sound. We will begin with an uncontroversial claim made by Kramer on the nature of ethical enquiry, namely that it must: '[Embrace] all the standards and normative implications articulable in statements that apply ethical predicates to objects of ethical assessment.'[73] One such normative implication is the mind-independence of moral principles: that they exist regardless of their recognition by those to whom they are addressed.[74] A second is what Kramer refers to as their determinate-correctness: '[t]he extent to which there are determinately correct answers to moral questions is inversely proportional to the extent of the leeway enjoyed by anybody who confronts those questions.'[75] Weak moral propositions can be overridden, whereas strong moral reasons such as a categorical imperative are obligatory and should be followed. Disagreements as to the bindingness of a directive are not evidence that the problem is incommensurable, as the mind-independence of the principle presupposes that a means of identifying its requirements must exist.[76] These preliminary points are necessary to see that Kramer is open to the mind-independence of a moral requirement that binds all to whom it is addressed, and that this presupposes the existence of a test to identify the requirements in question. As the PGC requires both of these predicates, he ought to be open to its existence and validity should the argument leading to it be valid.

It is against this preliminary observation that we can consider Kramer's argument to the contrary. There are two primary reasons that Kramer believes the argument for the PGC fails, and each will be addressed in turn. The first, in a pair of articles co-authored with Nigel Simmonds, concedes that Kramer has no issue with the dialectically necessary progression of the argument to universalise Gewirth's starting point;[77] rather, their claim concerns the nature of Gewirth's starting claim. Kramer and Simmonds believe that what Beyleveld identifies as stage two of the of the argument for the PGC, that an agent is required to make a claim-right that their GCAs ought not to be interfered with without their consent, is not a true 'ought' claim.[78] This is on their understanding that an 'ought' judgment needs to provide an addressee with a reason as to why they ought to accept it. As Gewirth's starting point is made from the

[72] M Kramer and N Simmonds, 'Reason Without Reasons: A Critique of Alan Gewirth's Moral Philosophy' (1996) 34(3) *The Southern Journal of Philosophy* 301; M Kramer and N Simmonds, 'No Better Reasons: A Reply to Alan Gewirth' (1998) 36(1) *The Southern Journal of Philosophy* 131; M Kramer, *In the Realm of Legal and Moral Philosophy* (Macmillan 1999), 174–199; M Kramer, *Moral Realism as a Moral Doctrine* (Wiley-Blackwell 2009) 290.

[73] Kramer, *Moral Realism as a Moral Doctrine* (n 72) 3.

[74] ibid 27.

[75] ibid 86.

[76] ibid 92.

[77] Kramer and Simmonds, 'Reason Without Reasons' (n 72) 302–03.

[78] See section 2 of Chapter 3; Alan Gewirth, *Reason and Morality* (University of Chicago Press 1978) 63–103.

internal viewpoint of the agent, it does not provide an addressee with a reason why they ought to accept the validity of the 'ought' claim being made against them. They conclude that the rights claim made by the agent is not a true 'ought'. They then argue that, if stage three is merely a universalised version of the same claim, and the rights claim made in stage two of the PGC is not a true 'ought', then whatever claim is universalised by stage three of the argument cannot be a true 'ought'.[79] They do note that both Beyleveld and Gewirth would suggest this conclusion misapprehends the claim being made by the agent in stages one and two: that the 'ought' here is merely pragmatic in that the agent is required, from their internal viewpoint, to accept that they have a good reason to see that they ought to protect their GCAs from non-interference.[80] They reject this by suggesting that, if true, then Beyleveld and Gewirth are claiming that the 'ought' claim made by agent X requires agent Y to refrain from a given action even though agent Y is unaware of, or might even reject, the reason given to them by agent X. They suggest this is clearly nonsense, thus justifying their starting assumption that a true 'ought' must provide a reason for its acceptance to any addressee.[81]

Gewirth responds directly to Kramer and Simmonds' article[82] and notes that their objection has both been raised[83] and addressed before.[84] He suggests that their location of the reason for seeing an 'ought'-claim as valid as being located with the addressee rather than addressor who claims the reason exists is an artificially narrow conception of the nature of an 'ought'-claim.[85] They, of course, reject this counter claim – but they are mistaken for two reasons. Firstly, their claim appears premised on a misunderstanding of the nature of the pragmatic claim necessarily made by the agent in stages one and two of the argument for the PGC. The claim is not one that is premised on a mere preference for a particular action but is made in relation to certain conditions that are necessary for any and all action to be undertaken. As such, the agent has the strongest possible reason to see that they must protect their GCAs against non-consensual interference as, without them, any action would be impossible. From their internal viewpoint, they are thus perfectly legitimate in claiming that pragmatism requires them to claim that their GCAs can be protected

[79] Kramer and Simmonds, 'Reason Without Reasons' (n 72) 303; Kramer and Simmonds, 'No Better Reasons' (n 72).

[80] ibid (n 72) 304–05.

[81] ibid 304, 306.

[82] A Gewirth, ''Ought' and Reasons for Action' (1997) 35(2) *The Southern Journal of Philosophy* 171.

[83] C McMahon, 'Gewirth's Justification of Morality' (1986) 50(2) *Philosophical Studies* 261.

[84] See sections 2.1 and 3.1 of Chapter 1. See also: A Gewirth, 'The Justification of Morality' (1988) 53(2) *Philosophical Studies* 245–62; J Scheuerman, 'Gewirth's Concept of Prudential Rights' (1987) 37(148) *Philosophical Quarterly* 291–304; D Beyleveld, *The Dialectical Necessity of Morality; An Analysis and Defense of Alan Gewirth's Argument to the Principle of Generic Consistency* (University of Chicago Press 1991) 201–31.

[85] Gewirth, ''Ought' and Reasons for Action' (n 82) 172–73.

against non-consensual interference – a claim that is analogous to a declaration that they perceive that the legitimacy of their rights claim to their GCAs is one that others ought to accept. That the 'ought' is here perceived by the addressor rather than the addressee is not a misuse of the term but is perfectly compatible with its normal usage to identify a proscriptive claim being made by an addressor against an addressee. If Kramer and Simmonds reject that this proscriptive normative claim made by the addressor is a true 'ought', then they must have in mind an alternative conception of the normative claim that would render it impossible in a literal sense for the addressee to reject the claim. Since this is clearly a mischaracterisation of the nature of moral claims, we must conclude that the 'ought' identified from the internal viewpoint of the agent is sound.

Secondly, even if they were to reject this conclusion, Kramer and Simmonds are incorrect to claim that the 'ought' that results from stage three of the argument for the PGC is not true because the thing being universalised was itself not an 'ought'. To attempt to make sense of this objection, we will remind ourselves that the reason why they reject the pragmatic 'ought' claim is that, to be valid, an 'ought' must contain a reason as to why an addressee ought to see it as a reason for them to act or refrain from acting.[86] Yet this is exactly what stage three of the PGC succeeds in providing. Their objection seeks to artificially separate the steps of the PGC into separate and distinct claims, and thus overlooks the dialectically necessary progression of the argument as a singular whole. The universalisation of the pragmatic claim that takes place in stage three simply provides the addressee with the reason for the need to accept it as a valid 'ought' claim on Kramer and Simmonds' own conception of what it means to be a true 'ought' claim. Its status before this point is simply irrelevant to the success of the argument. We can thus see that Kramer's first objection to the argument for the PGC, focused on the nature of the pragmatic 'ought' claim made by the agent fails.

His second objection, though stated more extensively elsewhere,[87] can be summarised in the following claim:

> What is so objectionable about the efforts to assimilate moral obligatoriness to logical requisiteness … is that they evince a dearth of trust in the solidity for moral principles and moral requirements.[88]

This claim seems to be grounded in the sentiment that to reduce moral principles to simple logical prerequisites is somehow improper, and that grounds other than rationality and consistency are preferable.[89] But this claim does not sit well with Kramer's earlier claims regarding the determinate-correctness of

[86] Kramer and Simmonds, 'Reason Without Reasons' (n 72) 304, 306.
[87] Kramer, *In the Realm of Legal and Moral Philosophy* (n 72) 174–99.
[88] Kramer, *Moral Realism as a Moral Doctrine* (n 72) 290.
[89] ibid.

moral standards, which hold that moral disagreements can be resolved with greater understanding of both the rule itself and the circumstances in which it is being applied. This presupposes that an acceptable test can be identified that can be used to ascertain both the nature of the rule and the relevance of the context in which it is being applied, which is precisely what Gewirth has done in outlining the argument for the PGC. Kramer's objection to grounding moral permissibility in ethical rationalism thus creates a contradiction in his position: he rejects ethical rationalism for its reliance on rationality in identifying moral claims, whilst simultaneously holding that rationality is vital to resolve moral uncertainty using the claim that such uncertainty can only be resolved by a test against which a rule and relevant context can be assessed for their moral relevance. Resolving this contradiction requires him to either abandon his rejection of ethical rationalism, or his claim to the determinate-correctness of moral standards.

It is not clear which of these seems preferable to Kramer. His scepticism of the Gewirthian claim that rationality can ground moral truth is deeply held, as can be seen in his claim that:

> Moral principles are of course in conformity with the laws of logic, but their distinctively moral force is not a species of logical necessity, and that force is in no way tarnished or diminished by not being such a specie.[90]

This is not to say that moral claims are not to be subject to the laws of logic, but that they must be more than this. Otherwise, they would be described as logical rather than moral truths.[91] Kramer does not offer further support for this claim, instead appearing to see this as self-evidently true. We can thus begin to interrogate the claim. If Kramer is correct that a moral precept should be in conformity with the laws of logic, this suggests that the opposite is also true: a moral principle which is not in conformity with the laws of logic cannot be a true moral principle. An irrational directive is thus prima facie incapable of serving as a true moral directive. A connection between irrationality and the validity of a moral directive is therefore present on Kramer's own understanding of the nature of moral claims, meaning his hostility to the ethical rationalist claim must be grounded in a conception of morality that is circular, insofar as it adopts a conception of morality as a necessary part of the argument by which it attempts to demonstrate the truth of that same conception. Yet, even if we were to concede this point to Kramer *arguendo*, a further problem arises in relation to the incommensurability of moral directives. If he is correct insofar as moral principles are mind independent, in that they are valid regardless of whether they are accepted, then we must return to the necessity of the existence of a means by which their validity can be assessed. Such a test must be rationally justifiable, as were this not the case then it could not succeed in providing

[90] ibid 290.
[91] ibid.

a reason for us to accept the validity of the moral directives in question. Thus, the mind independence of moral directives necessitates the following if absolute moral indeterminacy is to be avoided:

(a) a test exists against which the validity of moral directives can be assessed;
(b) this test must be capable of being rationally justified for us to accept it as valid; and
(c) if the test must be rationally justified to be accepted, moral directives it identifies as successful must also be rationally permissible.

Were this not true, then this would be analogous to the claim that mind-independent truths cannot or need not be rationally discernible, meaning we are required to question why we ought to accept a directive claiming to be a self-evident truth independent of its rational justifiability. We can therefore see a stronger connection between a directive's rationality and its moral content than Kramer would have us believe exists when he makes the claim that logical inconsistencies are possible in a moral norm.[92] This claim appears incompatible with his own commitment to both the mind-independent nature of moral directives and their determinate-correctness, thus identifying a problem in the argument proposed. The problem is one that would, of course, disappear entirely were he to abandon his objection to ethical rationalism and accept that the PGC is capable of producing mind-independent moral directives and a test for which action can be assessed for its determinate-correctness that he requires of a supreme moral principle. This is the preferable course of action for Kramer to take given that his objections to the principle have been shown to be unfounded.

4.2. Implications for Kramer's Theory of Law

In a recent monograph on the nature of moral claims, Kramer stated that 'one of the chief messages of this book is that nearly all non-tautological and non-self-contradictory claims about ethics or morality are ethical or moral in content.'[93] This work has shown that the PGC is neither tautological nor self-contradictory and the preceding analysis has shown not only that Kramer's substantive objections to the argument for the PGC are unfounded, but also that his own characterisation of the nature or moral claims requires him to accept it as valid. In light of this conclusion, this section will now move on to engage with his extensive writing on legal validity. It will do so in two parts, firstly addressing his dismissal of the Gewirthian natural law position of Beyleveld and Brownsword endorsed by this work before considering his own defence of the separation thesis.

[92] ibid.
[93] ibid 13.

Kramer's objection to the Gewirthian natural law position begins from his observation that pragmatism plays a key role in the deliberations of legal officials charged with using their discretion as part of any adjudicatory process. He makes this claim in direct opposition to the approach he claims Beyleveld and Brownsword would make should we instead adopt the natural law position endorsed by this thesis: that such officials would be bound by the PGC to recognise that the outcome of their deliberations must be morally permissible in order to be legally valid.[94] Kramer suggests that this could be accepted by a legal official not because they accept the PGC compliant natural law position, but because they wish to maintain their own privileged position; if this is true, then their pragmatic desires are ultimately the reason for their action. If moral considerations are merely a reason to act rather than the reason for action, such officials could hardly be described as acting morally.[95] Thus, he believes that Beyleveld and Brownsword's theory is not a true theory of natural law at all.

He reaches this conclusion over the course of several pages of engagement with their position in his *In Defense of Legal Positivism*;[96] but notable by its absence is any reference to the PGC or its operation within Beyleveld and Brownsword's theory. We can assume from this that his analysis grants the validity of the PGC *arguendo*, so his rejection of it on the grounds that pragmatism can be a reason for action that overrides moral reasons to act is one we ought to take seriously. It can, however, itself be rejected insofar as it mischaracterises the claim made by any PGC-compliant theory of natural law. This theory holds that, to be legally valid, any legal directive must be morally permissible. The motivation of judges in reaching such a conclusion is not immediately pertinent, as this test for moral permissibility is ultimately outcome-focused. That a judge might reach a PGC-compliant outcome for a pragmatic reason does not overshadow the only relevant consideration in assessing the legal validity of their decision: that it was morally permissible, regardless of how that outcome was reached. Kramer could, of course, offer a second potential outcome to his hypothetical scenario: that the legal officials were instead to believe that pragmatism required them to reach a non-PGC-compliant outcome to their deliberation. The positivist position would suggest that this conclusion would be legally valid, yet our discussion of positivist theories to this point has shown that this conclusion is untenable in light of the natural law claim defended by this work. Kramer's claim that a pragmatic reason to reach a particular outcome demonstrates the incorrectness of Beyleveld and Brownsword's claim therefore fails; such a decision would either be PGC compliant and legally valid, or not PGC compliant and incapable of possessing the normative force necessarily claimed by law.

[94] Kramer, *Law Without Trimmings* (n 71) 216.
[95] ibid 228–29.
[96] ibid 225–33.

Having rejected Kramer's attempted dismissal of our PGC-compliant theory of natural law, we are able to move on to consider his own theories with regard to the validity of legal norms. Our starting point ought to be a restatement of Kramer's commitment to the inclusive-positivist claim that moral permissibility and legal validity should be seen as concepts that are entirely separable. Overlaps are possible, but are contingent on being expressly provided for by the legal system under consideration.[97] We will firstly address Kramer's preference for what he labels a 'theoretical-explanatory' analysis of law over the normative approach he ascribes to proponents of theories of natural law, before considering his argument for a positivist conception of the Rule of Law in light of the point, previously argued, that his own characterisation of the nature of moral claims requires him to accept the validity of the PGC.

Kramer's writing is, on the whole, dismissive of substantive natural law theories such as that endorsed by this work. Central to this rejection is his belief that the most appropriate approach to questions of legal validity ought accurately to describe legal systems as they exist and that, as such, a descriptive 'theoretical-explanatory' analysis is preferable to the normative, moral-political approach preferred by proponents of theories of natural law.[98] Such a moral-political approach can be justified only insofar as it is contingently accepted by officials operating within a given legal system.[99] Yet Kramer's preference for a starting point that is based in empirical observation of practice and is therefore, to use our analysis from section 2 of Chapter 3, made in reference to an (F_c) conception rather than a neutral starting point grounded in (F_b) such as that proposed by our agreed referent. His methodology therefore begs the question and presupposes a positivist conception of legal validity. The only support he offers in justification of this position is the suggestion that the benefits of the incorporationist approach outweigh the existence of any 'regrettable moral-political effects.'[100] This positivist assumption demonstrates clearly that, instead of actively seeking to demonstrate the falsehood of the natural law position, Kramer instead seems content to talk over them. By failing to meaningfully engage with opposing views, his arguments simply cannot succeed in the way he suggests they do. This unwillingness to engage them head on can, to some extent, be explained by his earlier claim that a judge can be justified in prioritising prudential over moral reasoning when adjudicating disputes.

> Whenever I refer to reasons-for-action in this section, I am focusing not only on the considerations to which officials do give weight in deciding how they should be have, but also (and even more importantly) on the considerations to which they would give weight if they grasped the serviceability of those considerations for the furtherance of their general aims.[101]

[97] ibid 1.
[98] Kramer, *Where Law and Morality Meet* (n 1) 156–57.
[99] ibid 151.
[100] ibid 157.
[101] ibid, n 16.

In light of this claim, Kramer suggests that – as a matter of realism – judges simply do not reduce all issues of adjudication to questions of moral permissibility, and it would thus be wrong to conclude that this is what ought to be required of them. Should a natural lawyer argue against this point, that a judge should always consider the moral permissibility of a rule to be a requirement of its legal validity, Kramer would contend that they are describing the law as it ought to be rather than analysing the law as it is. Such a claim would end the debate if it were in any way supportable, but it does not engage in the slightest with the actual normative argument put forward by the substantive natural law claim endorsed here. If we were to begin from the neutral starting point of our agreed referent highlighted in section 2 of Chapter 3 rather than the positivist starting point favoured by Kramer, then we are required to accept that the unified hierarchy of practical reason necessitated by the PGC simply requires that a legal rule must be morally permissible to do the one thing that law must be capable of doing: claiming to be capable of guiding our actions. Nothing in Kramer's preference for a theoretical-explanatory approach directly engages with this claim, and thus gives us no reason to prefer his account of legal validity over our PGC-compliant natural law account that has so far been shown to be sound.

Kramer attempts to salvage his argument by responding to a similar line of natural law argumentation put to him by Dyzenhaus: that the internal perspective to which positivism commits itself necessitates that, if we accept a supreme moral principle can be identified that constrains all action, adjudication must be subject to its requirements as would any other action. It is thus conceptually impossible for moral deliberation to *not* take place during any process of deliberation. Kramer's response is to concede that this may be an accurate description of how judges in an individual legal system may respond to such a moral principle, but it does not follow that this is something that can be universalised to the very concept of law itself.[102] Such a response does not in any way, however, respond to Dyzenhaus' claim; if a supreme moral principle can be identified that applies to any and all action, and adjudication is a form of action, then the supreme moral principle must require that the outcome of adjudication be permissible if the resultant directive is to claim to be capable of guiding our action. The only way that Kramer's objection could defeat this claim is if he could hypothesise a legal system in which neither the legal officials charged with its oversight nor the subjects to whom its directives are addressed are agents. Yet such a hypothetical system would be impossible, as practical rationality is at the heart of all adjudication and it is axiomatic of the purpose of law that it exists to subject conduct to the governance of rules, thus necessitating agential subjects. The objection to Dyzenhaus' point thus misunderstands the nature of his claim and can be rejected for that reason.

[102] ibid 158–59.

Kramer is, of course, unlikely to accept this conclusion. His objection to the natural law claim may therefore shift to one that rejects the functional account of law upon which our natural law claim is constructed on the grounds that the nature of legal obligations is substantively different to, and thus distinguishable from, moral concerns. Such a claim is central to his rejection of Lon Fuller's natural law position: that a purposive approach to law need not result in morally permissible system, but could instead result in one that was either amoral or immoral[103] because:

> Legal rules do not normally trade on each citizen's agency or autonomy in the cognitive sense; they normally present requirements and prescriptions that are to be heeded by persons who are capable of choosing to heed them.[104]

Kramer concludes that these differences between legal and moral reasoning can justify his theoretical-explanatory approach. Assessing the validity of this claim when made against an expressly moral functional account of law such as that presented by Lon Fuller is beyond the scope of this book. Kramer's position does not hold, however, when we begin from the morally neutral agreed referent upon which our PGC-compliant theory of natural law is constructed: that the purpose of law is to subject human conduct to the governance of rules. This statement makes no reference as to whether any resultant legal system must be moral, amoral or immoral in nature. The only thing that can be said at this stage is that, if the purpose of law is to guide human conduct, the rules in question must be capable of succeeding in their task. From this it follows that they must be capable of claiming to provide a reason as to why they ought to be followed, locating legal obligations within the broader realm of a unified hierarchy of practical reason. It follows from this that if a supreme moral principle can be identified legal rules must be morally permissible with reference to that principle to be capable of providing us with a reason as to why they ought to be followed. Given that the PGC does serve as such a principle, we are forced to conclude – from our starting point of an amoral functional account of law – that a rule must be morally permissible with reference to the PGC to claim to be capable of guiding our action, and thus must be morally permissible with reference to the PGC to be legally valid. Kramer's shift in focus thus does not overcome the natural law claim presented in this book, even if it might be able to overcome others.

A final attempt by Kramer to reject this conclusion may take the following form: that even if the law needs to recognise the agency of its subject, this recognition need not result in directives that are normative in character. As such, recognising the agency of legal subjects need not create an obligation that substantively limits the range of legally permissible rules available to the system.

[103] Kramer, *Law Without Trimmings* (n 71) 42–43.
[104] ibid 60.

He gives the example of a bank robber, who allows his victim to engage their agency and choose whether they wish to comply with his demands or be shot. He suggests that this does not mean that the command given by the bank robber is normative in character, but that it remains a command that the victim is likely to respond to one way or another.[105] Such a claim may be true, but we cannot draw any conclusions with regard to whether a rule must be morally permissible for it to be legally valid from the example he provides. To translate the example to a legal system would require us to accept that the non-normative content of such a command is, prima facie, a valid legal directive. Such an assumption requires us to adopt a positivist conception of legal validity, and thus begs the question. Proceeding from the neutral starting point of our agreed referent, we would reach a different conclusion: that such a directive cannot be valid law as the choice presented to the agent in question is presented in a morally impermissible way. The objection Kramer raises cannot circumvent this conclusion and should be rejected.

This section has sought to demonstrate that Kramer's commitment to the separability thesis, informed by his preference for a theoretical-explanatory methodology, is incapable of rebutting the moral-political normative natural law claim that a rule's moral permissibility is a necessary condition of its legal validity. We will conclude with what might be a surprising claim: that his broader writing on the rule of law suggests that the natural law claim is one that he ought to be inclined to accept. Take the following excerpt from *Where Law and Morality Meet*, in which he claims that:

> [The] moral status of any particular procedural deviation [from the requirements of the rule of law] is often a complicated matter which we can ascertain only by keeping an eye out for the possible existence of several interacting substantive considerations.[106]

This short excerpt, if we are to take it at face value, has significant consequences with regard to his claimed commitment to the separability thesis. For in recognising that deviation from a fundamental tenet of the rule of law can only be justified by reference to substantive considerations, Kramer is conceding that the deliberative project must be located in practical reasoning. In introducing a hierarchy of norms which must be considered in order to justify deviation, we can imply that he would only accept a deviation should it be seen as preferable to compliance. A test is therefore required by which we can assess which course of action is the most reasonable. This test must take account of the normative weight claimed by each alternative course of action to properly identify which one we ought to take. Kramer's claim thus necessitates a test located within a unified hierarchy of practical reason, as only a test that considers all possible

[105] ibid 59.
[106] Kramer, *Where Law and Morality Meet* (n 1) 199.

reasons for action can complete the task he asks of it. He thus requires a test such as that provided by the PGC; and since he his objections to its validity have all been shown to fail, we can see this as something that ought to be integrated into the above statement so that it can remain internally coherent. Should he attempt to suggest that this conclusion is only true on a contingent basis, he is showing himself to be mistaken as to the scope of the operation of a supreme moral principle. By allowing for the possibility of moral deliberation in such an assessment, he must concede that – if a supreme moral principle can be located – then to claim its application is contingent does not make sense. Its status as a supreme moral principle requires that its application is necessary, meaning his incorporationism collapses into an orthodox natural law position. His commitment to the rule of law thus requires him to accept that the PGC, by its status as a valid supreme moral principle, must also necessarily serve as a test for the validity of any and all legal rules.

5. CONCLUSION

This chapter has demonstrated that inclusive positivism, in allowing for the permissibility of a moral foundation of law, concedes a point which is fatal to its own coherence. It is in the very nature of a supreme moral principle that it applies equally to all actions and the theories of Lyons, Coleman and Kramer have each been shown to be incapable of avoiding the necessary conclusion that a rule's moral permissibility with reference to the PGC is a necessary condition of its legal validity.

Formalism, it has been shown, is only a coherent explanation of the content of law if it rests on legitimate grounds. To hold otherwise would be to introduce the paradox of unjust justice into legal discourse, which would be an irrational concession. Lyons' attempt to fortify formalism with his minimal separation thesis has similarly been demonstrated to be flawed, in that it can only avoid an internal contradiction if the contingent relationship between law and morality which it allows for is instead characterised as necessary. A similar conclusion must also be reached with Coleman's incorporationism resting on the conventionality thesis; the creation of a legal system necessarily takes place in a pre-legal sphere, therefore it cannot rely on exclusionary reasons to reject moral compliance. Coleman's rejection of force as a justification for legal authority therefore means that any resultant legal system must be accepted as legitimate by its subjects and, as its creators are bound by the PGC to act within its constraints, this is only possible if the resulting system is itself comprised of PGC-compliant primary rules. The practical difference thesis has similarly been shown to be deficient, in that the exclusionary authority it ascribes to law is predicated on a misunderstanding of reasons, actions and the nature of a categorical imperative to act.

Lastly, Kramer's commitment to the separability thesis, informed by his theoretical-explanatory methodology, similarly fails. Kramer's own understanding of moral requirements precludes him from avoiding a claim if it can be proven to be morally necessary, and his rebuttals of the PGC have been repeatedly shown to be founded on a misunderstanding of ethical rationalism. The contingent acceptance of moral norms within a legal system has therefore been demonstrated to be the Trojan horse which has led to the downfall of inclusive positivism.

Conclusion

THIS WORK HAS defended a simple claim – that the PGC properly understood provides an inescapable reason to accept the strong natural law position that identifies a rule's moral permissibility is a necessary condition of its legal validity. In making this claim, the thesis builds on the previous work of Beyleveld and Brownsword in *Law as a Moral Judgment* by addressing developments within legal positivism which have emerged since its publication.[1] It has done so in two parts. The first sought to establish the philosophical soundness of the argument for the PGC, firstly by defending its validity against common arguments that might be made against it. It demonstrated that common attacks against the claim that it successfully establishes a supreme moral principle either fail to fully engage with the substantive argument advanced by Gewirth or operate on a misunderstanding of the claim put forward by the PGC. It then moved on to demonstrate why the PGC serves as an absolute and exclusionary reason against all non-permissible action using the framework of deliberative rationality advanced by Joseph Raz. The PGC thus sits at the top of a unified conception of practical reason and must override all non-compatible reasons for action – including legal directives. On its own, however, this is not enough to demonstrate the truth behind the natural law proposition. Part II of this book therefore took these conclusions and applied them to the debate between legal positivists and natural lawyers. Chapter 3 proceeded by identifying a starting point for the enquiry that is acceptable to both sides of the debate and demonstrated that this requires us to accept that – in order to claim to be capable of providing a reason for action – a legal directive must be compliant with the requirements of the PGC. This core natural law claim was then located within a justificatory norm, with examples as to why this must necessarily feature in such a norm being provided by the theories of both Hart and Kelsen before contemporary positivist theories were demonstrated to be incapable of accounting for the validity of a legal rule without conceding that its directive must be permissible with reference to the PGC. This is a concise summary of the steps taken during the book and will be expanded on to demonstrate the necessity of this conclusion.

Part I of the work comprises of two chapters, each of which was concerned with demonstrating that the PGC is capable of behaving as a supreme moral principle as claimed by Gewirth and Beyleveld and Brownsword. This groundwork is necessary as any successful theory of natural law first needs to identify

[1] D Beyleveld and R Brownsword, *Law as a Moral Judgment* (Sheffield Academic Press 1986).

a valid test against which a legal rule can be assessed for its moral permissibility; this test must be rationally identifiable to ensure that it is acceptable to all regardless of their own subjective moral beliefs. Chapter 1 began by laying out the argument for the PGC, adopting the three-step division as laid out by Beyleveld for the clarity that this presentation brings to the dialectically necessary progression of the argument. From a starting point of the inescapable fact of our agency, the PGC requires us to accept that we are required to respect the GCAs of all other agents or else we engage in a logical contradiction. The PGC thus behaves in a way that is analogous to a categorical imperative, in that it applies to all action carried out by all agents regardless of their subjective belief. This critical morality provides a minimum threshold of permissibility, with a plurality of action permissible – and thus a plurality of equally permissible collective moral standards – provided they do not fall below the minimum level required. Such a conclusion is necessary on the standard view of what it means to engage in practical reason, as per Korsgaard and a Kantian conception of the person. This claim was then defended against some initial objections from the sceptical philosophical tradition, beginning with Bernard Williams' primary objection that the level of abstraction required for the identification of morality through formal principles such as the PGC means that they ignore the lived experiences of their subjects and the necessary importance of interpersonal relationships that they formulate. If they ignore such essentials, Williams suggests, such principles are inapplicable to real-world moral dilemmas. This point was shown to fail in its attack against the claim to universal applicability made by the PGC insofar as it does not engage with the nature of the argument presented by Gewirth. It was also rendered empty by Williams' own reliance on a starting-point of bare agency in his other moral writings, and can therefore, be rejected. Secondly, it was demonstrated that the subjective morality often attributed to Nietzsche is nothing of the sort, and that his writings are, in fact, compatible with limitations on actions grounded in factors essential for universal human flourishing such as the GCAs that the PGC seeks to defend. Thirdly, the scepticism of Friedman and Foot were dealt with in turn. Friedman's argument mischaracterises the scope of the PGC and should be rejected accordingly. Equally, Foot's argument that we should reject the PGC because moral requirements can only exist at the level of a hypothetical imperative should be rejected, in that the PGC operates as a universally applicable instrumental reason, and is therefore compatible with her conception of moral requirements. Our discussion of philosophical objections to the PGC concluded with an overview of Enoch's objections that the PGC does not provide an adequate reason to follow its requirements; an agent could simply say that they do not care about their agential status to successfully justify non-compliance. He continued his attack, arguing that even if we did accept that the PGC provided adequate reasons for compliance, it would be improper to characterise their requirements as moral. Like those presented by previous sceptics, these arguments were shown to be deficient in that they either mischaracterise the claim of the PGC, or else endorse the starting point of the argument and are thus required to accept Gewirth's conclusion via the dialectically necessary progression of the argument.

Having shown the argument for the PGC to be defensible against common arguments to the contrary, chapter two turned to the writing of Joseph Raz to demonstrate why its moral directives necessarily sit at the top of any hierarchy of reasons for action. It did this by laying out Raz's account of different types of reasons. Since reasons necessarily conflict, a hierarchy of reasons must exist so that an agent is able to identify which reason should ultimately be one that succeeds in providing an absolute or conclusive reason upon which they should act. A hierarchy presupposes the existence of a test by which the weight of reasons can be identified, which is the role claimed by the PGC. Given the success of the argument for the PGC was demonstrated in Chapter 1, we are required us to view it as an absolute and exclusionary reason that overrides any non-compliant reasons for action. Raz ought to accept this conclusion given his theory of reasons for action relies on either the principle of instrumental reason or a potentially weaker 'facilitative principle'; both proceed from the same starting point as the PGC and thus require us to accept its validity. A unified hierarchy of practical reason is thus necessary, in which all reasons for action – including legal directives – are equally subject to the absolute and exclusionary reason against non-compliant behaviour provided by the argument for the PGC. Thus, an agent has an overriding reason to refuse to follow non-PGC-compliant directives that claim to be legal in nature. Yet at this point, the natural law claim has not yet been proven; a legal positivist could accept the argument to this point, claiming that all we have demonstrated is that a person ought to disregard an immoral rule and accept the punishment for doing so. A successful natural law claim must build on this conclusion and demonstrate instead why a non-PGC-compliant directive that claims to be a legal rule is not law at all. Only once this has been argued can we justify the claim that a rule's moral permissibility is a necessary condition of its legal validity, and it is to that task that Part II turned.

The purpose of Part II was to both establish a PGC-compliant natural law position and defend it against contemporary positivist theories. It began with Chapter 3, which attempted to fit together the pieces of the jigsaw to fully demonstrate the natural law position. The importance of identifying a starting point that ought to be acceptable to all sides in the debate was first addressed, as it was demonstrated that both sides in the debate presuppose that such an objective starting point exists through the fact their claims are advanced in a manner compliant with an (F_b) rather than an (F_c) position. What is thus needed is an agreed referent, which – in order to be acceptable – must acknowledge the normative claim made by law whilst remaining silent as to whether this normative claim is morally permissible. This is achieved by the claim that law is the enterprise of subjecting human conduct to the governance of rules. A legal rule must, therefore, be prima facie capable of successfully guiding our action which, given the PGC's status as an absolute and exclusionary reason as established in

Chapter 2, requires all legal directives to be morally permissible to be legally valid. The natural law claim is thus established and was then defended against some preliminary objections that might be raised against this conclusion. Firstly, it dismissed the orthodox characterisation of Kantian reasoning as necessitating a positivist conception of legal rules. It finally considered Leiter's argument that all enquiry into the nature of law is doomed to failure because law is essentially a human creation, and – as human purposes vary over time – human artefacts are incapable of being subsumed under a single definition. This argument can be rejected in that it overlooks the central purpose of a legal system – to direct the action of its subjects. The strong natural law claim endorsed by this work must be accepted as a logical necessity. The second part of the chapter took this claim and demonstrated how it is compatible with existing theories of legal validity, using the paradigmatic positivist theories of Hart and Kelsen as examples. It was shown that, not only is the PGC capable of featuring in Hart's secondary rule of recognition or Kelsen's basic norm, but its status at the top of any and all normative hierarchies means that both theories can only remain internally coherent if this contingent acceptance is instead seen to be necessary for the legal validity of the rule.

Chapter 4 then applied this conclusion to the positivist position adopted by Joseph Raz. Of primary interest is his 'Sources Thesis', which holds that law is a social fact and must, therefore, stem from non-moral social sources. Morality can influence the creation of law but must do so at the pre-legal stage and should therefore be seen as a separate normative hierarchy to legal obligations. Such a claim fails necessarily; if Raz accepts that a law-creating body is capable of creating law in compliance with moral requirements, it follows that if a moral principle can be shown to be categorically binding for all agents, then the law-creators – in their capacity as agents – are obliged to act in compliance with that principle. The law they create must also be in compliance with the universally binding moral principle – in this case, the PGC. As Chapter 2 demonstrated that the requirements of the PGC are ones that Raz ought to accept, it follows that his positivist stance is untenable. This claim is supported by Raz's further insistence that law necessarily claims legitimate authority; as non-PGC-compliant rules are irrational and therefore prima facie incapable of making claims to legitimacy, law must necessarily be PGC compliant. Raz's further objection that his Sources Thesis should be seen to operate on a systemic basis rather than at the level of individual norms should be dismissed as incoherent and contradictory for the same reason. The only way the Sources Thesis can remain an adequate description of the creation of legal norms is for it to be modified to exclude the possibility of creating non-PGC-compliant rules; Raz's positivism is therefore incapable of surviving the necessary requirements imposed upon it by the PGC.

The final chapter of this thesis grouped together three theories of Inclusive Positivism, further developing the point first made in connection to Raz; if a conception of law concedes that a law-creating body is capable of integrating moral requirements into that system at its discretion, then should a moral principle be identified which applies to all actions, law-creating bodies become obliged to incorporate its requirements into the system they create. Since the PGC operates as an absolute and exclusionary reason in this way, it obliges all agents to act in conformity with its requirements, meaning that the contingent connection between moral permissibility and legal validity allowed for by inclusive positivists becomes one of necessity. The theories of Lyons, Coleman and Kramer were considered in turn and shown to be incapable of overcoming this conclusion. Firstly, Lyons' formalism – like Raz's Sources Thesis – requires that law must make a claim to legitimate authority to survive; the chapter demonstrated that to claim otherwise would introduce a paradox into Lyons' work by which an objectively just act could also be substantively unjust in its content. Such a claim is irrational, therefore it should be rejected. The 'minimal separation thesis' which Lyons suggests can be used to escape this conclusion is itself unsound; it can only survive as a source of law which claims authority over our actions if the contingent moral requirements to which he alludes are replaced with a necessary compliance with the requirements of a supreme moral principle – the PGC.

Coleman's 'conventionality thesis' was then shown to be incapable of creating legal norms unless these norms are morally permissible with reference to the PGC. In attempting to locate the source of legal normativity in the shared cooperative action of system-creators in a pre-legal system of rules, and further recognising that these agents might be influenced by moral concerns in concretising their behaviour into law, Coleman depicts a scene remarkably similar to that present in Raz's sources thesis. The exercise therefore fails for the same reason; as the creators of a legal system are necessarily agents acting prior to the existence of any legal obligation, they must necessarily act in accordance with reasons they already possess. Since their agency requires them to recognise the PGC as imposing valid limits on the scope of their actions, any actions they undertake must be PGC compliant. As the creation of a legal system is an action, the system they create must also be capable of creating obligations only insofar as these obligations are PGC compliant; any contradictory system of norms would be incapable of possessing authority over the subjects of the legal system, or capable of possessing a reason to be established by the system-creators. The PGC must therefore be present in both the secondary rule of recognition in Coleman's system and within the primary rules that system creates; it is therefore the source of legal normativity. That this is in conflict with the 'practical difference thesis' is of minimal concern, in that Coleman himself argues that the thesis is not central to any conception of positivism; even if it were, the objection would rest on both a misunderstanding of the nature of exclusionary reasons within deliberative reasoning and a mischaracterisation of Raz's 'normal justification thesis' and still fail.

The last theorist to be subjected to scrutiny from the PGC was Matthew Kramer. Forcefully presented, his conclusions were shown to be inconsistent with his own understanding of the nature of moral claims. He commits himself to the position that if a moral action is required then it serves as an absolute and exclusionary reason against behaviour to the contrary, and – as such – concedes the possibility that a principle could act as a Categorical Imperative in this way. His dismissal of the PGC does not, however, successfully overcome the dialectically necessary argument; it instead either misunderstands the nature of the 'ought' claim presented, or skirts around the argument by claiming that rationalism alone is incapable of serving as a foundation for moral principles. This position is incompatible with his own characterisation of the mind-independence of moral principles, which presupposes a test that would be necessary for their identification. This, in turn, presupposes that a reason must exist for choosing the acceptability of one test over another, as it would be paradoxical to suggest that a test for the validity of a moral principle could be prima facie irrational. There is therefore no valid reason for Kramer to deny the rational foundation of moral principles, and he ought to accept the PGC in the absence of any successful reason not to. In light of the inclusive nature of his positivism, his acceptance of the claim that a rule's moral permissibility can be a condition of its legal validity on a contingent basis collapses into one where this criterion becomes necessary.

It is not anticipated that this thesis will conclusively end the debate as to whether a rule's moral permissibility is necessary condition of its legal validity. It does, however, go some way to clarifying some misconceptions which are present in much of contemporary positivism. It has demonstrated that disagreement between positivism and non-positivist theories is axiomatically normative rather than merely linguistic. It has further demonstrated that the dialectically necessary argument to the PGC is capable of withstanding many common assaults against it and should therefore be accepted as sound in the absence of a successful rebuttal to the contrary. It has also been demonstrated that the universally applicable instrumental reason produced by the argument is capable of acting similarly to a categorical imperative, which requires us to accept a unified theory of reasons for action within deliberative reasoning. As such, any theory of law which recognises that a rule's moral permissibility is capable of being incorporated into a test for its legal validity is forced, by the nature of the argument, to abandon claims to contingent incorporation in favour of a necessary connection. To claim otherwise is a simple misunderstanding of what it is to act and cannot overcome the natural law position advanced throughout this work.

Bibliography

Allen, P, '"Ought" from "Is"? What Hare and Gewirth Should Have Said' (1982) 3(3) *American Journal of Theology and Philosophy* 90.

Alexy, R, *The Argument from Injustice* (S Paulson and B Paulson tr, Oxford University Press 2009).

Archer, MS, *Being Human: The Problem of Agency* (Cambridge University Press 2000).

Arendt, A, *The Human Condition* (2nd edn, University of Chicago Press 1998).

Arnold, T, *The Symbols of Government* (Yale University Press 1935).

Aquinas, T, *Summa Theologiae* (T Gilby OP tr, Cambridge University Press 2006).

Austin, J, *The Province of Jurisprudence Determined* (first pub 1832, WE Rumble ed, Cambridge University Press 1995).

Bertea, S, *The Normative Claim of Law* (Hart 2009).

Beyleveld, D, *The Dialectical Necessity of Morality: An Analysis and Defense of Alan Gewirth's Argument to the Principle of Generic Consistency* (University of Chicago Press 1991).

Beyleveld, D, 'The Principle of Generic Consistency as the Supreme Principle of Human Rights' (2012) 13(1) *Human Rights Review* 1.

Beyleveld, D, 'Gewirth versus Kant on Kant's Maxim of Reason: Towards a Gewirthian Philosophical Anthropology' in P Bauhn (ed) *Gewirthian Perspectives on Human Rights* (Routledge 2016).

Beyleveld, D, and Brownsword, R, *Law as a Moral Judgment* (Sheffield Academic Press 1986).

Beyleveld, D, and Brownsword, R, 'Law as a Moral Judgment vs Law as the Rules of the Powerful' (1983) 28 *American Journal of Jurisprudence* 79.

Beyleveld, D, and Brownsword, R, 'The Practical Difference between Natural-Law Theory and Legal Positivism' (1985) 5 *Oxford Journal of Legal Studies* 32.

Beyleveld, D, and Brownsword, R, 'Principle, Proceduralism and Precaution in a Community of Rights' (2006) 19(2) *Ratio Juris* 141.

Bittner, R, 'Stronger Reasons' in LH Meyer et al. (eds), *Rights, Culture, and the Law: Themes from the Legal and Political Philosophy of Joseph Raz* (Oxford University Press 2003).

Bratman, ME, 'Shared Cooperative Activity' (1992) 101(2) *Philosophical Review* 327.

Bratman, ME, 'Shared Intentions' (1993) 104 *Ethics* 97.

Bratman, ME, 'Reflections on Law, Normativity and Plans' in S Bertea and G Pavlakos (eds) *New Essays on the Normativity of Law* (Hart 2011).

Brink, D, 'Kantian Rationalism: Inescapability, Authority, and Supremacy' in G Cullity and B Gaut (eds) *Ethics and Practical Reason* (Oxford University Press 1997).

Broome, J, 'Practical Reasoning' in J Bermúdez and A Millar (eds) *Reason and Nature: Essays in the Theory of Rationality* (Clarendon Press 2002).

Broome, J, 'Reasons' in Wallace, RJ et al (eds) *Reason and Value* (Oxford University Press 2004).

Capps, P, *Human Dignity and the Foundations of International Law* (Hart 2009).

Capps, P and Pattinson, SD, (eds) *Ethical Rationalism and the Law* (Hart 2017).

Cicero, *On the Commonwealth and On the Laws* (J Zetzel tr, first pub 1999, Cambridge University Press 2002).

Celano, B, 'Are Reasons for Action Beliefs' in LH Meyer et al. (eds), *Rights, Culture, and the Law: Themes from the Legal and Political Philosophy of Joseph Raz* (Oxford University Press 2003).

Coleman, J, *Markets, Morals and the Law* (Cambridge University Press 1988).

Coleman, J, *Risks and Wrongs* (Cambridge University Press 1992).

Coleman, J, 'Authority and Reason' in RP George (ed) *The Autonomy of Law: Essays on Legal Positivism* (Oxford University Press 1996).

Coleman, J, 'Incorporationism, Conventionality, and the Practical Difference Thesis' (1998) 4(4) *Legal Theory* 381.
Coleman, J, *The Practice of Principle: In Defence of a Pragmatist Approach to Legal Theory* (Oxford University Press 2001).
Coleman, J, 'The Architecture of Jurisprudence' in JF Beltrán al (eds) *Neutrality and Theory of Law* (Springer 2013).
Cumminsky, D, 'Gewirth's Kantian Consequentialism' in M Boylan (ed), *Gewirth: Critical Essays on Action, Rationality and Community* (Rowman & Littlefield 1998).
d'Entrèves, AP, *Natural Law; An Introduction to Legal Philosophy* (first pub 1951, Hutchinson & Co., 1970).
Enoch, D, 'Agency, Shmagency: Why Normativity Won't Come from What is Constitutive of Action' (2006) 115(2) *The Philosophical Review* 169.
Enoch, D, *Taking Morality Seriously* (Oxford University Press 2011).
Fish, S, *Doing What Comes Naturally: Change, Rhetoric, and the Practice of Theory in Literary and Legal Studies* (Duke University Press 1990).
Friedman, RB, 'The Basis of Human Rights: A Criticism of Gewirth's Theory' in JR Pennock and JW Chapman (eds), *Human Rights – Nomos XXIII* (New York University Press 1981).
Foot, P, 'Morality as a System of Hypothetical Imperatives' (1972) 81(3) *The Philosophical Review* 305.
Foot, P, 'Morality, Action and Outcome' in T Honderich (ed), *Morality and Objectivity: A Tribute to J.L.Mackie* (New York University Press 1981).
Frankfurt, H, *Necessity, Volition, and Love* (Cambridge University Press 1999).
Gewirth, A, 'The Normative Structure of Action' (1971) 25(2) *The Review of Metaphysics* 238.
Gewirth, A, 'The "Is-Ought" Problem Resolved' (1973) 43 *Proceedings and Addresses of the American Philosophical Association* 34.
Gewirth, A, *Reason and Morality* (University of Chicago Press 1978).
Gewirth, A, 'The Basis and Content of Human Rights' in JR Pennock and JW Chapman (eds), *Human Rights – Nomos XXIII* (New York University Press 1981).
Gewirth, A, *Human Rights: Essays on Justification and Applications* (University of Chicago Press 1982).
Gewirth, A, 'Replies to my Critics' in E Regis Jr (ed) *Gewirth's Ethical Rationalism* (University of Chicago Press 1984).
Gewirth, A, 'The Justification of Morality' (1988) 53(2) *Philosophical Studies* 245–262.
Gewirth, A, 'Is Cultural Pluralism Relevant to Moral Knowledge?' (1994) 11(1) *Social Philosophy & Policy* 22.
Gewirth, A, *The Community of Rights* (University of Chicago Press 1996).
Gewirth, A, '"Ought" and Reasons for Action' (1997) 35(2) *The Southern Journal of Philosophy* 171.
Gibbard, A, *Meaning and Normativity* (Oxford University Press 2012).
Grice, P, *Aspects of Reason* (Oxford University Press 2001).
Haffner, S, *Defying Hitler: A Memoir* (Phoenix 2003).
Hart, HLA, 'Positivism and the Separation of Law and Morals' (1958) 71(4) *Harvard Law Review* 593.
Hart, HLA, *Essays in Jurisprudence and Philosophy* (Clarendon Press 1983).
Hart, HLA, *The Concept of Law* (3rd edn, Oxford University Press 2012).
Hegel, G, *Elements of the Philosophy of Right* (HB Nisbet tr, A Wood ed, Cambridge University Press 1991).
Horwich, P, *Truth* (Oxford University Press 1990).
Jowitt, J, 'Legal Rights for Animals: Aspiration of Logical Necessity?' (2020) 11(2) *Journal of Human Rights and the Environment* 173.
Kant, I, *The Metaphysics of Morals* (Mary Gregor tr, Cambridge University Press 1996).
Kant, I, *Groundwork of the Metaphysics of Morals* (first published 1785, Mary Gregor tr, Cambridge University Press 1998).
Kant, I, *Critique of Pure Reason* (Paul Guyer and Allen Wood tr, Cambridge University Press 1998).

Kelsen, H, *Pure Theory of Law* (Max Knight tr., 2nd edn, University of California Press 1970).
Kelsen, H, *General Theory of Law and State* (Transaction 2005).
Korsgaard, C, 'Reflective Endorsement' in O O'Neill (ed) *The Sources of Normativity* (Cambridge University Press 1996).
Korsgaard, C, 'Reply' in O O'Neill (ed) *The Sources of Normativity* (Cambridge University Press 1996).
Korsgaard, C, *Self-Constitution: Agency, Identity, and Integrity* (Oxford University Press 2009).
Kramer, M, *In Defense of Legal Positivism: Law Without Trimmings* (Oxford University Press 1999).
Kramer, M, *In the Realm of Legal and Moral Philosophy* (Macmillan 1999).
Kramer, M, *Where Law and Morality Meet* (Oxford University Press 2008).
Kramer, M, *Moral Realism as a Moral Doctrine* (Wiley-Blackwell 2009).
Kramer, M, and Simmonds, N, 'Reason Without Reasons: A Critique of Alan Gewirth's Moral Philosophy' (1996) 34(3) *The Southern Journal of Philosophy* 301, 303.
Kramer, M, and Simmonds, N, 'No Better Reasons: A Reply to Alan Gewirth' (1998) 36(1) *The Southern Journal of Philosophy* 131.
Kripke, SA, *Wittgenstein on Rules and Private Language* (Harvard University Press 1982).
Laurence, B, 'Juridical Laws as Moral Laws in Kant's The Doctrine of Rights' in G Pavlakos and V Rodriguez-Blanco (eds), *Reasons and Intentions in Law and Practical Agency* (Cambridge University Press 2015).
Leiter, B, 'The Demarcation Problem in Jurisprudence: A New Case for Scepticism' (2011) 31(4) *Oxford Journal of Legal Studies* 663.
Lucas, J, *The Principles of Politics* (Oxford University Press 1966).
Lucy, W, 'Natural Law Now' (1993) 56(5) *Modern Law Review* 745.
Lyons, D, 'Moral Aspects of Legal Theory' (1982) 7 *Midwest Studies in Philosophy* 223.
Lyons, D, *Moral Aspects of Legal Theory: Essays on Law, Justice, and Political Responsibility* (Cambridge University Press 1993).
McBride, M, 'Raz on the Internal Point of View' (2011) 17 *Legal Theory* 227.
McMahon, C, 'Gewirth's Justification of Morality' (1986) 50(2) *Philosophical Studies* 261.
Marmor, M, *Positive Law and Objective Values* (Oxford University Press 2001).
May, S, *Nietzsche's Ethics and his War on 'Morality'* (Clarendon Press 1999).
Mill, JS, *Utilitarianism* (R Crisp ed, Oxford University Press 1998).
Moore, M, 'Authority, Law, and Razian Reasons' (1989) *Southern California Law Review* 827.
Murphy, N, *Natural Law in Jurisprudence and Politics* (Cambridge University Press 2006).
Nagel, T, 'Universality and the Reflective Self' in O O'Neill (ed) *The Sources of Normativity* (Cambridge University Press 1996).
Nietzsche, F, *The Will to Power* (Walter Kaufman and R. J. Hollingdale tr, Vintage 1968).
Nietzsche, F, *Beyond Good and Evil* (Marion Faber tr, Oxford University Press 1998).
Parfit, D, 'Reason and Motivation' (1997) *Aristotelian Society*, suppl. 71.
Penner, JE, 'Legal Reasoning and the Authority of Law' in LH Meyer et al. (eds), *Rights, Culture, and the Law: Themes from the Legal and Political Philosophy of Joseph Raz* (Oxford University Press 2003).
Postema, GJ, 'Coordination and Convention at the Foundations of Law' (1982) 11 *Journal of Legal Studies* 165.
Postema, GJ, 'Law as Command: The Model of Command in Modern Jurisprudence' in E Sosaand and E Villanueva (eds), *Social, Political and Legal Philosophy* (Blackwell 2001).
Radbruch, G, 'Statutory Lawlessness and Supra-Statutory Law (1946)' (2006) 26 (1) *Oxford Journal of Legal Studies* 1.
Raz, J, *The Concept of a Legal System: An Introduction to the Theory of a Legal System* (2nd edn, Oxford University Press 1980).
Raz, J, 'Hart on Moral Rights and Legal Duties' (1984) 4 *Oxford Journal of Legal Studies* 123.
Raz, J, *The Morality of Freedom* (Oxford University Press 1986).
Raz, J, 'Facing Up: A Reply' (1989) 62 *Southern California Law Review* 1153.

Raz, J, *Ethics in the Public Domain: Essays in the Morality of Law and Politics* (Rev. ed. Oxford University Press 1994).
Raz, J, 'Intention in Interpretation' in RP George (ed) *The Autonomy of Law: Essays on Legal Positivism* (Oxford University Press 1996).
Raz, J, 'Two Views on the Nature of the Theory of Law: A Partial Comparison.' (1998) 4(3) *Legal Theory* 249.
Raz, J, *Engaging Reason: On the Theory of Value and Action* (Oxford University Press 1999).
Raz, J, *Practical Reason and Norms* (2nd edn Oxford 1999).
Raz, J, *Value, Respect, and Attachment* (Cambridge University Press 2001).
Raz, J, 'About Morality and the Nature of Law' (2003) 48 *American Journal of Jurisprudence* 1.
Raz, J, 'Incorporation by Law' (2004) 10 *Legal Theory* 1.
Raz, J, *Between Authority and Interpretation: On the Theory of Law and Practical Reason* (Oxford University Press 2009).
Raz, J, *The Authority of Law* (2nd edn, Oxford University Press 2009).
Raz, J, 'Human Rights Without Foundations' in S Besson and J Tasioulas (eds) *The Philosophy of International Law* (Oxford University Press 2010).
Raz, J, *From Normativity to Responsibility* (Oxford University Press 2011).
Rodriguez-Blanco, V, 'The Moral Puzzle of Legal Authority: A Commentary on Shapiro's Planning Theory of Law' in S Bertea and G Pavlakos (eds) *New Essays on the Normativity of Law* (Hart 2011).
Schaubroeck, K, 'Legal Normativity and the Instrumental Principle' in S Bertea and G Pavlakos (eds) *New Essays on the Normativity of Law* (Hart 2011).
Scheuerman, J, 'Gewirth's Concept of Prudential Rights' (1987) 37(148) *Philosophical Quarterly* 291–304.
Sidgwick, H, *Methods of Ethics* (7th edn, Macmillan 1907).
Sigmund, P, 'Law and Politics' in N Kretzmann and E Stump (eds), *The Cambridge Companion to Aquinas* (Cambridge University Press 1993).
Spaak, T, 'Kelsen and Hart on the Normativity of Law' in P Wahlgren, (ed) *Perspectives on Jurisprudence; Essays in Honour of Jes Bjarup* (Stockholm Institute for Scandinavian Law 2005).
Stephen, L, *The Science of Ethics* (first published 1882, Cambridge University Press 2011).
Tamanaha, B, *A Realistic Theory of Law* (Cambridge University Press 2017).
Timmons, M, *Significance and System: Essays on Kant's Ethics* (Oxford University Press 2017).
Toddington, S, *Rationality, Social Action and Moral Judgment* (Edinburgh University Press 1993).
Weinrib, EJ, 'Law as a Kantian Idea of Reason.' (1987) 87 *Columbia Law Review* 472.
Willaschek, M, 'Which Imperatives for Right? On the Non-prescriptive Character of Juridical Laws in Kant's Metaphysics of Morals' in M Timmons (ed) *Kant's Metaphysics of Morals: Interpretive Essays* (Oxford University Press 2002).
Williams, B, *Morality: An Introduction to Ethics* (Cambridge University Press 1972).
Williams, B, *Moral Luck* (Cambridge University Press 1981).
Williams, B, 'Ethics and the Fabric of the World' in T Honderich (ed), *Morality and Objectivity: A Tribute to J.L.Mackie* (New York University Press 1981).
Williams, B, 'History, Morality, and the Test of Reflection' in O O'Neill (ed) The Sources of Normativity (Cambridge University Press 1996).
Williams, B, *Ethics and the Limits of Philosophy* (Routledge 2006).
Williams, G, 'The Controversy Surrounding the Word "Law"' in P Laslett (ed), *Philosophy, Politics and Society*, (Basil Blackwell 1970).
Wittgenstein, L, *Philosophical Investigations* (GEM Anscombe tr, 3rd edn, Blackwell 1953).

Index

Lightning Source UK Ltd.
Milton Keynes UK
UKHW020108260123
415990UK00004B/172

9 781509 947683